Poems by Augusta Webster and Amy Levy

AUGUSTA WEBSTER was born in 1837, [...]
She taught herself Greek, Italian and S[...]
French while living in Paris and Geneva. Her first collections of poetry, *Blanche Lisle and Other Poems* (1860) and *Lilian Gray* (1864) were published under the name of Cecil Home. In 1863 she married Thomas Webster, a fellow of Trinity College, Cambridge. Their only child was the subject of her sonnet sequence *Mother and Daughter* (1895). In addition to her major collections *Dramatic Studies* (1866), *A Woman Sold and Other Poems* (1867) and *Portraits* (1870), she also wrote essays, a novel and verse dramas, and reviewed for *The Athenaeum*. She died in 1894.

MATHILDE BLIND was born in Mannheim in 1841. After the death of her father, her mother married Karl Blind; his involvement in revolutionary politics caused the family to flee to England in 1848. She moved in radical circles throughout her life, maintaining friendships with Garibaldi and Mazzini, as well as with writers and artists of the Pre-Raphaelite group. Her work includes translations and a biography of George Eliot (1883). She published two long poems, *The Heather on Fire* (1886), about the Highland Clearances, and *The Ascent of Man* (1888), an account of evolution, as well as shorter verses, later collected by Arthur Symons in her *Complete Poetical Works* (1900). She died in 1896.

AMY LEVY was born in London in 1861 and became the first Jewish student to study at Newnham College, Cambridge. Her first book, *Xantippe and Other Poems*, was published in 1880. After she had left university, she began to earn her living as a writer in London. Oscar Wilde admired her work and published her journalism in his *Woman's World* magazine. She wrote three novels, one of which, *Reuben Sachs* (1888; translated into German by Eleanor Marx), was controversial for its attack on contemporary Jewish life. She committed suicide in 1889 at the age of twenty-seven; her last collection of poems, *A London Plane-Tree and Other Verse*, was published posthumously.

JUDITH WILLSON studied English at Newnham College, Cambridge and the University of York. She has been a teacher, and has worked in publishing since 1989. Carcanet publish her edition of *Selected Poems of Charlotte Smith* (2003).

FyfieldBooks aim to make available some of the great classics of British and European literature in clear, affordable formats, and to restore often neglected writers to their place in literary tradition.

FyfieldBooks take their name from the Fyfield elm in Matthew Arnold's 'Scholar Gypsy' and 'Thyrsis'. The tree stood not far from the village where the series was originally devised in 1971.

> *Roam on! The light we sought is shining still.*
> *Dost thou ask proof? Our tree yet crowns the hill,*
> *Our Scholar travels yet the loved hill-side*

from 'Thyrsis'

Out of My Borrowed Books

Poems by
Augusta Webster, Mathilde Blind and Amy Levy

Edited with introductions by
JUDITH WILLSON

...teaching myself out of my borrowed books
Augusta Webster, 'A Castaway'

FyfieldBooks

CARCANET

Acknowledgements

I am grateful to Michael Schmidt and Stephen Procter of Carcanet Press for their comments on drafts of the text, to the editor Helen Tookey, and to Stella Halkyard, Modern Literary Archivist of the John Rylands University Library of Manchester.

First published in Great Britain in 2006 by
Carcanet Press Limited
Alliance House
Cross Street
Manchester M2 7AQ

A CIP catalogue record for this book is available from the British Library
ISBN 1 85754 854 X
978 1 85754 854 9

The publisher acknowledges financial assistance from Arts Council England

Typeset by XL Publishing Services, Tiverton
Printed and bound in England by SRP Ltd, Exeter

CONTENTS

ILLUSTRATIONS

INTRODUCTION

Her mother wants to make of her such a woman as she is herself
– a woman of dark and dreary duties; and Rose has a mind full-
set, thick-sown with the germs of ideas her mother never knew.
It is agony to her often to have these ideas trampled on and
repressed. She has never rebelled yet, but if hard driven she will
rebel one day, and then it will be once for all. [Her father] some-
times fears she will not live, so bright are the sparks of intelligence
which, at moments, flash from her glance and gleam in her
language... Now, behold Rose, two years later... unknown birds
flutter round the skirts of that forest; no European river this, on
whose banks Rose sits thinking. The little quiet Yorkshire girl is
a lonely emigrant in some region of the southern hemisphere.
(from Charlotte Brontë, *Shirley* (1849), Ch. 9)

Rose Yorke's rebellious intelligence allows her only two possible life-
stories: it may kill her, irreconcilable as it is with the inherited burden
of female duties, or it may exile her to the precarious future of an
empty land. Two narratives, literal and metaphorical, that formed the
warp and weft of women's thinking about their lives. 'I see the
numbers of my kind who have gone mad for want of something to
do', writes Florence Nightingale in 1867, torn between the contrary
costs of dutiful conformity and self-fulfilment.[1] The conflict is
embodied in Jane Eyre and Dorothea Brooke; it is voiced in Augusta
Webster's monologues, in Mathilde Blind's epics of historical process
and in Amy Levy's reinterpretation of exclusion. For all three poets,
this is their imaginative territory: the remaking of 'such a woman as
she is herself', the redefinition of independence and isolation, compli-
ance and transgression, the articulation of new voices. Above all, there
is for each a new sense of what happiness might be, not granted as a
reward for duty, but created by a spark of intelligence and a gleam of
language.

Augusta Webster was born in 1837, which makes her childhood
almost contemporaneous with that of the fictional Rose; Amy Levy,
the youngest of the poets in this anthology, in 1861. None lived to
a great age: Mathilde Blind, born in 1841, lived furthest into the
century, dying in 1896. Webster had died two years earlier, and by
1896 Levy had been dead for seven years. And yet the roughly fifty
years spanned by their three lives encompassed profound and extraor-
dinary changes in what was possible for women, changes which form

both the context and the content of their writing. Located between the death of Letitia Landon and the publication of Virginia Woolf's first novel, their lives and their work embody the transition from the Victorians to the modern.

All three would have been significant figures, at least on the margins of social history, had they never written a word of poetry: in different ways, each was involved in public life, engaging in debate, contributing to the century's changing landscape. An awareness of the distance that could be travelled in one lifetime, from the radical campaigners of the 1850s who were Webster's colleagues, to Levy and her friends, the emergent New Women of the 1880s, reveals why this public aspect to their lives is so significant. In 1839, when Augusta Webster was an infant, Sarah Stickney Ellis published her popular work *The Women of England, Their Social Duties, and Domestic Habits*. It was a thoughtful discussion of how women might live, and it went into eleven editions. Ellis was an educated, professional writer whose publications contributed to the family income, but, she argues, 'there is a voice in woman's heart too strong for education'. Women's quality of 'disinterested kindness' fits them for the highest roles as guardians of morality and shapers of future generations; few girls 'are ever called upon for their Latin, their Italian, or even for their French; but all women in this sphere of life are liable to be called upon to visit and care for the sick'.[2] Born in 1812, Ellis is part of a growing sense of change in what is possible for women, but she makes no connection between women's idealised role and their actual intellectual dissatisfactions and practical poverty. Nor is she troubled by the disparity between social need and women's individual, domestic skills in responding to it. By 1866, when Emily Davies published her briskly argued book *The Higher Education of Women*, the terms of reference had changed:

> Women who think at all can scarcely help thinking about the condition of the poor, and to arrive at sound conclusions on so vast a subject involves an acquaintance more or less complete with almost every consideration which comes within the range of the politician... And the moment [women] attempt in any way to alleviate the sufferings of the poor, they find that a strong, clear head is as necessary as a warm heart.[3]

Solutions to social ills, Davies spells out with some exasperation, involve women in matters that demand competence and education.

Webster was part of the circle of campaigners for suffrage and education that included Emily Davies, and to which Mathilde Blind and, more distantly, Amy Levy, also had connections.[4] When Blind died, she left a bequest to Newnham College, Cambridge, where Amy Levy had been a student seventeen years earlier. There is a symbolic significance in the link. Webster's generation imagined institutions into being, building the physical and social structures that made change possible. Her poetry is not explicitly polemical, but it is grounded in social demands, for recognition, for a voice and a purpose. By the end of the century, the structures, however fragile, are in place. The emphasis shifts: Levy's writing is framed by the pressures of improvising a new kind of life, creating a new sense of self. The social change is one of the central public narratives of the nineteenth century, but it is also a change in an inner landscape. It is this contested space between suppression of self and exile from community that is the imaginative territory explored in the work of each poet.

As writers of this historical moment, Webster, Blind and Levy are at once part of mainstream literary culture and consciously outside it. Webster was a prolific reviewer whose judgements carried weight; William Rossetti did not find it ridiculous to suggest that she could be considered a possible Poet Laureate following the death of Tennyson. Blind was a significant presence in artistic and intellectual circles, an important biographer of George Eliot, a translator of substance. Even Levy, for whom marginality is a defining theme, was a respected professional writer, a journalist, novelist and translator as well as a poet. And yet they stand apart from the mainstream, aware of difference of gender, inheritance and expectation. For Webster and Blind, radical politics and aesthetics implied a stance as outsiders. Blind and Levy were even more conspicuously set apart by foreignness, real or, in Levy's case, perceived. Levy's religion and sexuality compounded the distance.

Each, though, redefined the meaning of this separation, realigning the literature she inherited to a conscious sense of a female tradition of writing, the 'grandmothers' in Elizabeth Barrett Browning's phrase. Christina Rossetti held Webster's poetry in very high regard; Amy Levy, in her turn, wrote insightfully on Rossetti's poetry.[5] Webster's monologues were a direct influence on Levy's early writing. All three shared a sense of indebtedness to Barrett Browning. Her work recurs as a point of reference, her life as a model of how a woman might succeed as a poet. *Aurora Leigh* (1856), Barrett Browning's celebration of a woman's rebellious creativity that neither destroys her nor is silenced into acquiescence, is a presence behind Augusta Webster's dramatic monologues, behind Blind's claim to the freedom and power of the poet's voice, behind Levy's exploration of the relationship between integrity and community. Moreover, in different ways each was conscious of inheriting a link to Barrett Browning's own models – Mme de Staël's *Corinne*, Felicia Hemans, Letitia Landon. Nor were they writing in social isolation: the networks within which they moved – their friendships with the Rossettis and the Garnetts, Swinburne and William Morris and Eleanor Marx, with half a century of female activists, from the campaigners for women's education to the social reformers of the *fin de siècle* – form recurring, overlapping patterns, as do the institutions whose development was woven into the course of their own lives – the colleges and committees and lobbying groups.

Above all, what links Webster, Blind and Levy is their engagement with the meaning of Rose Yorke's silence. In the figure of the non-compliant woman whose 'strong, clear head' is unconstrained by conventional definitions of femininity lies, for each, a means of voicing the relationship between imaginative, moral independence and self-destructive isolation. The anomalous and marginal are made central: in the transgressive women of Webster's monologues, in the huge solitudes of Blind's epics, in Levy's claim for the centrality of the marginal, there is an insistence on the authority of the voice of the woman writing, not the woman written about.

Notes

1   *Selected Letters*, ed. Martha Vicinus and Bea Nergaard, Virago Press, London 1989, p. 39. It is striking how closely emigration becomes associated with women from the mid-nineteenth century. A number of schemes promoted female emigration as a solution whereby 'surplus women' might be rescued from destitution and temptations to immorality to make new lives in the colonies, in a kind of geographical parallel to the the social exile of transgression.

2   Sarah Stickney Ellis, *The Women of England, Their Social Duties, and Domestic Habits*, Fisher, Son and Co., London 1839, pp. 65, 76–7. Available at the Victorian Women Writers Project, www.indiana.edu/~letrs/vwwp/ellis/womeneng.html.

3   Emily Davies, *The Higher Education of Women*, Alexander Strahan, London 1866, Chapter IV, p. 71.

4   Webster was closely associated with the Langham Place circle of women campaigners and reformers, with whom Mathilde Blind had links through her half-sister Ottilie; Amy Levy's early poem 'Run to Death' was first published in one of the group's journals (see p. 259 below).

5   Christina Rossetti wrote of Augusta Webster that she was 'by far the most formidable of those [poetesses] known to me' (letter to William Rossetti 1890, *Letters of Christina Rossetti*, vol. 4, ed. Antony H. Harrison, University of Virginia Press, Charlottesville and London 2004, p. 180). William Rossetti recorded that his sister shared his 'very high admiration' of Webster's work, in particular her verse drama *The Sentence* (ibid., n. 2). Levy's 'The Poetry of Christina Rossetti' was published in Oscar Wilde's magazine *The Woman's World* in February 1888, pp. 178–80.

Note on the Texts

The text of the poems is based on that of the first edition in each case (see Further Reading, pp. 266–8, for bibliographic details.)

The modern edition of Augusta Webster's poetry is Christine Sutphin, *Augusta Webster: Portraits and Other Poems* (Broadview Press, Peterborough, Ontario 2000); although this is only a (substantial) selection. It includes a detailed introduction and bibliography, along with some of Webster's prose writings, none of which have been otherwise reprinted. There is currently no biography of Webster; the *DNB* remains the main source for details about her life.

There is no modern edition of Blind's works. The standard collected edition is the *Poetical Works* edited by Arthur Symons (T. Fisher Unwin, London 1900), which includes Richard Garnett's memoir, the main source of biographical information. Symons followed the texts of Blind's published collections, but reordered poems to fit thematic patterns. I have kept to the original chronology of the collections, although as Blind did frequently reprint poems in different collections, this is in itself not a neutral editorial decision.

A selection of Levy's poetry is included in Melvyn New's *Complete Novels and Selected Writings of Amy Levy* (University Press of Florida, Gainesville, FL 1993). Linda Hunt Beckman, *Amy Levy: Her Life and Letters* (Ohio University Press, Athens, OH 2000), includes almost all Levy's letters in her critical biography.

The complete texts of the original collections of all three are available on the Web at the Victorian Women Writers Project, www.indiana.edu/~letrs/vwwp/. Where possible, references to letters and prose writings are to the modern editions, to whose editors' scholarship I am indebted.

Both Webster and Blind wrote long poems which are not easily accommodated within a selection. Where it has not been possible to include the whole poem, I have aimed to include extracts that are substantial enough to be representative of the whole. Omissions are indicated by a row of asterisks (single asterisks are as the original texts). A few very minor editorial changes have been made to the texts, in relation to conventions for punctuation and quotation marks and in modernising the spelling of a small number of words. Obvious typographic errors in the original texts have been silently corrected

AUGUSTA WEBSTER

1837–94

Photographed by Ferrando, Roma.

Augusta Webster

Augusta Webster was recognised by contemporaries as one of the foremost poets of her day; in 1870 a reviewer of her *Portraits* considered that 'with this volume before us, it would be hard to deny her the proud position of the first living English poetess. Elizabeth Barrett Browning has passed away, and her mantle seems to have fallen on Mrs Webster'.[1] Moreover, she was close to the centre of movements for social reform; she was a pioneer in taking public office and she was an intelligent and incisive literary critic. And yet her life has almost vanished from the record, to be glimpsed only at an angle in others' memoirs, biographies and letters.

Some of the reasons for this are clear. She died relatively young; few of her letters and papers survive; her long poems (like those of Mathilde Blind) are not easily accommodated in anthologies, and the first selection of her verse, published in 1893, gave disproportionate space to her unrepresentative shorter poems. Although she did make influential literary connections, particularly in Pre-Raphaelite circles, the feminist writers, reformers and philanthropists with whom she was most closely connected were consciously outside and at odds with the mainstream (Christina Rossetti suspected that her politics were the reason for Gladstone's omission of Webster's name from his list of 'leading poetesses').[2] Moreover, such networks were still in the process of invention, not yet consolidated into the institutions that supported Amy Levy's generation.

What can be retrieved of Webster's life amounts to little more than a chronology of tantalising details. She was born Augusta Davies in 1837, in Dorset, the daughter of a naval officer, and spent part of her early childhood on her father's ship as well as in Scotland and Cornwall, before the family settled in Cambridge in 1851. According to Theodore Watts-Dunton's obituary in the *Athenaeum*, she was 'one of the brilliant daughters of Admiral Davies', and it is often asserted that she taught herself Greek in order to help her brother with his studies – like Elizabeth Barrett Browning and Christina Rossetti's sister Maria, piecing together a classical education at second-hand. However she managed it, she learned Greek well enough to publish respected translations of Aeschylus's *Prometheus Bound* (1866) and Euripides' *Medea* (1868) and, in 1877, an authoritative critical study of two translations of the *Agamemnon* of Aeschylus, by Browning and the scholar Edmund Morshead. In this she coolly dissects a number of Browning's mistranslations before letting him off the hook with a lethal kindness: 'There is no need of multiplying instances; we have noted down a long list of them, but our object is merely to illustrate a general criticism, not to pursue the ungracious task of hunting down imperfections for a catalogue'.[3] This, from a woman who had never been initiated into what George Eliot called 'the Eleusinian mysteries of a University education'. She also learned Italian, Spanish and French, and seems to have spent some time as a young woman living in Paris and Geneva, as well as studying at the Cambridge School of Art.

In 1863 she married Thomas Webster, a Fellow of Trinity College Cambridge; their only child, Margaret Davies Webster, was born the following year. Around 1870 the Websters moved to London, where they lived in Cheyne Walk, neighbours of Dante Gabriel Rossetti. Following an anecdote in Watts–Dunton's *Life and Letters* (1916), it is often asserted that Thomas Webster was persuaded by his wife to abandon his Cambridge Fellowship and law practice for the sake of her literary career, though it is impossible to know whether this is true or simply a construction that seemed the only feasible interpretation to contemporaries, who tended to characterise her poetry as having a rather daunting 'strength'.

In London, her life became increasingly public and political. During the 1870s she worked for the National Committee for Women's Suffrage, and was writing on literary and social matters for *The Examiner*, pieces collected as *A Housewife's Opinions* in 1879. The housewife had incisive and well-informed opinions, on Greek verse and the dramatic monologue, on working-class housing and the influence of William Morris on design, on education and female suffrage, and expressed them with an urbane logic and humour:

It is a hard law, however gently meant, which can stand in the way of a woman earning for her needs and those dependent on her. Nor should even earning beyond needs be made impossible. To do that is to put hope of bettering herself entirely out of a woman's life. Why may not an energetic and intelligent young woman, old enough to be a free agent, work hard – overwork if she please, as everybody does who gets on in the world – to set aside a sum of money for a given purpose, for learning a better trade, for starting a shop, for educating talents of which she is conscious or were it but for the humbler hope of buying a smart warm winter suit new for herself...[4]

Her journalism flies off the page with an ease and energy that suggests the competence and good sense she must have brought to her service on the London School Board, to which she was twice elected, in

1879 and 1885. It was a more radical commitment than it may appear, and implies much about Webster's involvement in both educational reform and the suffrage movement. Women had been granted the municipal vote in 1869, decades before they gained a voice in national politics: when the 1870 Education Act established elected school boards, they seized opportunities to stand for office at local government level, fully aware that this was a step towards opening up wider possibilities.[5]

At the heart of Webster's literary achievement are her four mature volumes of poetry: *Dramatic Studies* (1866), *A Woman Sold* (1867), *Portraits* (1870) and *A Book of Rhyme* (1881). In these collections Webster explores the selves that women inherit and create, and the languages that define them. Like Mathilde Blind, she is at her surest in the expansive, public forms of dramatic and narrative verse, rather than the private, contemplative shapes of lyric. Webster's poems, as a contemporary reviewer recognised, 'exhibit, in a high degree, that power of going out of oneself and thinking the thoughts of others, which is, of course, the essential function of the dramatist. There is an amount of force, too, as well as tenderness and beauty, about some of these self-portraitures.'[6] It is a perceptive reading: Webster takes readers out of themselves in order to discover a self-portrait after all. Eulalie, the prostitute of 'A Castaway', looks back to the girl she was, who darned her stockings and went out to tea and, turning to her mirror, finds no discontinuity:

> And what is that? My looking glass
> Answers it passably; a woman sure,
> No fiend, no slimy thing out of the pools,
> A woman with a ripe and smiling lip
> That has no venom in its touch I think...

In the voices of Eulalie, the woman sold; Eleanor, the woman who sells herself; Medea, the woman who murders her children; even in the eloquent silence of the woman in 'Tired', constructed by her husband out of his expectations and feminine miracles of pink gauze, Webster blurs distinctions between women who conform and those who transgress, finding the common themes in the script of women's lives. Eva, who becomes the nun Sister Annunciata, is betrayed into the convent by her family as much as Eulalie is betrayed by the very ordinariness of the lack of expectations for her life: 'Was I this good girl, / This budding colourless young rose of home?' (Such drifting, compliant girls who accept their music and embroidery as 'part of woman's mission to anybody or nobody'[7] are a recurrent theme of

A Housewife's Opinions, as they are of Emily Davies's demands for purposeful education.) In 'A Woman Sold', Eleanor, as corrupt and pitiable as Eulalie, has negotiated a different set of possibilities, buying wealth and independence through a loveless marriage, 'my mother pressing me'. Webster insists on the home as the source of the contracts that women make with the world, the place that keeps girls in ignorant dependence as much as safety. Her characters, women who would never be acknowledged in respectable households, are revealed as living by common transactions that cut across class and appearance. Sister Annunciata's vigil brings visions of her renounced lover; Eulalie is a careworn and commonplace woman, as unseductive as Annunciata is disturbingly sexual. Both, in the end, are fallen women, and both are disruptive figures, the one in making the body, the original Eva, present in a place that acknowledges only the soul, the other by being so unremarkable in a world that would rather be reassured that she was a creature who belonged to a different order of experience, like Dante Gabriel Rossetti's 'Jenny':

> Like a rose shut in a book
> In which pure women may not look.

The more we read of Eulalie, the closer we become to her; Jenny, 'fond of a kiss and fond of a guinea', constructed in the poet's gaze from allure and shame, sleeps through the poem with golden coins in her hair, and the longer we share in the guilty pleasure of looking, the less she is anyone, and the safer we are:

> Yet, Jenny, looking long at you,
> The woman almost fades from view.

In addition to her dramatic poetry, Webster was writing verse drama during the 1870s and early 1880s: *The Auspicious Day* (1872), *Disguises* (1879), *In a Day* (1882) and *The Sentence* (1887). Of these, only *In a Day* ever seems to have been performed, at Terry's Theatre in London in 1890. Margaret Davies Webster, who had become an actress, played the leading role. As Webster's plays were written primarily for reading, 'closet dramas', the lack of public performance is not necessarily evidence of her failure as a dramatist (though adopting the form may indicate that even Webster could not conceive of occupying the public territory of the theatre). Closet drama had its own qualities, drawing into poetry some of the externality of the theatre to explore conflicts and relationships, and demanding a correspondingly alert responsiveness from readers.[8] It was a poetic form used by George Eliot and Barrett Browning, too, enabling each to write on an ambitious scale that rejected the assumption that women's natural poetic voice was the intimate confessional lyric. Although Webster's plays themselves have long been forgotten, the qualities of drama are crucial to her poetry's claim to intellectual substance. In her *Examiner* article 'Poets and Personal Pronouns' she defines her position with a light touch:

> [The poet] is taken as offering his readers the presentment of himself, his hopes, his sorrows, his guilts and remorses, his history and psychology generally... We have only to try to imagine what, if I meant I, must be the mental state of these writers of many emotions, to see, in the fact of their being able to correct their proofs and get their books through press, consoling evidence that, as a rule, I does not mean I.[9]

It is notable that many of Webster's verse dramas and dramatic poems enact situations of extremity and violence: in these hybrid forms she literally gives voices to otherwise unspeakable feelings. *The Sentence* is a tragedy about Caligula; she had translated *Medea*; 'Sister Annunciata', 'A Woman Sold', 'Circe', 'A Castaway', are dramatic poems in which the most transgressive female archetypes demand recognition as compromised, nuanced characters finding a way through the narratives they have been given. (These poems were almost certainly an important influence on Amy Levy's writing. She too would use the dramatic poem as a means of enabling Medea, Xantippe and Magdalen to step out of their traditional definitions and have their say: women owning their language, not women as they are written.)

From 1884 until her death ten years later Webster was a poetry reviewer for *The Athenaeum*. Watts-Dunton, her colleague on the magazine, considered that 'as a critic... she had no superior, scarcely an equal'.[10] To a modern reader, her reviews speak with a confident authority grounded in a precise technical understanding. She analyses the effects of metrics and diction with a care that reflects her training in languages and her skill as a translator: Coventry Patmore, she writes, 'uses the pause as a sudden dead stop in the rhythm instead of as a rhythm punctuation'.[11] She praises poetic craft and has a sharp ear for falsity of technique and sentiment. The 'weary damsels of so many plaintive lyrics' of the fashionable poet Agnes Mary F. Robinson (1857–1949) bore her: Robinson is wasting her talent on 'vagueness and dreamings and sweetly told conceits'; 'we would have Miss Mary Robinson come into the real world – away from dreaming in enchanted gardens'. The critical rigour of her review is the more marked, because she knew Robinson personally.[12] Reviewing put her at the centre of literary life as a shaper of opinions and maker of reputations, but it is a role whose influence is difficult to measure because of reviewers' anonymity. Paradoxically, this gave Webster (and other women reviewers such as Mary Robinson herself) a space in which to wield cultural power but it also ensured that in many cases their contribution has remained hidden.

Webster's last work was the sonnet sequence *Mother and Daughter*, published posthumously in 1895 with an introduction by William Rossetti. To Rossetti, the subject was unproblematic: '[as] natural a one as any poetess could select'. To modern readers, the sequence can seem a disappointing end to Webster's writing, an innocuous collection of lyrics on a conventional feminine theme. But although there is no way of knowing the process of the sequence's composition, it is worth bearing in mind that Webster's daughter was around thirty years old in 1895. Unless the sonnets had been accumulating since the early 1860s, they are a conscious work of art by a mature writer exploring new subject matter, rather than the spontaneous responses of a new mother – 'as a rule, I does not mean I'. The sequence is notably suffused with an imagery of ageing and loss, as much as of new life. This too is a closet drama. Webster claims a form in which traditionally the woman is the object of love, brought into being through the poet–lover's definition of the relationship, guaranteed her share of immortality through his undying art. She also inherits the conventions of poems in which the child is beloved object: evocations of the fragility of innocence, moments captured before they are lost to time and change, or death. What she makes of these static forms is a multiple narrative. The momentariness of a sonnet sequence contains the development of the individual mother–child relationship; of retrospection and continuity; and of the larger narrative of art:

> And how could I grow old while she's so young?
>   Methinks her heart sets tune for mine to beat,
>   We are so near; her new thoughts, incomplete,
>   Find their shaped wording happen on my tongue;
> Like bloom on last year's winterings newly sprung...

The child is mother to the woman, the creation that ensures her self-creation as both mother and poet – as the poet is validated in the 'shaping-wording' in which the child lives. The sequence becomes a drama of process, another stage in Webster's exploration of the nature of female experience and of the language that shapes it.

Incomplete at Webster's death, *Mother and Daughter* is another loss in a record full of silences. As so often in Webster's life, there is a void where one searches for the live connections of relationships and responses. An occasional detail animates the chronology with a vividness and colour that suggest the woman. In Ray Strachey's early history of the women's movement, *The Cause*, Webster flares into life as a student in her twenties 'for whom admission to the Art School in South Kensington was secured, [who] nearly dashed the prospects of women art students for ever by being expelled for whistling'.[13] But how her place was secured and how the incident played out are unknown. The story has been repeated in a number of discussions of Webster, a rare personal detail that remains without context. For a poet whose writing is so attentive to the complexities of the identities women and writers create, the almost casual erasure of her life story is both loss and resolution: it leaves only the self of her writing.

Notes

1 *Examiner and London Review*, 21 May 1870, in Christine Sutphin, ed., *Augusta Webster: Portraits and Other Poems*, Broadview Press, Ontario 2000, pp. 418–21.

2 Letter to William Rossetti, 1890, *Letters of Christina Rossetti*, vol. 4, ed. Antony H. Harrison, University of Virginia Press, Charlottesville and London 2004, p. 180. Webster herself wrote of her politics in a letter to William Morris's daughter May, 'I feel a very great interest in Socialism and find myself in sympathy with it on many points but I am not a Socialist and never shall be unless a form of Socialism is developed which leaves... a larger room for Individualism than is generally connected with the idea of Socialism' (17 May 1886; BL Add 45346 f. 25).

3 *The Examiner*, 17 November 1877 and 24 November 1877, in Sutphin, pp. 353–66.

4 'Protection for the Working Woman', in *A Housewife's Opinions: Essays Reprinted from The Examiner*, Macmillan, London 1879, p. 174.

5 School boards were responsible for enforcing bye-laws, planning the provision of new schools, engaging contractors to build and maintain schools, and overseeing the general management of schools in their districts; serving on them involved women in demanding professional responsibilities, far removed from ad hoc philanthropy (see Patricia Hollis, *Women in Public: The Women's Movement 1850–1900*, George Allen and Unwin, London 1979, pp. 228, 266–7).

6 Review of *Dramatic Studies* in *The Nonconformist*, 27 June 1866, in Sutphin, pp. 403–4.

7 'Pianist and Martyr', in *A Housewife's Opinions*, p. 23.

8 '*We* have to study, as well as Mrs Webster', noted a contemporary reviewer of the 'intricacies and subtleties of character' unfolded in 'A Woman Sold' (*The Month*, March 1876, p. 276, in Susan Brown, 'Determined Heroines: George Eliot, Augusta Webster and Closet Drama by Victorian Women', *Victorian Poetry* 33, 1995, pp. 89–109).

9 'Poets and Personal Pronouns', *The Examiner*, 2 March 1878, in Sutphin, pp. 366–72.

10 'Mrs Augusta Webster', *The Athenaeum*, 15 September 1894, p. 355.

11 On *The Unknown Eros*, *The Athenaeum*, 22 November 1890, p. 693.

12 *Athenaeum*, 17 April 1886, p. 517, review of Robinson's *An Italian Garden*, quoted in 'Augusta Webster and the Lyric Muse: *The Athenaeum* and Webster's Poetics', *Victorian Poetry* 42, 2004, pp. 135–64. Mary Robinson was a celebrated poet and literary hostess; she knew, and effected introductions between, most of the writers and artists of 1880s London. Her Kensington salon was attended by Mathilde Blind and Amy Levy, as well as by Webster herself. Her poetry was often praised for its lyricism, delicacy and charm, terms that contrast significantly with reviewers' more nervous admiration for Webster's tougher qualities.

13 G. Bell and Sons, London 1928, repr. Virago Press, London 1978, p. 96.

from *Blanche Lisle and Other Poems* (1860)

from *Blanche Lisle*

The gold-barred shadows slumber on the grass,
Unstirred by breathing of the languid day,
Seldom and slow the lazy cloudlets pass,
Flecking the blue sky with their silvered grey,
And faintly floating on to fade away.
The noontide hush has come: with closed beak
Sits the small minstrel voiceless on the spray,
Silence, so silent that it seems to speak,
Broods in that strange, weird stillness laughter dares not break.

For there is voice in silence when it rests
Upon the quiet earth like a rapt sleep,
A speechless voice that brings to many breasts
The feeling of a mystic presence deep
With unshaped thoughts, and wordless hopes that keep
No hold save in the shrine of such repose,
When the lulled mind holds all life's turmoils cheap
As myths that pass, how it scarce recks or knows,
But wandering through high dreams to greater stature grows.

Such silence shadows now the lonely glade:
The gossip grasshopper has not a word,
The early morning's whispering wind is laid,
No breath awakes the broad trees ancient-yeared,
On sleeping slopes the light oats droop unstirred,
The sluggish river sweeps unmurmuring by;
The one dull sound that through the hush is heard,
Of tedious booming bees that homeward fly,
But makes the unmarred stillness brood more heavily.

Far back the old red house seems all asleep,
No hum of being stirring through its walls,
It frowns like some enchanted ancient keep
Where drowsiness on whoso enters falls,
And with the might of sloth its captives thralls;
Two cedar giants, glooming at each side,
Throw dull dark shadows on the dull dark walls;
In front the sombre ilex branches wide,
And massive, mournful yews the light of heaven hide.

She gazes at it, resting in the shade
Of a wide-branching many-belted oak –
Its huge-zoned trunk with thick green moss enlaid –
Tracing the coilings of the slow blue smoke
With dreamy wistful eye of discontent,
Such as the vague complaint may best express
Of a young spirit in its yearnings pent,
Too curbed for joy, too care-free for distress,
Wearied of all things, most of its own weariness.

Thus wearied gazed she on the silent hall,
Wherein the heavy months like years crept by
Ever unchanged, each listless day like all;
So had she grown to youth from infancy,
No other thing of youth or brightness nigh,
Her guides the spinster aunt demure and sage,
Counting her knitting with a time-dimmed eye,
And the sick uncle querulous with age,
Studious of pedigrees and dull heraldic page.

And cloistered thus she grew to girlhood's grace
Mid calm home joys, yet, as her soul outspread,
She tired of the old legends of her race,
Tired of a life that seemed spent with the dead,
Looked into coming time with a vague dread
That all her morrows should be yesterdays,
Each morrow, like the long day that had fled,
Waking and dying in the selfsame ways,
Like long-repeated melody's too tedious phrase.

The Foolish Weaver

I wove myself a golden web,
    And oh! it shone so bright and fair
That I went weaving fearless on,
    Although my heart lay in its snare.

Still weaving on until my life
    Had light alone from its rich sheen,
And all things else, unseen for me,
    Became as though they had not been.

Still weaving, until grief and care
        Seemed but the myths of legends old,
And what had I to do with them! –
        So wove I still my web of gold.

Ah! what has touched the golden links,
        That they have grown an iron chain?
Oh! cruel fetters round my heart!
        Oh God! I faint beneath the pain.

Woe! for 'twas sorrow's death-cold hand,
        And I am hers for evermore –
Woe! for my life has scarce begun,
        And the youth of my soul is o'er.

Woe! for the golden web I wove
        Dull death alone can burst apart;
Woe! for the rust of iron links
        Eats deep into my aching heart.

Ah! how, poor weaver, should I speak,
        How dare I speak to comfort thee!
The knotted web thyself hast wrought
        Will not unravelled be by me.

I can but marvel at its strength,
        I can but sorrow at thy pain,
And I will weave no golden web,
        So shall I know no deathful chain.

from *Dramatic Studies* (1866)

from *Sister Annunciata*

I   An Anniversary

My wedding day! A simple happy wife,
Stolen from her husband's sight a little while
To think how much she loved him, might so kneel
Alone with God and love a little while
(For if the Church bless love, is love a sin?),
And, coming back into the happy stir
Of children keeping the home festival,

Might bring the Heaven's quiet in her heart;
Yes, even coming to him, coaxing him
With the free hand that wears his fetter on it,
Sunning her boldly in his look of love,
And facing him with unabashed fond eyes
Might, being all her husband's, still be God's
And know it — happy with no less a faith
Than we who, ever serving at His shrine,
Know ourselves His alone.
        Am I sinning now
To think it? Nay, no doubt I went too far:
The bride of Christ is more than other women;
I must not dare to even such to me.
They have their happiness, I mine; but mine
Is it not of Heaven heavenly, theirs of earth,
And therefore tainted with earth's curse of sin?
Did Mary envy Martha? Oh my Lord
Forgive thy handmaid if her spirit lone,
A little lone because the clog of flesh
That sunders it from Thee still burdens it
With the poor human want of human love,
Hungry a moment and by weakness snared,
Has dared, with the holy manna feast in reach,
To think on Egypt's fleshpots and not loathe.
Oh! Virgin Mother, pray thou for thy child,
That I who have escaped the dangerous world,
Rising above it on thy altar steps,
May feel the heavens round me lifting me,
Lifting me higher, higher, day by day,
Until the glory blinds me, and my ears
Hear only Heaven's voices, and my thoughts
Have passed into one blending with His will,
And earth's dulled memories seem nothingness!
        Ah me! poor soul, even here 'tis a hard fight
With the wiles of Satan! Was the Abbess wise
To set me, in the night too when one most
Is tempted to let loose forbidden dreams
And float with them back to the far-off life
Of foolish old delights — yes, was she wise
To set me in the night-hush such a watch,
Wherein 'to think upon my ancient life
With all its sins and follies, and prepare
To keep my festival for that good day

That wedded me out of the world to Christ?'
She has forgotten doubtless, 'tis so long
Since she came here, how, trying to recall
Girl sins and follies, some things of the past
Might be recalled too tenderly, and so
The poisonous sad sweet sin of looking back
Steal on one unawares.

★★★★★

   Ah! I remember me
In the first days – when I was sad and restless
And seemed an alien in a hopeless world,
All form and pious parrot-talk, a home
For stunting dull despair shut from the sun,
A nursery to bloat the sick self in
To a misshapen God to feed whose fires
The loves and hopes and faiths, the very life
Of the young heart must perish, and I knew
For the best future nothing but a blank,
For then the present bitterness of death,
The horrible death in life – my first belief
In any comfort earlier than the grave's
Came from a touch of tenderness in her,
Only a tone, a look as she passed by
Where I was sitting by the broken well,
Looking at the green growth that overslimed
The never heaven waters, thinking 'this,
The image of the thing my life becomes,
Unlighted, unlightgiving, ignorant
Of sunflash and of shadow, with the slime
Of utter foul stagnation hiding heaven
As surely as its narrow walls fair earth,
And under all, chill, chill!' 'God bless you daughter,'
She said; her usual greeting, but it came
With the kind of sound one likes to dwell upon –
A little trivial phrase in the right tone
Makes music for so long. 'God bless you daughter'
As if she meant it – and there was the touch
Of a mere womanly pity in her eyes.
So her blessing loosed the bands about my heart,
And the passion of tears broke out.
   'Twas the first time

Since the night before they brought me to my vows
In a passive dream; I think because since then
I had been hopeless, and it must have been
That the feeling of a human tenderness
Still folding me, made something like a hope,
Feeding my withering heart like water drops
Given the poor plant brought from the fresh free air
And natural dewings of the skyward soil,
Where its wild growth took bent at the wind's will,
To learn indoors an artificial bloom
Or die. Before it had been too near death
For weeping – and the comfort of those tears!
I almost wish that I could weep so now!
      No, no, I take again my wish, which was a sin;
It was no wish, a fancy at the most;
Lord, let it not be numbered with my sins!
      What mere mad sin against the spirit, that,
If I could wish to lose my hard-won state
Of holy peace. And wherefore should I weep?
For what endurance? I who have inhaled
The rich beatitude of my spousalship,
To the heart's core.
      But *then* I only saw
The human side, knew but the present loss
Of the outer bloom of life, and did not know
That, stripped of the flower-wings, the fruit grew on,
Yea, and to ripe to immortality,
In this sure shelter. Or I knew it, say,
As I know that bye and bye, when I am dead,
I shall be sunned in the grave on summer days,
While, if one now were standing in the frosts,
The chariest winter beam were something, all;
And what such summers waiting for the time
Of silence and of change? A sorry mocking
Of hungering hope with bitter dead sea fruit.
      She preached to me, good woman, when she turned,
Catching the breath of my outswelling grief,
And, with the softened smile some mothers rest
Upon their children, came to me quietly,
And sat beside me there. No doubt she ran
Her whole small simple round of eloquence;
I have heard it all since then, I think; but then
I did not hear – a murmur in my ears

That hummed on, soothing, like a lullaby.
And through it I perceived some scraps of texts,
And godly phrases, and examples drawn
From the lives of the saints, and wise encouragements;
And I wept on. But the warm touch of her hands
Nursing my right hand in them motherly,
And the feeling of her kindly neighbourhood,
These spoke a language that I understood
And thrilled to in my desolate mood. Through them
That heavy sense of prison loneliness,
Whether I moved alone or companied,
Was lifted from my heart, broken away
In the rushing of my tears; and even from then,
Wherefore I know not, I was moved to grope
Up from the dark towards the light of Heaven.
        But ah the long ascent! It was enough
At first to learn the patience that subdued
My throbbing heart to its new quiet rule,
The hope of Heaven that bore down earth's despair –
But these were comfort, and the craving grew
As natural for them as the sick man's
For the pain-soothing draught he learned perforce
To school his palate to. But then the effort
To be another self, to know no more
The fine-linked dreams of youth, the flying thoughts
Like sparkles on the wave-tops changing place
And all one scattered brightness, the high schemes
And glorious wild endeavours after good,
Fond, bubble-soaring, but how beautiful!
The sweet unreal reveries, the gush
Of voiceless songs deep in the swelling heart,
The dear delight of happy girlish hopes –
Of, ah my folly! some hopes too strange sweet
That I dare think of them even to rebuke –
Ah not to be forgotten though they lie
Too deep for even memory. Alas!
Even if I would, how could I now recall
To their long-faded forms those phantasies
Of a far, other, consciousness which now
Beneath the ashes of their former selves
Lie a dead part of me, but still a part,
Oh evermore a part.

★★★★★

Nay, it must not be.
Oh once my own beloved, now a mere name,
A name of something that one day was dear,
In an old world, to one who is no more,
Vex me no more with idle communings –
Love me, love her, what matters it to me?
I stand as far apart as angels are
From earthly passion – not by my own strength,
But by the grace shewn in me, and the bar
Of my divine espousal. Stand far off
Even in thought.
      Yes, though this was thy word,
That long fond evening when we stole apart
Out of the music and the talking, when
We stood below the orange-boughs abloom,
And the sweet night was silent, and the waves
Were rocking softly underneath the moon,
Asleep in the white calm, and we, alone,
Were whispering all our hearts each into each:
'Eva, my Eva, darling of my life,
If they should part us still you are my all.
I will not love the other. She might bear
My name, gild with the purchase money for it
Our houses' tarnished splendours, rear the heirs
Of its new greatness – you, you, only you,
In your cold prison, would be wife to me,
Wife of my soul. Are we not one, love, so?
They could not beat down that; and I would live
In a secret world with you, so that in Heaven
I could claim you boldly, "This was my own wife"
And all the angels know it true.'
      Ah me!
How long that wild rapt promise hindered me
In my first struggles for the Saints' cold peace,
Because he spoke it in a certain tone –
Sometimes he used it – that had a strange power
To thrill me with strange pleasure through and through
And leave long after echoes still possessed
Of something more than most tones, even his,
And easier to recall at will; and these
Remained with me; I could not quite forego
      Their dangerous sweetness.

★★★★★

Oh, only love, I never broke my truth
By questionings of yours, and you, I know,
Had in me that blind trust that was my right –
And yet we are apart. Oh! it is hard!
Has God condemned all love except of Him?
Will He have only market marriages
Or sprung from passion fancies soon worn out,
Lest any two on earth should partly miss
The anger and distrust that haunt earth's homes
And cease to know there is no calm till death?
     None for who lives the outside waking life:
We are calm here, calm enough. Oh Angelo
Why am I here in the ceaseless formal calm
That makes the soul swell to one bursting self
And seem the whole great universe, the while
It only sees itself, learns of itself,
Hopes for itself, feeds, preys upon itself
And not one call comes to it from without
'Think of me too, a little live for me,
Take me with thee in growing nearer God'?
Why am I –?
     Am I mad? Am I mad? I rave
Some blasphemy which is not of myself!
What is it? Was there a demon here just now
By me, within me? Those were not my thoughts
Which just were thought or spoken – which was it?
Oh not my thoughts, not mine! All saints of heaven
Be for me, answer for me; I am yours,
I am your Master's, how can I be Satan's?
I have not lost my soul by the wild words.
Not yet, not yet.
     Oh this was what I feared.
The night-watch is a long one and I flag,
My head is hot, I feel the fever fire
Of weariness before the languor comes.
I am left prey to Satan's snares for those
Who too much live again the former life
In the dangerous times of unwatched loneliness.
He lurks in those retrodden paths, he makes
His snaky coils of all these memories,
Clogging them round my spirit. Is the work
Of long long months, of years, undone in a night?
     Alas! the ordeal is too hard for me.

I am shut out in the dark! where is the oil
To feed the virgin's lamp? What! are these tears
Only of water? They should be of blood
Fitter to weep my sin in.

★★★★★

My uncle's words, denouncing, terrible,
Made my soul's bitter portion once. But now
That dread is past. I was not guilty thus.
I know it, in my inmost heart I know it.
Good Father Andrea – you who, with your gift
Of patient comforting, first lighted me,
From that dim horror – you whose pastoral hand
Came, while I seemed to wait and care no more,
Lone on the dead sea of despondency,
And the chill waters lapping round their prey
Bore me indifferent to the shores of Hell,
Came heaven-blessed and stayed me – I know now
With fuller certainty than you could give,
By God's own comforting I think. I look
Clear-eyed upon *that* past. The fault was theirs
Who thought it wise to rate as purposes
The fanciful longings of an almost child
Let fall at fluent moments, wise to call
Her natural yearnings for some scope beyond
The round of foolish struttings petty forms,
And petty prides and petty policies
Vocation for a ministry to Heaven.
What knew I of vocation? I was galled
By the bird-snare fetters round me, longed to fly
On wild young wings towards the freer Heaven;
And, seeing, that the cage hung on the tree
Was higher than the nest upon the ground,
Said sometimes 'Yet at least if I were there',
Because I so might reach a purer sky
And breathe untainted air; but most of all
Because I longed to soar.
        An almost child:
Ah yes, how young I was until my love
Awaked me woman. What had I perceived
Of the world's earnest? I could lose myself
In the high rhapsodies of eager youth,

Flame at the wrongs and weakness of the times,
And shudder at the sin; could dream the while
Of heroisms I no more understood
In their plain natures than those names of evils
I hurled my angers at; could hope and plan
Impossible better things and, imaging
A present Paradise of the whole world
If men would only think a few new thoughts,
Talk reasoning unreason, fiery-tongued,
On its blurred good and bad. But what knew I
Of its bad or of its good? My reasonings,
Silent or spoken in unguarded bursts,
What were they but a fluent ignorance
Nursed upon dreams?
              They said, 'She is early ripe:
Fifteen, and yet she judges of the world
As one who has all things tried and found them vain
In a grave experience: 'tis a happy thing
That she accepts the convent: we are borne clear:
She accepts it freely, being mature to choose.'
And the deep world I thought I weighed and spurned
As wanting in the balance, nevertheless
Had shown me nothing of its meaning yet:
And I had not seen its brightness, had not known
What pleasure meant, when saying 'It is naught',
Nor happiness, when saying 'Heaven's is all';
And had not known the triumphs of sweet praise
On the general tongue and ringing to the ears
Of one dear over all, and had not known
The gladness of dear hope, and had not known,
Had not conceived, what love was, love-sought love,
When saying 'Life is weary every day
And the wide world is barren to the heart.'
They were too prompt to take my girlish fits
Of dream enthusiasm for the dream I made
Of an ideal perfectness withdrawn
From reach of sin and sorrow in the hush
Of convent calm, and turn them to their will.
The fault was theirs. But I, knowing my God
Hears me and judges, say I never framed
A set intention, spoke one purposed word
Pledging me to the life I ranked so high.

★★★★★

What was I pondering
Before this drowsy languor stole my will?
Let me remember.
Yes the sins and follies
Of my vain youth. But I had almost done –
Or had I? Where was I in the blurred page
Whose half-forgotten fragment-facts from days
That were no more all faults than all good deeds
I am bidden read in the dusk that time has made?
Ah me! how to bethink me? When there grows
The counterfeit of some large landscape known
In past familiar days upon that sense
Which seems an inward memory of the eye –
Grows, at the plainest even, half as if
One looked upon it with the former sight –
If one were bidden break the vivid whole
Into its several parts traced point by point,
Or more, if one were bidden duly note
The rocks that broke the smoothness of the lake,
Or the black fissures on the great snow-hills,
Or say the pools along the marshy wastes,
How the thought-picture would become perplexed
Into a shifting puzzle, and the sight
Would ache that vainly tried to scan by units.
Even so it seems to me when I essay
To singly look upon the marring flaws
That foiled my youth's best virtues, or on those
That of its evil made the blackest scars.
Weary, so weary of the effort! Nay
I *will* remember! Well, my girlish days
Were full of faults – were doubtless full of faults –
Were full of faults: but what were the faults' names?
I am forgetting what I seek – their names?
Why there was many a paltry selfishness –
Many no doubt, for I was often shamed
To be so much below the self I dreamed –
Only I cannot call them singly back.
And there were pettish quarrels, girlish-wise,
With one or other of the rest at home,
Oftenest with Leonora, though, I think,
We chose each other most, and she has kept
My memory dearest of them; she alone
Remembers my old name-day, comes to me,

As if it still were festival to me,
With flowers, and calls me Eva.
                    Does she guess,
I wonder, that I could have stolen her greatness?
Poor Leonora, would she have lost much?
Wife's sister to the prince instead of wife;
That dowry he designed her for amends,
To make her welcome to some simpler home –
Perhaps with love with it, such as *we* hoped
When we were lovers – yes, perhaps with some one
Who could have taught her smiles: she only laughs.
I would I knew her happy now! She says
She is most happy: but she says she knows
Nothing worth sorrow.
                    Nothing! Nothing worth
The weeping out one's life for! Nothing worth
The wearying after in a waking dream
Of all one's days, the straining to one's heart
As a mother her one child, her one dead child,
Although a plague had stricken it and the end
Were her own dying! Nothing worth a sorrow
Dearer than any future joy could be,
Stronger than love, oh! longer lived than love,
Than love itself, a sorrow to be lived for
Liked love itself, to be one's closest life!
If only one were free to sorrow thus!
Oh to be left my sorrow for a while,
Only a little while! to weep at will!
Oh let me weep a while if but for shame
Because I cannot check the foolish passion,
Because I weep despite myself. Alas!
Oh Lord my helper, when shall I find rest?

By the Looking-Glass

Alone at last in my room –
How sick I grow of the glitter and din,
Of the lips that smile and the voices that prate
To a ballroom tune for the fashion's sake:
Light and laughters without, but what within?
Are these like me? Do the pleasure and state

Weary them under the seeming they make?–
But I see all through my gloom.

For why should a light young heart
Not leap to a merry moving air,
Not laugh with the joy of the flying hour
And feed upon pleasure just for a while?
But the right of a woman is being fair,
And her heart must starve if she miss that dower,
For how should she purchase the look and the smile?
And I have not had my part.

A girl, and so plain a face!
Once more, as I learn by heart every line
In the pitiless mirror, night by night,
Let me try to think it is not my own.
Come, stranger with features something like mine,
Let me place close by you the tell-tale light;
Can I find in you now some charm unknown,
Only one softening grace?

Alas! it is I, I, I,
Ungainly, common. The other night
I heard one say 'Why, she is not so plain.
See, the mouth is shapely, the nose not ill.'
If I could but believe his judgement right!
But I try to dupe my eyesight in vain,
For I, who have partly a painter's skill,
I cannot put knowledge by.

He had not fed, as I feed
On beauty, till beauty itself must seem
Me, my own, a part and essence of me,
My right and my being – Why! how am I plain?
I feel as if this were almost a dream
From which I should waken, as it might be,
And open my eyes on beauty again
And know it myself indeed.

Oh idle! Oh folly! Look,
There, looking back from the glass, is my fate,
A clumsy creature smelling of earth,
What fancy could lend her the angel's wings?

OUT OF MY BORROWED BOOKS

She looks like a boorish peasant's fit mate.
Why! what a mock at the pride of birth,
Fashioned by nature for menial things,
With her name in the red-bound book.

Oh! to forget me a while,
Feeling myself but as one in the throng,
Losing myself in the joy of my youth!
Then surely some pleasure might lie in my reach.
But the sense of myself is ever strong,
And I read in all eyes the bitter truth,
And fancy scorning in every speech
And mocking in every smile.

Ah! yes, it was so tonight,
And I moved so heavily through the dance,
And answered uncouthly like one ill taught,
And knew that ungentleness seemed on my brow,
While it was but pain at each meeting glance,
For I knew that all who looked at me thought
'How ugly she is! One sees it more now
With the other young faces so bright.'

I might be more like the rest,
Like those that laugh with a girlish grace
And make bright nothings an eloquence;
I might seem gentler and softer souled;
But I needs must shape myself to my place,
Softness in me would seem clumsy pretence,
Would they not deem my laughters bold?
I hide in myself as is best.

Do I grow bitter sometimes?
They say it, ah me! and I fear it is true,
And I shrink from that curse of bitterness,
And I pray on my knees that it may not come;
But how should I envy – they say that I do –
All the love which others' young lives may bless?
Because *my* age will be lone in its home
Do I weep at the wedding chimes?

Ah no, for they judge me ill,
Judging me doubtless by that which I look,

Do I not joy for another's delight?
Do I not grieve for another's regret?
And I have been true where others forsook
And kind where others bore hatred and spite,
For there I could think myself welcome – and yet
My care is unpitied still.

Yes, who can think it such pain
Not to be fair 'Such a trifling thing'.
And 'Goodness may be where beauty is not'
And 'How weak to sorrow for outward show!'
Ah! if they knew what a poisonful sting
Has this sense of shame, how a woman's lot
Is darkened throughout! – Oh yes I know
How weak – but I know in vain,

    I hoped in vain, for I thought,
When first I grew to a woman's days,
Woman enough to feel what it means
To be a woman and not be fair,
That I need not sigh for the voice of praise
And the beauty's triumph in courtly scenes
Where she queens with her maiden – royal air
Ah! and so worshipped and sought.

But I, oh my dreaming! deemed
With a woman's yearning and faith in love,
With a woman's faith in her lovingness,
That that joy might brighten on me, even me,
For which all the force of my nature strove,
Joy of daily smiles and voices that bless,
And one deeper other love it might be –
Hush, *that* was wrong to have dreamed.

I thank God, I have not loved,
Loved as one says it whose life has gone out
Into another's for evermore,
Loved as I know what love might be
Writhing but living through poison of doubt,
Drinking the gall of the sweetness before,
Drinking strange deep strength from the bitter lee –
Love, love in a falsehood proved!

              OUT OF MY BORROWED BOOKS

Loving him on to the end,
Through the weary weeping hours of the night,
Through the wearier laughing hours of the day;
Knowing him less than the love I gave,
But this one fond dream left my life for its light
To do him some service and pass away;
Not daring, for sin, to think of the grave
Lest it seemed the only friend.

Thank God that it was not so,
And I have my scatheless maidenly pride,
But it might have been – for did he not speak
With that slow sweet cadence that seemed made deep
By a meaning – Hush! he has chosen his bride.
Oh! happy smile on her lips and her cheek,
My darling! And I have no cause to weep,
I have not bowed me so low.

But would he have wooed in vain?
Would not my heart have leaped to his will,
If he had not changed? – How, *changed* do I say?
Was I not mocked with an idle thought,
Dreaming and dreaming so foolishly still?
By the sweet glad smile and the winning way
And the grace of beauty alone is love bought.
He woo me! Am I not plain?

But yet I was not alone
To fancy I might be something to him.
They thought it, I know, though it seems so wild
Now, in this bitterer Now's hard light.
Vain that I was! could his sight grow dim?
How could he love me? But she, when she smiled
Once, the first once, by her beauty's right
Had made all his soul her own.

It is well that no busy tongue
Has vexed her heart with those bygone tales.
But I think he fears he did me some wrong,
I see him watch me at times, and his cheek
Crimsons a little, a little pales,
If his eye meets mine for a moment long.
But he need not fear, I am not so weak
Though I *am* a woman and young.

I had not grown to my love,
Though it might have been. And I give no blame:
Nothing was spoken to bind him to me,
Nothing had been that could make him think
My heart beat stronger and fast when he came,
And if he *had* loved me, was he not free,
When the fancy passed, to loose that vague link
That only such fancy wove?

No he has done no such ill
But that I can bear it, nor shame in my heart
To call him my brother and see her his,
The one little pearl that gleams through our gloom:
He has no dishonour to bar them apart.
I loving her so, am rested in this;
Else I would speak though I spoke her doom,
Though grief had the power to kill.

When she came a while ago,
My young fair sister bright with her bloom,
Back to a home which is little glad,
I thought 'Here is one who should know no care,
A little wild bird flown into a room
From its far free woods; will she droop and grow sad?
But, here even, love smiles upon one so fair.
And I too might feel that glow.'

But now she will fly away!
Ah me! And I love her so deep in my heart
And worship her beauty as he might do.
If I could but have kept her a little time!
Ah she will go! So the sunbeams depart
That brightened the winter's sky into blue,
And the dews of the chill dusk freeze into rime,
And cold cold mists hang grey.

I think she loved me till now –
Nay doubtless she loves me quietly yet,
But his lightest fancy is more, far more,
To her than all the love that I live.
But I cannot blame (as if love were a debt)
That, though I love, he is held far before;
And is it not well that a bride should give
All, all her heart with her vow?

But ah, if I smiled more sweet
And spoke more soft as one fairer could,
Had not love indeed been more surely mine?
Folly to say that a woman's grace
Is only strong o'er a man's light mood!
Even the hearts of the nearest incline
With a gentler thought to the lovely face,
And the winning eyes that entreat.

But I – yes flicker pale light,
Fade into darkness and hide it away,
The poor dull face that looks out from the glass,
Oh wearily wearily back to me!
Yes, I will sleep, for my wild thoughts stray
Weakly, selfishly – yes let them pass,
Let self and this sadness of self leave me free,
Lost in the peace of the night.

from *A Woman Sold and Other Poems* (1867)

from *A Woman Sold*

I   Eleanor Vaughan

LIONEL   Then it is true!

ELEANOR   Oh Lionel, you look
So strangely at me. Think, I all alone,
So many reasons, all my friends so fain,
My mother pressing me, Sir Joyce so good,
So full of promises, he who could choose
No bride among the highest ladies round
But she would smile elate and all her kin
Bow low and thank him and go swelled with pride –
You cannot wonder that my friends declare
They'll hear no noes, but force me to my good.

LIONEL   No, 'tis at you I wonder. Eleanor,
When first I heard this lie – I called it so
In anger for you, I will call it so,
Though your lips contradict me, till the last
Worst proof have sworn it other, 'tis so strange,

So recklessly untrue to that pure self
Of my love Eleanor – when first I heard
That lie on you, as if you, a young thing
In the bud of stainless girlhood, you the like
Of babies in your fond grave innocence,
You proud as maidens are who do not know
What sin and weariness is like in lives
Smirched by the pitch that seethes, they've told you, far
From your balm-scenting nostrils, but perceive
Yourselves are as the high accessless snows
Whose blushings do but prove their perfect white,
And so look coldly down on something base,
You know not what, beneath you – you whose smiles
Are gladder than most laughters, and whose voice
Rings like the wild birds' singing in the wood,
Because you are so young and new in heart,
You who to me –
                    But say, to put the least,
You, the Miss Vaughan we men agree to think
Worth anyhow such common reverence
As good girls like our sisters have from us –
That you were bought like any lower thing
Our Croesus fancies, like the horse that won
The Derby last, the picture of the year,
The best bred pointer, or the costliest ring;
You bought by such a buyer, a cold fool
Whose very vices, like his polished airs,
His tastes and small-talk, were acquired by dint
Of callous perseverance; one who'll own,
With a feigned yawn, he's something bored with life,
Meaning by life stale sins and selfishness;
A dried up pithless soul, who, having lacked
The grace to have a youngness in his youth,
Now lacks the courage to be old – You bought
For laces, diamonds, a conspicuous seat
In country ballrooms, footmen, carriages,
A house in town and so on – and no doubt
Most liberal settlements, that is but just.
A man past youth and practised out of tune
For loving should not haggle at the price
When he buys girlhood, blushes, sentiment,
Grace, innocence, aye even piety
And taste in decking churches, such fawn eyes

As yours are, Eleanor, and such a bloom
Of an unfingered peach just newly ripe.
Aye, when a modest woman sells herself
Like an immodest one, she should not find
A niggard at the cheque book.
              Eleanor,
Can I not *taunt* you even to a no?
Look up; defend yourself. Oh! you sit there
Languid and still, and grow a little pale,
And flush a little, and will not reply
Even by a look. Be angry with me, child,
Cry out that I misjudge you to my shame;
Say I, like a rough lawyer, questioned you
Into a maze, and twisted me a yes
Out of your shifting coil of noes, while you
Were dimly pondering what I asked. Speak, speak;
Say anything, but do not let me break
My passion on you while you droop and give
Like a rock-rooted seaweed in the surf.
Say anything, except that I do well
To speak to you as I have spoken now.

ELEANOR   Ah well! you do no ill that I can chide.
I, who have gladly let you give me praise
Far past my merit in the foolish time
When I believed I could grow like your praise
Must bear in patience now if you give blame
Perhaps a little harder than you know.

LIONEL   So humble, Eleanor! How you are changed –
What is it? Are you ill? You were so proud.

ELEANOR   Yes, that was long ago before I knew
I could be *tempted* even to do wrong.
You know my boast was that I never broke
The lightest merry promise. Long ago
I could be proud.

LIONEL   Be proud again, my love,
My Eleanor! I know you are yourself
When you speak so. Be proud again, too proud
Not to atone. Stay, shall I tell you, dear,
How I received the tidings that Miss Vaughan

Was pricked for Lady Boycott? Why, I laughed,
Laughed, Eleanor, as any schoolboy might
Who heard his awful doctor had been caught
Picking a small boy's pocket for his pence.
It was not long ago. Young Polwarth came
To town, dined with me at our club, and there
Tossed out his precious news quite innocent
Of where it touched. 'Miss Vaughan!' I laughed, 'The joke
Is too far-fetched. You do not know her well.'
Till he, abashed, recanted, 'Well, no doubt
The rumour is not true; but so it runs.'
And later that same evening Pringle came,
And he – I think he knew he stung me – yes
He'd guessed why his sweet speeches forced a clash
Of discord in your ears, where other words
Were making your love music – he was loud
With the same story. 'Aye,' he said, 'she's wise,
That coy Miss Eleanor, she knows her worth.
All very well to lure on you or me
With her odd ways, half peacock and half dove,
Strutting and cooing – but, for marriage, why
We come to business then. She's a shrewd girl.'
And *he* would not recant: he'd swear 'twas true.
But I said, 'You'd not play fool's trumpeter
To the idiot gossips who invent such trash:
No surely: you and I both know her well.'
And, Eleanor, even now I say to you,
It is not true – I know it who know you.

ELEANOR   Yes, long ago you knew me, but not now.

LIONEL   And when was long ago? A second time
You talk of long ago. Not three months past
Since we last parted, and I took your word
Of sorrow-sweet good bye away with me
To be my sweetest memory, and thought,
'I shall succeed because she loves me so,'
And turned me to my crabbed toil, as if
It had been some romance of a true love
That thrills the reader through – some rare romance
With your name in it, Eleanor, and mine,
And a glad end. You call this long ago,
And I still live in it, live in the life

Your love – the dream of your love was it? – gave.
What long ago? Not all a year by days
Has passed since first a sudden moment broke
My silence – ours. You looked me a reproach,
Not knowing how you looked, how pleadingly,
For a light word I spoke – as a man speaks
Who plays with his own heart and pricks at it
To prove because he laughs it does not feel –
A jest as if I thought gay scorn of love
And prized a woman as we prize a rose,
Meaning all roses and the one in hand,
All liked with just a difference for taste
In perfumes and in tints. You looked at me:
And I at you. How could I help it, child?
I had remembered on for weeks and months
That I was a poor man and should not speak,
But I forgot it just a moment long,
Because you had forgotten, and my eyes,
Hungry for one love look, met yours so full
That you grew red and trembled, and I knew
In a quick impulse that you were my own,
And that I had no life which was not you.
And I said, breathless – what, I do not know,
But something that meant 'love me', and you raised
Your quivering face with a strange radiance on it
Of tenderness and promise and grave joy,
And looked into my eyes, and said no word,
But laid your hand in mine. And then you wept
Because – 'twas you that said it, Eleanor –
Because you were so happy. And I drew
Your head against my breast, and whispered 'wife',
And you – oh sweet and simply loving girl
And natural – you put your lips to mine
And kissed me. Oh! my wife that was to be,
My Eleanor, was that day long ago,
That day which always is my yesterday?

ELEANOR   No, no, you must not talk to me of that,
You must not. There are things one must forget –
One should at least. But ah! it is so hard.
One must be happier than I can be
To be able to forget past happiness.
But, Lionel, what you call yesterday

Seems to me parted from my present self
By a whole other life lived in the dark,
I know not when. Ah! surely yesterday
Is long ago when all its hopes are dead,
And Eleanor is dead who lived in it
And loved you – oh *did* love you. Do not think
I am all heartless. I *did* love you more
Than you will know now ever.
       Let me go,
Let go my hand – not now – oh! Lionel,
We are not each other's now.

LIONEL   *Did* love me, *did*?
Is *that* a long ago too? My own love
You love me now. Yes love me. Look at me.
You'll keep your faith. You dare not say again
We are not each other's now.

ELEANOR   You hold my hand;
Look what you hold with it – it hurts me now
In your tight gasp, and it has hurt ere now
With another kind of pain. But bye and bye
I shall grow used to it. It means, you know,
My fetter to the hus – to him, Sir Joyce,
Who will be soon – I suppose I am his now,
Marked by his ring.

LIONEL   There, take your hand again.
It *is* his for the moment. It was mine
By a less unholy bargain. Answer me,
Do you love your happy lover, Eleanor Vaughan?

ELEANOR   He is kind. A good wife always gives her love
To a kind husband.

★★★★★

II Lady Boycott

LADY BOYCOTT   Mary, you need not play now at belief
That the happiness of wifely love was mine –
Such love as we believed in when we talked
In our dear wont here, oh! so long ago,

In such soft dusk as this, of what should be
And what should not to make up that pure good
Of loving and of being loved again.
Mary, you know I never loved Sir Joyce.

MARY   Oh Eleanor! I feared it. But indeed
I think you should not say it — even now.

LADY B.   Oh let me say it, friend, sweet secret friend,
Who will not babble it to the four winds
To have them blow it through the neighbours' homes.
Let me speak but to you, I who have smiled
A cheating silence for so many years.
You do not know the penance to be good
And pretty-mannered dull day by dull day,
Lapping one's heart in comfortable sloth
Lest it should fever for its work, its food
Of free bold loving. No, you cannot dream
How one may suffer just by doing right
When in one's heart one knows how under right,
For base of it, there lies a stifled wrong
Which is not dead. Ah me! wrong never dies.
You lay it underground, you tread your path
Smoothly above it, then you build new hopes,
New duties, new delights, upon its grave —
It stirs and breaks up all. And, worse than this,
Mary, you cannot kill old happiness —
No not except by heaping new upon it —
And you remember in your heavy heart
The sweetness of delicious unwise days
Left with your young girl follies — with your doll,
Your poetry, your dreamings, and your love;
Irrational light pastimes.

MARY   Hush, oh! hush.
I never like you in your flouting moods.
You shall not scorn yourself so. Weep, dear, weep,
If you are sad, and bid me comfort you,
But let be with that jarring heartlessness.
'Tis bitter acting, dear, when grief puts on
A show of laughters and makes mirth by scoffs.

LADY B.   Aye, you were right to hush me. Let me have

The ease of free complaining. There's no fault
If I look dull-eyed now, no secret told.
'Tis only loveless wives who must not fret,
For fear of being understood – indeed
For fear of understanding their own selves.
But I, alas! there has a new thing chanced,
And forced myself upon me. I have burst
My serious due disguise of widowhood.
I am bold now with my sorrow. Why indeed
Should I talk shadows to myself or you
Who know the shape of truth behind them? Yes,
You read my secret, Mary, years ago:
You, with your show of taking me at what
I should have been, an easy-minded wife
Who loved her lord in quiet and was pleased
To have her comforts with him... or without;
You, with your silent tenderness, your talk
Of making duty dear by loving it
For God's sake, if not man's – you knew the while,
I saw it, you kind prudent hypocrite,
That I was wearier than the worn drudge
Who toils past woman's strength the hard day through
And cowers at evening to the drunken boor
Who strikes her with a curse because she's his
And that's his right upon her – wearier
Because my labour was to love against
The longings and the loathings of my heart,
Because the price I earned was only smiles
And too familiar fondlings. Ah! he had
His rights upon me. And he meant me well.
He was not often hard to me; he gave
With an unstinting hand for all my whims,
And tricked me with the costliest fineries
Almost beyond my wish; was proud of me
And liked to look at me, and vaunted me,
My beauty and my grace and stateliness,
My taste and fashion. What could he do more?
We were not suited; some more fitting wife –
Say one who could have loved him, for that makes
The only fitness – one whom years or care
Had brought a little nearer to his age,
Enough to crave no more than was in him
Of sympathies and high ideal hopes;

One who had never loved, or could forget
How the young love, and could bestow on him
A fond contented kindness for the sake
Of his meant kindness to her; such a wife
Might have enjoyed in him a better calm
Of meet companionship than I could find,
Might have shared with him little daily thoughts
And answered when he talked and not felt dull,
Nor missed – you do not know him I *did* love;
You do not know all that there was to miss.
I cannot make you feel that for me. Well,
As for Sir Joyce, doubtless if he had used
A cruel tongue against me, cruel smiles
And frowns, or cruel hands, I must have been
Only more wretched; though I'd wildly think
Often and often I could draw free breath
Rather beneath a bad harsh tyranny,
Coming from him, than kindness and his smile
And condescending husbandly caress.
He made me feel so abject and so false
When he approved me so! Why, I have longed
To shriek 'No, hate me, I am false to you',
And have him think me fouler than my fault.
And yet I dreamed, not loving him, I loved
No other then. I thought my heart at least
Had numbed to an unsinning deadness. Yes,
I did in truth believe I had full learned
The difficult strange lesson to forget,
Because I would not, could not think of *him*.
Because I had no lover, I believed
I had no love.

MARY   Oh! my poor Eleanor,
I stop you once again. You run too wild
In your regrets. I know you had no love,
Except as one may love the dead. You were
A weary woman plodding on alone,
Thinking sometimes 'Alas I might have gone
A fairer way and held a guiding hand
Warm within mine', and sometimes looking back
Too sadly on the old bright time of love,
As in your age you might look back on youth;
But you had no fond passion quick in you

To make a fever in your heart. That pulsed
Too slow and chilly. You were faint because
You had foregone the love on which it lived,
And you knew that. But, dear, you let the love
Go with the lover, mourning for them both.
I could read that much, plainly.

LADY B.   Well, may be
You read it rightly, and I did not dash
My forced cold wifely duty with that blot.
I'll hope it. But there has a new life come
And joined on to the old that was before
My bargain with Sir Joyce, and now it seems
As if there had been scarce a break between –
Only a troubled rest, as when one tries
To wake and cannot, and yet does not sleep.
I cannot count you 'Look, so many days,
Or years, or moments even, I was pure
From present loving.' I feel only this:
There is a man I know whose whisper was
To me all promise of the future days,
All sweetness of the present; and there is
A man who with one cold and civil look
Has broken me, has made me sick of hope
Because he is not in it, made my life
Too flickering to be worth the care it costs;
And they are one, and they are my one love.
Oh! Mary, darling, comfort, comfort me.
Yes, hold me to you, let my head lie so.
Yes, soothe me, love me, darling – Oh my friend
I need another love than yours, *his* love.
I want it, want it.

★★★★★

LADY B.   Yet let me tell you. While my husband lived
In seeming strength I had a creeping fear
Would haunt my conscience like bad memories there,
As if, if he should die, I should perceive
A sense of freedom, and go lighter stepped,
And not be sad at all as I must seem.
But while I nursed him dying that was changed.
I did not feign the tenderness I showed,

Nor wear my care for ornament. I seemed
To love him since he suffered. And I felt
That to *his* best he loved me. So I wept
Because we were to part with such an awe,
And he was scared at dying, *not* because
It seemed the wife's right way. And then, he dead,
The irretrievable strange going hence,
And something too the still dread show of death,
Struck me with such a sadness as made tears
A natural comfort to me, made the calm
Of one who has been grieving hush my life.
And while I still was sad a good kind soul —
If she had but grown dumb as well as deaf!
Came with her cordial chatter. 'So, my dear,
The widow's weeds put by. Well, quite time too:
You've worn them past the fashion for wives now.
I'm glad too; for my nephew's coming soon.
Don't think I did not know that naughty work —
You were too bad. But he could never bear
A word against you. Ah! he's true to you,
Like lovers in old times. You never heard
I think of that bad fever that he had
And raved of you long after you were wed.
Ah he raves now of you another way,
Poor boy. You'll not desert him now again.'
I thought she knew. I had not seen him then
Since he had made me promise, but some months
Before my marriage, to be true to him,
And strong. — Strong! I who was too weak to stand
Against some breaths of anger and the stress
Of long persuasions and the paltry lure
Of being the great lady all ablow
With insolent wealth and fashion. Strong! and I —
Why did he trust me? He should have staid near,
If but to look at me the silent look
That made me feel my purpose confident
Because he trusted.
              Well, to tell my tale:
I played the cheat to him and to Sir Joyce:
Loved one and left him, did not love the other
And married him. But, foolishly enough,
It was the one I left who made complaint
As if I had been worth it. Laugh with me;

How foolish men will be! Aye you hold up
A warning finger. Well, I'll be sedate,
And pity my own sorrows decorously.
He was angry, had some bickering with Sir Joyce,
(They never told me what nor why), and so
They broke acquaintance and we never met.
How could I tell that the good cackler's talk
Was... what it was?

       Alas! for many weeks
It chimed in like rich music when I thought,
Growing sweeter, sweeter, sweeter, day by day,
As never surely the good woman's words
Were heard in any ears before. I framed
My hopes, my fancies, purposes, to them,
And, since the time seemed long till he should come,
Spent my full heart in daydreams.

       Did I say,
A while ago, I'd dream here now with you
As we were wont? Ah! Mary, weariness
Can never dream. It sleeps, or is afire
With fever of a visionary toil
Over the trodden way that was so long.
I know no dreamings now.

       Oh, foolish me!
I saw one bar, and only one. I thought.
'He'd never take me with my clog of lands,
Houses, and shares, and so forth, which are mine
Because I was another man's. He's proud,
He will not be beholden to Sir Joyce.'
And so among my dreams I saw the joy
Of sacrificing what I once prized far
Beyond its worth, and still prized something well,
To him, to our new-blossomed love. And then
I fancied how he'd thank me, and forgive,
And praise me as in old days.

       Well, we met.
I woke, at the first moment woke. He smiled,
And I could have shrieked, weeping out aloud,
But I smiled too. And bye and bye I tried
To fool myself a little: but 'twas vain.
We have talked often − always pleasantly,
Appropriately to the occasion too −
And I could hate myself who looked to him

       OUT OF MY BORROWED BOOKS

For more than that. I heard a while ago
That he was new betrothed. I never asked
Was the news true or false. To me 'tis one.
Nothing could make me less to him than now,
Or more. To him I'm – Talk of something else,
Of anything but me. 'Tis your turn now.

Going

The ripples break upon the beach,
  And sway the shadow of the heights;
The long slant beams that shoreward reach
  Are fretted in a thousand lights.

But on the shore the stillness dreams,
  In the blue sky the hill-tops sleep,
And through the haze of golden gleams
  The quiet shadows show more deep.

Oh silent hills! Oh sleeping shore!
  Soon shall I lose you in the grey
Of stealthy evening creeping o'er,
  Of evening darkening o'er the bay.

Oh silent hills! Oh sleeping shore!
  The waning light will come again,
But I shall look on you no more,
  For me morn wakens you in vain.

Sleep on, fair shore and sun-loved hills –
  I seek the land where I was born;
I seek the grey north with its chills;
  I shall not look on you at morn.

from *Portraits* (1870)

Medea in Athens

Dead is he? Yes, our stranger guest said dead –
said it by noonday, when it seemed a thing
most natural and so indifferent
as if the tale ran that a while ago
there died a man I talked with a chance hour
when he by chance was near me. If I spoke
'Good news for us but ill news for the dead
when the gods sweep a villain down to them,'
'twas the prompt trick of words, like a pat phrase
from some one other's song, found on the lips
and used because 'tis there: for through all day
the news seemed neither good nor ill to me.

And now, when day with all its useless talk
and useless smiles and idiots' prying eyes
that impotently peer into one's life,
when day with all its seemly lying shows
has gone its way and left pleased fools to sleep,
while weary mummers, taking off the mask,
discern that face themselves forgot anon
and, sitting in the lap of sheltering night,
learn their own secrets from her – even now
does it seem either good or ill to me?
No, but mere strange.

      And this most strange of all
that I care nothing.

      Nay, how wild thought grows.
Meseems one came and told of Jason's death:
but 'twas a dream. Else should I, wondering thus,
reck not of him, nor with the virulent hate
that should be mine against mine enemy,
nor with that weakness which sometimes I feared
should this day make me, not remembering Glaucè,
envy him to death as though he had died mine?

Can he be dead? It were so strange a world
with him not in it.

            Dimly I recall
some prophecy a god breathed by my mouth.
It could not err. What was it? For I think –
it told his death.

            Has a god come to me?
Is it thou, my Hecate? How know I all?
For I know all as if from long ago:
and I know all beholding instantly.
Is not that he, arisen through the mists? –
a lean and haggard man, rough round the eyes,
dull and with no scorn left upon his lip,
decayed out of his goodliness and strength;
a wanned and broken image of a god;
dim counterfeit of Jason, heavily
wearing the name of him and memories.

And lo, he rests with lax and careless limbs
on the loose sandbed wind-heaped round his ship
that rots in sloth like him, and props his head
on a half-buried fallen spar. The sea,
climbing the beach towards him, seethes and frets,
and on the verge two sunned and shadowed clouds
take shapes of notched rock-islands; and his thoughts
drift languid to the steep Symplegades
and the sound of waters crashing at their base.
And now he speaks out to his loneliness
'I was afraid and careful, but she laughed:
"Love steers" she said: and when the rocks were far,
grey twinkling spots in distance, suddenly
her face grew white, and, looking back to them,
she said, "Oh love, a god has whispered me
'twere well had we died there, for strange mad woes
are waiting for us in your Greece": and then
she tossed her head back, while her brown hair streamed
gold in the wind and sun, and her face glowed
with daring beauty, "What of woes," she cried,
"if only they leave time for love enough?"
But what a fire and flush! It took one's breath!'
And then he lay half musing, half adoze,
shadows of me went misty through his sight.

And bye and bye he roused and cried 'Oh dolt!

Glaucè was never half so beautiful.'
Then under part-closed lids remembering her,
'Poor Glaucè, a sweet face, and yet methinks
she might have wearied me': and suddenly,
smiting the sand awhirl with his angry hand,
scorned at himself 'What god befooled my wits
to dream my fancy for her yellow curls
and milk-white softness subtle policy?
Wealth and a royal bride: but what beyond?
Medea, with her skills, her presciences,
man's wisdom, woman's craft, her rage of love
that gave her to serve me strength next divine,
Medea would have made me what I would;
Glaucè but what she could. I schemed amiss
and earned the curses the gods send on fools.
Ruined, ruined! A laughing stock to foes!
No man so mean but he may pity me;
no man so wretched but will keep aloof
lest the curse upon me make him wretcheder.
Ruined!'

        And lo I see him hide his face
like a man who'll weep with passion: but to him
the passion comes not, only slow few tears
of one too weary. And from the great field
where the boys race he hears their jubilant shout
hum through the distance, and he sighs 'Ah me!
she might have spared the children, left me them –
no sons, no sons to stand about me now
and prosper me, and tend me bye and bye
in faltering age, and keep my name on earth
when I shall be departed out of sight.'

And the shout hummed louder forth: and whirring past
a screaming seabird flapped out to the bay,
and listlessly he watched it dip and rise
till it skimmed out of sight, so small a speck
as a mayfly on the brook; and then he said
'Fly forth, fly forth, bird, fly to fierce Medea
where by great Aegeus she sits queening it,
belike a joyful mother of new sons;
tell her she never loved me as she talked,
else had no wrong at my hand shewn so great:

tell her that she breaks oaths more than I broke,
even so much as she seemed to love most —
she who fits fondling in a husband's arms
while I am desolate.' And again he said
'My house is perished with me — ruined, ruined!'

At that he rose and, muttering in his teeth
still 'ruined, ruined', slowly paced the sands:
then stood and, gazing on the ragged hulk,
cried 'Oh loathed tool of fiends, that, through all storms
and sundering waters, borest me to Medea,
rot, rot, accursed thing,' and petulant
pashed at the side —

          Lo, lo! I see it part!
a tottering spar —it parts, it falls, it strikes!
He is prone on the sand, the blood wells from his brow,
he moans, he speaks, 'Medea's prophecy.'
See he has fainted.

          Hush, hush! he has lain
with death and silence long: now he wakes up —
'Where is Medea? Let her bind my head.'
Hush, hush! A sigh — a breath — He is dead.

                    ★

          Medea!
What, is it thou? What, thou, this whimpering fool,
this kind meek coward! Sick for pity art thou?
Or did the vision scare thee? Out on me!
do I drivel like a slight disconsolate girl
wailing her love?

          No, not one foolish tear
that shamed my cheek welled up for any grief
at his so pitiful lone end. The touch
of ancient memories and the woman's trick
of easy weeping took me unawares:
but grief! Why should I grieve?

          And yet for this,
that he is dead. He should still pine and dwine,

hungry for his old lost strong food of life
vanished with me, hungry for children's love,
hungry for me. Ever to think of me –
with love, with hate, what care I? hate is love –
Ever to think and long. Oh it was well!
Yea, my new marriage hope has been achieved:
for he *did* count me happy, picture me
happy with Aegeus; he *did* dream of me
as all to Aegeus that I was to him,
and to him nothing; and *did* yearn for me
and know me lost – we two so far apart
as dead and living, I an envied wife
and he alone and childless. Jason, Jason,
come back to earth; live, live for my revenge.

But lo the man is dead: I am forgotten.
Forgotten; something goes from life in that –
as if oneself had died, when the half self
of one's true living time has slipped away
from reach of memories, has ceased to know
that such a woman is.

       A wondrous thing
to be so separate having been so near –
near by hate last and once by so strong love.
Would love have kept us near if he had died
in the good days? Tush, I should have died too:
we should have gone together, hand in hand,
and made dusk Hades glorious each to each.

Ah me, if then when through the fitful seas
we saw the great rocks glimmer, and the crew
howled 'We are lost! lo the Symplegades!'
too late to shun them, if but then some wave,
our secret friend, had dashed us from our course,
sending us to be shivered at the base,
well, well indeed! And yet what say I there?
Ten years together were they not worth cost
of all the anguish? Oh me, how I loved him!
Why did I not die loving him?

★

What thou!
Have the dead no room, or do they drive thee forth
loathing thee near them? Dost thou threaten me?
Why, so I saw thee last, and was not scared:
think not to scare me now; I am no babe
to shiver at an unavailing shade.
Go, go, thou canst not curse me, none will hear:
the gods remember justice. Wrongs! thy wrongs!
the vengeance, ghost! What hast thou to avenge
as I have? Lo, thy meek-eyed Glaucè died,
and thy king-kinsman Creon died: but I,
I live what thou hast made me.
          Oh smooth adder,
who with fanged kisses changedst my natural blood
to venom in me, say, didst thou not find me
a grave and simple girl in a still home,
learning my spells for pleasant services
or to make sick beds easier? With me went
the sweet sound of friends' voices praising me:
all faces smiled on me, even lifeless things
seemed glad because of me; and I could smile
to every face, to everything, to trees,
to skies and waters, to the passing herds,
to the small thievish sparrows, to the grass
with sunshine through it, to the weed's bold flowers:
for all things glad and harmless seemed my kin,
and all seemed glad and harmless in the world.
Thou cam'st, and from the day thou, finding me
in Hecate's dim grove to cull my herbs,
didst burn my cheeks with kisses hot and strange,
the curse of thee compelled me. Lo I am
The wretch thou say'st; but wherefore? By whose work?
Who, binding me with dreadful marriage oaths
in the midnight temple, led my treacherous flight
from home and father? Whose voice when I turned,
desperate to save thee, on my own young brother,
my so loved brother, whose voice as I smote
nerved me, cried 'Brave Medea'? For whose ends
did I decoy the credulous girls, poor fools,
to slay their father? When have I been base,
when cruel, save for thee, until – Man, man,
wilt thou accuse my guilt? Whose is my guilt?
mine or thine, Jason? Oh, soul of my crimes,

how shall I pardon thee for what I am?

Never. And if, with the poor womanish heart
that for the loving's sake will still love on,
I could let such a past wane as a dream
and turn to thee at waking – turn to thee!
I, put aside like some slight purchased slave
who pleased thee and then tired, still turn to thee!
Yet never, not if thou and I could live
thousands of years and all thy years were pain
and all my years were to behold thy pain,
never could I forgive thee for my boys;
never could I look on this hand of mine
that slew them and not hate thee. Childless thou,
what is thy childlessness to mine? Go, go,
thou foolish angry ghost, what wrongs hast thou?
would I could wrong thee more. Come thou sometimes
and see me happy.

      Dost thou mock at me
with thy cold smiling? Aye, can I not love?
What then? am I not folded round with love,
with a life's whole of love? There doth no thought
come near to Aegeus save what is of me:
am I no happy wife? And I go proud,
and treasure him for noblest of the world:
am I no happy wife?

      Dost mock me still?
My children is it? Are the dead so wise?
Why, who told thee my transport of despair
when from the Sun who willed me not to die
nor creep away, sudden and too late came
the winged swift car that could have saved them, mine,
from thee and from their foes? Tush, 'twas best so;
If they had lived, sometimes thou hadst had hope:
for thou wouldst still have said 'I have two sons,'
and dreamed perchance they'd bring thee use at last
and build thy greatness higher: but now, now,
thou hast died shamed and childless, none to keep
thy name and memory fresh upon the earth,
none to make boast of thee 'My father did it.'

Yea, 'twas best so: my sons, we are avenged.
Thou, mock me not. What if I have ill dreams
to see them loathe me, fly from me in dread,
when I would feed my hungry mouth with kisses?
what if I moan in tossing fever thirsts,
crying for them whom I shall have no more,
here nor among the dead, who never more,
here nor among the dead, will smile to me
with young lips prattling 'Mother, mother dear'?
what if I turn sick when the women pass
that lead their boys, and hate a child's young face?
what if —

      Go, go, thou mind'st me of my sons,
and then I hate thee worse; go to thy grave
by which none weeps. I have forgotten thee.

Circe

The sun drops luridly into the west;
darkness has raised her arms to draw him down
before the time, not waiting as of wont
till he has come to her behind the sea;
and the smooth waves grow sullen in the gloom
and wear their threatening purple; more and more
the plain of waters sways and seems to rise
convexly from its level of the shores;
and low dull thunder rolls along the beach:
there will be storm at last, storm, glorious storm.

Oh welcome, welcome, though it rend my bowers,
scattering my blossomed roses like the dust,
splitting the shrieking branches, tossing down
my riotous vines with their young half-tinged grapes
like small round amethysts or beryls strung
tumultuously in clusters, though it sate
its ravenous spite among my goodliest pines
standing there round and still against the sky
that makes blue lakes between their sombre tufts,
or harry from my silvery olive slopes
some hoary king whose gnarled fantastic limbs
wear crooked armour of a thousand years;

though it will hurl high on my flowery shores
the hostile wave that rives at the poor sward
and drags it down the slants, that swirls its foam
over my terraces, shakes their firm blocks
of great bright marbles into tumbled heaps,
and makes my preached and mossy labyrinths,
where the small odorous blossoms grow like stars
strewn in the milky way, a briny marsh.
What matter? Let it come and bring me change,
breaking the sickly sweet monotony.

I am too weary of this long bright calm;
always the same blue sky, always the sea
the same blue perfect likeness of the sky,
one rose to match the other that has waned,
tomorrow's dawn the twin of yesterday's;
and every night the ceaseless crickets chirp
the same long joy and the late strain of birds
repeats their strain of all the even month;
and changelessly the petty plashing surfs
bubble their chiming burden round the stones;
dusk after dusk brings the same languid trance
upon the shadowy hills, and in the fields
the waves of fireflies come and go the same,
making the very flash of light and stir
vex one like dronings of the spinning wheel.

Give me some change. Must life be only sweet,
all honey-pap as babes would have their food?
And, if my heart must always be adrowse
in a hush of stagnant sunshine, give me then
something outside me stirring; let the storm
break up the sluggish beauty, let it fall
beaten below the feet of passionate winds,
and then tomorrow waken jubilant
in a new birth: let me see subtle joy
of anguish and of hopes, of change and growth.

What fate is mine who, far apart from pains
and fears and turmoils of the cross-grained world,
dwell, like a lonely god, in a charmed isle
where I am first and only, and, like one
who should love poisonous savours more than mead,

long for a tempest on me and grow sick
of resting, and divine free carelessness!
Oh me, I am a woman, not a god;
yea, those who tend me even are more than I,
my nymphs who have the souls of flowers and birds
singing and blossoming immortally.

Ah me! these love a day and laugh again,
and loving, laughing, find a full content;
but I know nought of peace, and have not loved.

Where is my love? Does some one cry for me,
not knowing whom he calls? does his soul cry
for mine to grow beside it, grow in it?
does he beseech the gods to give him me,
the one unknown rare woman by whose side
no other woman, thrice as beautiful,
should once seem fair to him; to whose voice heard
in any common tones no sweetest sound
of love made melody on silver lutes,
or singing like Apollo's when the gods
grow pale with happy listening, might be peered
for making music to him; whom once found
there will be no more seeking anything?

Oh love, oh love, oh love, art not yet come
out of the waiting shadows into life?
art not yet come after so many years
that I have longed for thee? Come! I am here.

Not yet. For surely I should feel a sound
of his far answering, if now in the world
he sought me who will seek me – Oh ye gods
will he not seek me? Is it all a dream?
will there be never never such a man?
will there be only these, these bestial things
who wallow in my styes, or mop and mow
among the trees, or munch in pens and byres,
or snarl and filch behind their wattled coops;
these things who had believed that they were men?

Nay but he *will* come. Why am I so fair,
and marvellously minded, and with sight

which flashes suddenly on hidden things,
as the gods see who do not need to look?
why wear I in my eyes that stronger power
than basilisks, whose gaze can only kill,
to draw men's souls to me to live or die
as I would have them? why am I given pride
which yet longs to be broken, and this scorn
cruel and vengeful for the lesser men
who meet the smiles I waste for lack of him
and grow too glad? why am I who I am,
but for the sake of him whom fate will send
one day to be my master utterly,
that he should take me, the desire of all,
whom only he in the world could bow to him?

Oh sunlike glory of pale glittering hairs,
bright as the filmy wires my weavers take
to make me golden gauzes; oh deep eyes,
darker and softer than the bluest dusk
of August violets, darker and deep
like crystal fathomless lakes in summer noons;
oh sad sweet longing smile; oh lips that tempt
my very self to kisses; oh round cheeks,
tenderly radiant with the even flush
of pale smoothed coral; perfect lovely face
answering my gaze from out this fleckless pool;
wonder of glossy shoulders, chiselled limbs;
should I be so your lover as I am,
drinking an exquisite joy to watch you thus
in all a hundred changes through the day,
but that I love you for him till he comes,
but that my beauty means his loving it?

Oh, look! A speck on this side of the sun,
coming – yes, coming with the rising wind
that frays the darkening cloud-wrack on the verge
and in a little while will leap abroad,
spattering the sky with rushing blacknesses,
dashing the hissing mountainous waves at the stars.
'Twill drive me that black speck a shuddering hulk
caught in the buffeting waves, dashed impotent
from ridge to ridge, will drive it in the night
with that dull jarring crash upon the beach,

and the cries for help and the cries of fear and hope.

And then tomorrow they will thoughtfully,
with grave low voices, count their perils up,
and thank the gods for having let them live,
and tell of wives or mothers in their homes,
and children, who would have such loss in them
that they must weep, and may be I weep too,
with fancy of the weepings had they died.
And the next morrow they will feel their ease
and sigh with sleek content, or laugh elate,
tasting delights of rest and revelling,
music and perfumes, joyaunce for the eyes
of rosy faces and luxurious pomps,
the savour of the banquet and the glow
and fragrance of the wine-cup; and they'll talk
how good it is to house in palaces
out of the storms and struggles, and what luck
strewed their good ship on our accessless coast.
Then the next day the beast in them will wake,
and one will strike and bicker, and one swell
with puffed up greatness, and one gibe and strut
in apish pranks, and one will line his sleeve
with pilfered booties, and one snatch the gems
out of the carven goblets as they pass,
one will grow mad with fever of the wine,
and one will sluggishly besot himself,
and one be lewd, and one be gluttonous;
and I shall sickly look, and loathe them all.

Oh my rare cup! My pure and crystal cup,
with not one speck of colour to make false
the passing lights, or flaw to make them swerve!
My cup of Truth! How the lost fools will laugh
and thank me for my boon, as if I gave
some momentary flash of the gods' joy,
to drink where I have drunk and touch the touch
of my lips with their own! Aye, let them touch.

Too cruel am I? And the silly beasts,
crowding around me when I pass their way,
glower on me and, although they love me still,
(with their poor sorts of love such as they could,)

call wrath and vengeance to their humid eyes
to scare me into mercy, or creep near
with piteous fawnings, supplicating bleats.
Too cruel? Did I choose them what they are?
or change them from themselves by poisonous charms?
But any draught, pure water, natural wine,
out of my cup, revealed them to themselves
and to each other. Change? There was no change;
only disguise gone from them unawares:
and had there been one right true man of them
he would have drunk the draught as I had drunk,
and stood unchanged, and looked me in the eyes,
abashing me before him. But these things –
why, which of them has even shown the kind
of some one nobler beast? Pah, yapping wolves
and pitiless stealthy wild-cats, curs and apes
and gorging swine and slinking venomous snakes
all false and ravenous and sensual brutes
that shame the Earth that bore them, these they are.

Lo, lo! the shivering blueness darting forth
on half the heavens, and the forked thin fire
strikes to the sea: and hark, the sudden voice
that rushes through the trees before the storm,
and shuddering of the branches. Yet the sky
is blue against them still, and early stars
glimmer above the pine-tops; and the air
clings faint and motionless around me here.

Another burst of flame – and the black speck
shows in the glare, lashed onwards. It were well
I bade make ready for our guests tonight.

A Castaway

Poor little diary, with its simple thoughts,
its good resolves, its 'Studied French an hour',
'Read Modern History', 'Trimmed up my grey hat',
'Darned stockings', 'Tatted', 'Practised my new song',
'Went to the daily service', 'Took Bess soup',
'Went out to tea'. Poor simple diary!
And did *I* write it? Was I this good girl,

this budding colourless young rose of home?
did I so live content in such a life,
seeing no larger scope, nor asking it,
than this small constant round – old clothes to mend,
new clothes to make, then go and say my prayers,
or carry soup, or take a little walk
and pick the ragged-robins in the hedge?
Then for ambition (was there ever life
that could forego that?), to improve my mind
and know French better and sing harder songs;
for gaiety, to go, in my best white
well washed and starched and freshened with new bows,
and take tea out to meet the clergyman.
No wishes and no cares, almost no hopes,
only the young girl's hazed and golden dreams
that veil the Future from her.

     So long since:
and now it seems a jest to talk of me
as if I could be one with her, of me
who am... me.

     And what is that? My looking-glass
answers it passably; a woman sure,
no fiend, no slimy thing out of the pools,
a woman with a ripe and smiling lip
that has no venom in its touch I think,
with a white brow on which there is no brand;
a woman none dare call not beautiful,
not womanly in every woman's grace.

Aye let me feed upon my beauty thus,
be glad in it like painters when they see
at last the face they dreamed but could not find
look from their canvass on them, triumph in it,
the dearest thing I have. Why, 'tis my all,
let me make much of it: is it not this,
this beauty, my own curse at once and tool
to snare men's souls – (I know what the good say
of beauty in such creatures) – is is not this
that makes me feel myself a woman still,
some little pride, some little –

Here's a jest!
What word will fit the sense but modesty?
A wanton I but modest!

    Modest, true;
I'm not drunk in the streets, ply not for hire
at infamous corners with my likenesses
of the humbler kind; yes, modesty's my word –
'twould shape my mouth well too, I think I'll try:
'Sir, Mr What-you-will, Lord Who-knows-what,
my present lover or my next to come,
value me at my worth, fill your purse full,
for I am modest; yes, and honour me
as though your schoolgirl sister or your wife
could let her skirts brush mine or talk of me;
for I am modest.'

    Well, I flout myself:
but yet, but yet –

    Fie, poor fantastic fool,
why do I play the hypocrite alone,
who am no hypocrite with others by?
where should be my 'But yet'? I am that thing
called half a dozen dainty names, and none
dainty enough to serve the turn and hide
the one coarse English worst that lurks beneath:
just that, no worse, no better.

    And, for me,
I say let no one be above her trade;
I own my kindredship with any drab
who sells herself as I, although she crouch
in fetid garrets and I have a home
all velvet and marqueterie and pastilles,
although she hide her skeleton in rags
and I set fashions and wear cobweb lace:
the difference lies but in my choicer ware,
that I sell beauty and she ugliness;
our traffic's one – I'm no sweet slaver-tongue
to gloze upon it and explain myself
a sort of fractious angel misconceived –
our traffic's one: I own it. And what then?

I know of worse that are called honourable.
Our lawyers, who, with noble eloquence
and virtuous outbursts, lie to hang a man,
or lie to save him, which way goes the fee:
our preachers, gloating on your future hell
for not believing what they doubt themselves:
our doctors, who sort poisons out by chance,
and wonder how they'll answer, and grow rich:
our journalists, whose business is to fib
and juggle truths and falsehoods to and fro:
our tradesmen, who must keep unspotted names
and cheat the least like stealing that they can:
our – all of them, the virtuous worthy men
who feed on the world's follies, vices, wants,
and do their businesses of lies and shams
honestly, reputably, while the world
claps hands and cries 'good luck,' which of their trades,
their honourable trades, barefaced like mine,
all secrets brazened out, would shew more white?

And whom do I hurt more than they? As much?
The wives? Poor fools, what do I take from them
worth crying for or keeping? If they knew
what their fine husbands look like seen by eyes
that may perceive there are more men than one!

But, if they can, let them just take the pains
to keep them: 'tis not such a mighty task
to pin an idiot to your apron-string;
and wives have an advantage over us,
(the good and blind ones have), the smile or pout
leaves them no secret nausea at odd times.
Oh they could keep their husbands if they cared,
but 'tis an easier life to let them go,
and whimper at it for morality.

Oh! those shrill carping virtues, safely housed
from reach of even a smile that should put red
on a decorous cheek, who rail at us
with such a spiteful scorn and rancourousness,
(which maybe is half envy at the heart),
and boast themselves so measurelessly good
and us so measurelessly unlike them,

what is their wondrous merit that they stay
in comfortable homes whence not a soul
has ever thought of tempting them, and wear
no kisses but a husband's upon lips
there is no other man desires to kiss —
refrain in fact from sin impossible?
How dare they hate us so? What have they done,
what borne, to prove them other than we are?
What right have they to scorn us — glass-case saints,
Dianas under lock and key — what right
more than the well-fed helpless barn-door fowl
to scorn the larcenous wild-birds?

        Pshaw, let be!
Scorn or no scorn, what matter for their scorn?
I have outfaced my own — that's harder work.
Aye let their virtuous malice dribble on —
mock snowstorms on the stage — I'm proof long since:
I have looked coolly on my what and why,
and I accept myself.

        Oh I'll endorse
the shamefullest revilings mouthed at me,
cry 'True! Oh perfect picture! Yes, that's I!'
and add a telling blackness here and there,
and then dare swear you, every nine of ten,
my judges and accusers, I'd not change
my conscience against yours, you who tread out
your devil's pilgrimage along the roads
that take in church and chapel, and arrange
a roundabout and decent way to hell.

Well, mine's a short way and a merry one:
so says my pious hash of ohs and ahs,
choice texts and choicer threats, appropriate names,
(Rahabs and Jezebels), some fierce Tartuffe
hurled at me through the post. We had rare fun
over that tract digested with champagne.
Where is it? where's my rich repertory
of insults biblical? '*I prey on souls*' —
only my men have oftenest none I think:
'*I snare the simple ones*' — but in these days
there seem to be none simple and none snared,

and most men have their favourite sinnings planned
to do them civilly and sensibly:
'*I braid my hair*' – but braids are out of date:
'*I paint my cheeks*' – I always wear them pale:
'*I –*'

     Pshaw! the trash is savourless today:
one cannot laugh alone. There, let it burn.
What, does the windy dullard think one needs
his wisdom dovetailed on to Solomon's,
his threats out-threatening God's, to teach the news
that those who need not sin have safer souls?
We know it, but we've bodies to save too;
and so we earn our living.

     Well lit, tract!
it least you've made me a good leaping blaze.
Up, up, how the flame shoots! and now 'tis dead.
Oh proper finish, preaching to the last –
no such bad omen either; sudden end,
and no sad withering horrible old age.
How one would clutch at youth to hold it tight!
and then to know it gone, to see it gone,
be taught its absence by harsh, careless looks,
to live forgotten, solitary, old –
the cruellest word that ever woman learns.
Old – that's to be nothing, or to be at best
a blurred memorial that in better days
there was a woman once with such a name.
No, no, I could not bear it: death itself
shews kinder promise... even death itself,
since it must come one day –

     Oh this grey gloom!
This rain, rain, rain, what wretched thoughts it brings!
Death: I'll not think of it.

     Will no one come?
'Tis dreary work alone.

     Why did I read
that silly diary? Now, sing song, ding dong,
come the old vexing echoes back again,

church bells and nursery good-books, back again
upon my shrinking ears that had forgotten –
I hate the useless memories: 'tis fools' work
singing the hackneyed dirge of 'better days':
best take Now kindly, give the past goodbye,
whether it were a better or a worse.

Yes, yes, I listened to the echoes once,
the echoes and the thoughts from the old days.
The worse for me: I lost my richest friend,
and that was all the difference. For the world
would not have that flight known. How they'd roar:
'What! Eulalie, when she refused us all,
"ill" and "away", was doing Magdalene,
tears, ashes, and her Bible, and then off
hide her in a Refuge... for a week!'

A wild whim that, to fancy I could change
my new self for my old, because I wished!
since then, when in my languid days there comes
that craving, like homesickness, to go back
to the good days, the dear old stupid days,
to the quiet and the innocence, I know
'tis a sick fancy and try palliatives.

What is it? You go back to the old home,
and 'tis not *your* home, has no place for you,
and, if it had, you could not fit you in it.
And could I fit me to my former self?

If I had had the wit, like some of us,
to sow my wild-oats into three per cents,
could I not find me shelter in the peace
of some far nook where none of them would come,
nor whisper travel from this scurrilous world,
that gloats and moralises through its leers,
to blast me with my fashionable shame?
There I might – oh my castle in the clouds!
and where's its rent? – but there, were there a there,
I might again live the grave blameless life
among such simple pleasures, simple cares:
but could they be my pleasures, be my cares?
The blameless life, but never the content –

OUT OF MY BORROWED BOOKS

never. How could I henceforth be content
in any life but one that sets the brain
in a hot merry fever with its stir?
what would there be in quiet rustic days,
each like the other, full of time to think,
to keep one bold enough to live at all?
Quiet is hell, I say – as if a woman
could bear to sit alone, quiet all day,
and loathe herself, and sicken on her thoughts.

They tried it at the Refuge, and I failed:
I could not bear it. Dreary hideous room,
coarse pittance, prison rules, one might bear these
and keep one's purpose; but so much alone,
and then made faint and weak and fanciful
by change from pampering to half-famishing –
good God, what thoughts come! Only one week more
and 'twould have ended: but in one day more
I must have killed myself. And I loathe death,
the dreadful foul corruption, with who knows
what future after it.

       Well, I came back,
Back to my slough. Who says I had my choice?
Could I stay there to die of some mad death?
and if I rambled out into the world,
sinless but penniless, what else were that
but slower death, slow pining shivering death
by misery and hunger? Choice! what choice
of living well or ill? could I have that?
and who would give it me? I think indeed
some kind hand, a woman's – I hate men –
had stretched itself to help me to firm ground,
taken a chance and risked my falling back,
could have gone my way not falling back:
but, let her be all brave, all charitable,
how could she do it? Such a trifling boon,
little work to live by, 'tis not much,
and I might have found will enough to last:
but where's the work? More sempstresses than shirts;
and defter hands at white work than are mine
drop starved at last: dressmakers, milliners,
too many too they say; and then their trades

need skill, apprenticeship. And who so bold
as hire me for their humblest drudgery?
not even for scullery slut; not even, I think,
for governess, although they'd get me cheap.
And after all it would be something hard,
with the marts for decent women overfull,
if I could elbow in and snatch a chance
and oust some good girl so, who then perforce
must come and snatch her chance among our crowd.

Why, if the worthy men who think all's done
if we'll but come where we can hear them preach,
could bring us all, or any half of us,
into their fold, teach all us wandering sheep,
or only half of us, to stand in rows
and baa them hymns and moral songs, good lack,
what would they do with us? what could they do?
Just think! with were't but half of us on hand
to find work for... or husbands. Would they try
to ship us to the colonies for wives?

Well, well; I know the wise ones talk and talk:
'Here's cause, here's cure': 'No, here it is and here':
and find society to blame, or law,
the Church, the men, the women, too few schools,
too many schools, too much, too little taught:
somewhere or somehow someone is to blame:
but I say all the fault's with God himself
who puts too many women in the world.
We ought to die off reasonably and leave
as many as the men want, none to waste.
Here's cause; the woman's superfluity:
and for the cure, why, if it were the law,
say, every year, in due percentages,
balancing them with men as the times need,
to kill off female infants, 'twould make room;
and some of us would not have lost too much,
losing life ere we know what it *can* mean.

The other day I saw a woman weep
beside her dead child's bed: the little thing
lay smiling, and the mother wailed half mad,
shrieking to God to give it back again.

OUT OF MY BORROWED BOOKS

I could have laughed aloud: the little girl
living had but her mother's life to live;
there she lay smiling, and her mother wept
to know her gone!

My mother would have wept.

Oh mother, mother, did you ever dream,
you good grave simple mother, you pure soul
no evil could come nigh, did you once dream
in all your dying cares for your lone girl
left to fight out her fortune all alone
that there would be *this* danger? – for *your* girl,
taught by you, lapped in a sweet ignorance,
scarcely more wise of what things sin could be
than some young child a summer six months old
where in the north the summer makes a day,
of what is darkness... darkness that will come
tomorrow suddenly. Thank God at least
for this much of my life, that when you died,
that when you kissed me dying, not a thought
of this made sorrow for you, that I too
was pure of even fear.

Oh yes, I thought,
still new in my insipid treadmill life,
(my father so late dead), and hopeful still
here might be something pleasant somewhere in it,
some sudden fairy come, no doubt, to turn
any pumpkin to a chariot, I thought then
that I might plod, and plod, and drum the sounds
of useless facts into unwilling ears,
tease children with dull questions half the day,
then con dull answers in my room at night
ready for next day's questions, mend quill pens
and cut my fingers, add up sums done wrong
and never get them right; teach, teach, and teach –
what I half knew, or not at all – teach, teach
for years, a lifetime – *I*!

And yet, who knows?
it might have been, for I was patient once,
and willing, and meant well; it might have been

had I but still clung on in my first place –
a safe dull place, where mostly there were smiles
but never merrymakings; where all days
jogged on sedately busy, with no haste;
where all seemed measured out, but margins broad:
a dull home but a peaceful, where I felt
my pupils would be dear young sisters soon,
and felt their mother take me to her heart,
motherly to all lonely harmless things.
But I must have a conscience, must blurt out
my great discovery of my ignorance!
And who required it of me? And who gained?
What did it matter for a more or less
the girls learnt in their schoolbooks, to forget
in their first season? We did well together:
they loved me and I them: but I went off
to housemaid's pay, six crossgrained brats to teach,
wrangles and jangles, doubts, disgrace... then this;
and they had a perfection found for them,
who has all ladies' learning in her head
abridged and scheduled, speaks five languages,
knows botany and conchology and globes,
draws, paints, plays, sings, embroiders, teaches all
on a patent method never known to fail:
and now they're finished and, I hear, poor things,
are the worst dancers and worst dressers out.
And where's their profit of those prison years
all gone to make them wise in lesson books?
who wants his wife to know weeds' Latin names?
who ever chose a girl for saying dates?
or asked if she had learned to trace a map?

Well, well, the silly rules this silly world
makes about women! This is one of them.
Why must there be pretence of teaching them
what no one ever cares that they should know,
what, grown out of the schoolroom, they cast off
like the schoolroom pinafore, no better fit
for any use of real grown-up life,
for any use to her who seeks or waits
the husband and the home, for any use,
for any shallowest pretence of use,
to her who has them? Do I not know this,

I like my betters, that a woman's life,
her natural life, her good life, her one life,
is in her husband, God on earth to her,
and what she knows and what she can and is
is only good as it brings good to him?

Oh God, do I not know it? I the thing
of shame and rottenness, the animal
that feeds men's lusts and preys on them, I, I,
who should not dare to take the name of wife
on my polluted lips, who in the word
hear but my own reviling, I know that.
I could have lived by that rule, how content:
my pleasure to make him some pleasure, pride
to be as he would have me, duty, care,
to fit all to his taste, rule my small sphere
to his intention; then to lean on him,
be guided, tutored, loved – no not that word,
that *loved* which between men and women means
all selfishness, all putrid talk, all lust,
all vanity, all idiocy – not loved
but cared for. I've been loved myself, I think,
some once or twice since my poor mother died,
but *cared for*, never: that a word for homes,
kind homes, good homes, where simple children come
and ask their mother is this right or wrong,
because they know she's perfect, cannot err;
their father told them so, and he knows all,
being so wise and good and wonderful,
even enough to scold even her at times
and tell her everything she does not know.
Ah the sweet nursery logic!

             Fool! Thrice fool!
Do I hanker after that too? Fancy me
infallible nursery saint, live code of law!
Me preaching! Teaching innocence to be good!
A mother!

             Yet the baby thing that woke
and wailed an hour or two, and then was dead,
was mine, and had he lived... why then my name
would have been mother. But 'twas well he died:

I could have been no mother, I, lost then
beyond his saving. Had he come before
and lived, come to me in the doubtful days
when shame and boldness had not grown one sense,
for his sake, with the courage come of him,
I might have struggled back.

   But how? But how?
His father would not then have let me go:
his time had not yet come to make an end
of my 'for ever' with a hireling's fee
and civil light dismissal. None but him
to claim a bit of bread of if I went,
child or no child: would he have given it me?
He! no; he had not done with me. No help,
no help, no help. Some ways can be trodden back,
but never our way, we who one wild day
have given goodbye to what in our deep hearts
the lowest woman still holds best in life,
good name — good name though given by the world
that mouths and garbles with its decent prate,
and wraps it in respectable grave shams,
and patches conscience partly by the rule
of what one's neighbour thinks but something more
by what his eyes are sharp enough to see.
How I could scorn it with its Pharisees,
if it could not scorn me: but yet, but yet —
oh God, if I could look it in the face!

Oh I am wild, am ill, I think, tonight:
will no one come and laugh with me? No feast,
no merriment tonight. So long alone!
Will no one come?

   At least there's a new dress
to try, and grumble at — they never fit
to one's ideal. Yes, a new rich dress,
with lace like this too, that's a soothing balm
for any fretting woman, cannot fail,
I've heard men say it... and they know so well
what's in all women's hearts, especially
women like me.

No help! No help! No help!
How could it be? It was too late long since —
even at the first too late. Whose blame is that?
there are some kindly people in the world,
but what can they do? If one hurls oneself
into a quicksand, what can be the end,
but that one sinks and sinks? Cry out for help?
Ah yes, and, if it came, who is so strong
to strain from the firm ground and lift one out?
And how, so firmly clutching the stretched hand,
as death's pursuing terror bids, even so,
how can one reach firm land, having to foot
the treacherous crumbling soil that slides and gives
and sucks one in again? Impossible path!
No, why waste struggles, I or any one?
what is must be. What then? I, where I am,
sinking and sinking; let the wise pass by
and keep their wisdom for an apter use,
let me sink merrily as I best may.

Only, I think, my brother — I forgot
he stopped his brotherhood some years ago —
but if he had been just so much less good
as to remember mercy. Did he think
how once I was his sister, prizing him
as sisters do, content to learn for him
the lesson girls with brothers all must learn,
to do without?

        I have heard girls lament
that doing so without all things one would,
but I saw never aught to murmur at,
for men must be made ready for their work,
and women all have more or less their chance
of husbands to work for them, keep them safe
like summer roses in soft greenhouse air
that never guess 'tis winter out of doors:
no, I saw never aught to murmur at,
content with stinted fare and shabby clothes
and cloistered silent life to save expense,
teaching myself out of my borrowed books,
while he for some one pastime (needful true
to keep him of his rank, 'twas not his fault),

AUGUSTA WEBSTER

spent in a month what could have given me
my teachers for a year.

   'Twas no one's fault:
for could he be launched forth on the rude sea
of this contentious world and left to find
oars and the boatman's skill by some good chance?
'Twas no one's fault: yet still he might have thought
of our so different youths, and owned at least
'tis pitiful when a mere nerveless girl,
untutored, must put forth upon that sea,
not in the woman's true place, the wife's place,
to trust a husband and be borne along,
but impotent blind pilot to herself.

Merciless, merciless – like the prudent world
that will not have the flawed soul prank itself
with a hoped second virtue, will not have
the woman fallen once lift up herself...
lest she should fall again. Oh how his taunts,
his loathing fierce reproaches, scarred and seared,
like branding iron hissing in a wound!
And it was true – *that* killed me: and I felt
a hideous hopeless shame kill out my heart,
and knew myself for ever that he said,
that which I was – Oh it was true, true, true.

No, not true then. I was not all that then.
Oh, I have drifted on before mad winds
and made ignoble shipwreck, not today
could any breeze of heaven prosper me
into the track again, nor any hand
snatch me out of the whirlpool I have reached;
but then?

   Nay he judged very well: he knew
repentance was too dear a luxury
for a beggar's buying, knew it earns no bread –
and knew me a too base and nerveless thing
to bear my first fault's sequel and just die.
And how could he have helped me? Held my hand,
owned me for his, fronted the angry world
clothed with my ignominy? Or maybe

taken me to his home to damn him worse?
What did I look for? For what less would serve
that he could do, a man without a purse?
He meant me well, he sent me that five pounds,
much to him then; and, if he bade me work
and never vex him more with news of me,
we both knew him too poor for pensioners.
I see he did his best; I could wish now
sending it back I had professed some thanks.

But there! I was too wretched to be meek:
it seemed to me as if he, every one,
the whole great world, were guilty of my guilt,
abettors and avengers: in my heart
I gibed them back their gibings; I was wild.

I see clear now and know one has one's life
in hand at first to spend or spare or give
like any other coin; spend it or give
or drop it in the mire, can the world see
you get your value for it, or bar back
the hurrying of its marts to grope it up
and give it back to you for better use?
And if you spend or give that is your choice;
and if you let it slip that's your choice too,
you should have held it firmer. Yours the blame,
and not another's, not the indifferent world's
which goes on steadily, statistically,
and count by censuses not separate souls —
and if it somehow needs to its worst use
so many lives of women, useless else,
it buys us of ourselves, we could hold back,
free all of us to starve, and some of us,
(those who have done no ill and are in luck),
to slave their lives out and have food and clothes
until they grow unserviceably old.

Oh I blame no one — scarcely even myself.
It was to be: the very good in me
has always turned to hurt; all I thought right
at the hot moment, judged of afterwards,
shows reckless.

Why, look at it, had I taken
the pay my dead child's father offered me
for having been its mother, I could then
have kept life in me (many have to do it,
that swarm in the back alleys, on no more,
cold sometimes, mostly hungry, but they live);
I could have gained a respite trying it,
and maybe found at last some humble work
to eke the pittance out. Not I, forsooth,
I must have spirit, must have womanly pride,
must dash back his contemptuous wages, I,
who had not scorned to earn them, dash them back
the fiercer that he dared to count our boy
in my appraising: and yet now I think
I might have taken it for my dead boy's sake;
it would have been *his* gift.

　　　　　But I went forth
with my fine scorn, and whither did it lead?
Money's the root of evil do they say?
money is virtue, strength: money to me
would then have been repentance: could I live
upon my idiot's pride?

　　　　　Well, it fell soon.
I had prayed Edward might believe me dead,
and yet I begged of him – that's like me too,
beg of him and then send him back his alms!
What if he gave as to a whining wretch
that holds her hand and lies? I am less to him
than such a one; her rags do him no wrong,
but I, I, wrong him merely that I live,
being his sister. Could I not at least
have still let him forget me? But 'tis past:
and naturally he may hope I am long dead.

Good God! to think that we were what we were
one to the other... and now!

　　　　　He has done well;
married a sort of heiress, I have heard,
a dapper little madam, dimple cheeked
and dimple brained, who makes him a good wife –

No doubt she'd never own but just to him,
and in a whisper, she can even suspect
that we exist, we other women things:
what would she say if she could learn one day
she has a sister-in-law! So he and I
must stand apart till doomsday.

        But the jest,
to think how she would look! – Her fright, poor thing!
The notion! – I could laugh outright... or else,
for I feel near it, roll on the ground and sob.

Well, after all, there's not much difference
between the two sometimes.

        Was that the bell?
Some one at last, thank goodness. There's a voice,
and that's a pleasure. Whose though? Ah I know.
Why did she come alone, the cackling goose?
why not have brought her sister? – she tells more
and titters less. No matter; half a loaf
is better than no bread.

        Oh, is it you?
Most welcome, dear: one gets so moped alone.

Faded

Ah face, young face, sweet with unpassionate joy,
Possessful joy of having all to hope –
Rich, measureless, nameless, formless, *all* to hope –
Fair, happy, face with the girl's questioning smile
Expectant of an answer from the days,
Fair, happy, morning, face who wast myself,
Talk with me, with this later drearier self.
Oftenest I dare not see thee: but alone,
Thou and I in the quiet, while, without,
Dim eve goes dwindling her hushed, hueless, light
And makes the leaden dusk before the stars –
While, if my duller eyes through envious tears
Reply to shine, there's none at hand to note,
Nor yet thyself, in the sad and pensive calm,

Wilt flout me for my faded look of thee,
As when thou mock'st me in the untender noon –
While now we two a little time are one,
Elder and girl, the blossoming and the sere,
One blended, dateless, woman for an hour –
Thou and I thus alone, I read from thee
My lesson what I was; which (ah, poor heart!)
Means trulier my lesson, bitter to learn,
Of what I cease to be.

> Fie, cruel face!
Too comely, thou. Thy round curves shame my cheeks;
Thy gloss of almond-bloom in the March sun
Affronts my hardened reds; thy satiny brow,
Like smooth magnolia petals warmly white,
Enforces all my tale of fretted lines;
The quivering woof of sunshine through thy hairs
Shows mine's spent russets deader. All in thee
That's likest me today is proof the more
Of my today's unlikeness. Ah! I have waned.
As every summer wanes, that, all the while,
Seems to grow still more summer, till, one day,
The first dead leaves are falling and all's past.
Myself has faded from me; I am old.

Well, well, what's that to fret for? Yet, indeed,
'Tis pity for a woman to be old.
Youth going lessens us of more than youth:
We lose the very instinct of our lives –
Song-birds left voiceless, diswinged flies of the air.
And the loss comes so soon; and ere we know:
We have so many many after years,
To use away (the unmarried ones at least)
In only withering leisurely. Ah me!
Men jeer us clinging, clinging pitiably,
To that themselves account whole all for us:
Aye, but what man of them could bear, as we must,
To live life's worth a stinted dozen years.
And the long sequel all for learning age.
Why, if we try to cheat the merciless world
That bids us grow old meekly and to the hour
(Like babes that must not cry when bed-time comes)
And, being old, be nothing – try, maybe,

OUT OF MY BORROWED BOOKS

To cheat our lingering selves as if Time lingered –
Is our fault other than the toil in vain
Of any shipwrecked swimmer who, miles from land,
No sail in sight, breasts the resistless sea,
And perishing will not perish? Oh, 'tis known
How bankrupt men will hopelessly, impotent,
Battle each inch with unforgiving ruin,
Waste their tired brains on schemes a child should laugh at,
Befool their hearts with more unbodied hopes
Than shadows flung by momentary spray,
Tease their unwilling faces into smiles
And loathingly look contentment – but, at best,
To gain some futile hour from certainty:
But we in our utter loss, outlawed from life,
Irretrievable bankrupts of our very selves,
We must give ruin welcome, blaze our fact
Of nothingness – 'good friends, perceive I am old;
Pray laugh and leave me.' We are fools, we sin,
Abjectly, past all pardon, past all pity,
We women, if we linger, if, maybe,
We use our petty melancholy arts
And are still women some filched year or two –
Still women and not ghosts, not lifeless husks,
Spent memories that slink through the world and breathe,
As if they lived, and yet they know they are dead.

Once, long ago, I dreamed I had truly died:
My numb void body, in its winding-sheet,
Lay ignorant, but I, grown viewlessness,
Met my home's dear ones still; I spoke, methought,
Words which they marked not, smiled unanswered smiles,
And then I wept, and clung about their necks,
Closer, with vain embracing; and one said
(Another ghost, a voice, I searched not what)
'Thou art all dead for them; they cannot know,'
And still replied 'They felt not,' or 'They heard not,'
'They cannot, thou being dead,' until ere long
The anguish of it waked me – to be thus,
With them yet so forlorn of sense of theirs!
'Twas in my happiest days, when, like new fronds
Uncurling coil by coil on ferns in May
And widening to the light and dews and air,
The girl grows woman gladly, but, untold,

That dream clung like a sorrow, and, for pity,
I hoped the poor lone dead should bide apart,
Never among their living. Like that dream,
Lost and alone, I haunt our world today.

How strange life is! − a woman's − if, I mean,
One miss a woman's destiny and sole hope,
The wife's dear service with its round of tasks
And sweet humilities and glad fatigues,
And anxious joy of mothers − strange indeed!
To wait and wait, like the flower upon its stalk,
For nothing save to wither! And the while
Knows she that she is waiting? Maybe, yes:
And maybe, no. That new-made shallow lake,
Asleep there in the park, knows not, asleep,
It waits the brook next rainfall shall let loose
To brim it with full waters, bear it on
Filling its further channel: girls so wait,
Careless and calm, not judging what shall be;
Only they know life has not reached them yet,
And till life come they'll dream and laugh in the sun.
And the sun shines, and the dumb days flit by
And make no sign for working... till, at time,
To her whom life and love need the voice comes
Which names her wife among the happier many:
And till to her, maybe, who not again
Shall know rest and sweet dreams, nor in the world
Call anywhere her home, nor laugh at ease,
Nor spend her toils on those who'll love her for them,
Dawns change and the hour of wonder while she wakes
Alone in the eastwinds of a barren world:
And till to her to whom life never comes,
Whether by joy or sorrows or by toil,
The sunshine has grown drought, the calm, decay; ·
And there's the woman old.
                              Poor imaged mock,
Thou art more than I today; thou hast my right,
My womanhood's lost right to meet pleased eyes
And please by being happy. Many a time
I note, forgotten, how thy youth, that lasts,
Earns thee companionship of lingering looks,
Thy smile a tenderness whereof nought's mine.
Thou hast a being still; but what am I?

OUT OF MY BORROWED BOOKS

A shadow and an echo – one that was.

Well, Time's thy tyrant too: there waits for thee
In the sure end the day thou wilt have faded.
Carelessly thou'lt be lifted from thy place,
Too long usurped, where there'll, room being given,
Bloom some such other face, nor shine be missed –
As a newer rose, alike as roses are,
Makes us the self-same sweet as yesterday's –
As in the river's stream an on-come wave,
That is to pass, fills all the other filled
That took the drift before it and has passed –
As we have our succession, woman to woman,
And so no smiles are missed, there being enough.
I shall not know it: winters of many years
Before then long may have annulled my grave,
My date may be so back past household talk
'Tis out of guess whose the vague counterfeit
That on the canvas has past memory
Smiled peering through the dirt-crust and the cracks.
Yes; after me thou'lt years and years be thus,
Be young, be fair, be, dumb unconscious toy,
Beloved for youth and fairness; but at the end
Age and decay for thee too. Face of mine,
Forgotten self, thou art woman after all:
Sooner or later we are one again:
Both shall have had our fate... decay, neglect,
Loneliness, and then die and never a one
In the busy world the poorer for our loss.

How dusk it is! Have I sat indeed so long?
I had not marked. Time to have been long since
In the merry drawing-room with its lights and talk
And my young sisters' music. Hark! that's sweet.
Maudie's clear voice sends me my favourite song,
Filling my stillness here. She sings it well.

Exit.

Tired

No not tonight, dear child; I cannot go;
I'm busy, tired; they knew I should not come;
you do not need me there. Dear, be content,
and take your pleasure; you shall tell me of it.
There, go to don your miracles of gauze,
and come and show yourself a great pink cloud.

So, she has gone with half a discontent;
but it will die before her curls are shaped,
and she'll go forth intent on being pleased,
and take her ponderous pastime like the rest —
patient delightedly, prepared to talk
in the right voice for the right length of time
on any thing that anybody names,
prepared to listen with the proper calm
to any song that anybody sings;
wedged in their chairs, all soberness and smiles,
one steady sunshine like an August day:
a band of very placid revellers,
glad to be there but gladder still to go.
She like the rest: it seems so strange to me,
my simple peasant girl, my nature's grace,
one with the others; my wood violet
stuck in a formal rose box at a show.

Well, since it makes her happier. True I thought
the artless girl, come from her cottage home
knowing no world beyond her village streets,
come stranger into our elaborate life
with such a blithe and wondering ignorance
as a young child's who sees new things all day,
would learn it my way and would turn to me
out of the solemn follies 'What are these?
why must we live by drill and laugh by drill;
may we not be ourselves then, you and I?'
I thought she would have nestled here by me
'I cannot feign, and let me stay with you.'
I thought she would have shed about my life
the unalloyed sweet freshness of the fields
pure from your cloying fashionable musks:
but she 'will do what other ladies do' —

my sunburnt Madge I saw, with skirts pinned up,
carrying her father's dinner where he sat
to take his noonday rest beneath the hedge,
and followed slowly for her clear loud song.

And she did then, she says, as others did
who were her like. 'Tis logical enough:
as every woman lives (tush! as we all,
following such granted patterns for our souls
as for our hats and coats), she lived by rules
how to be as her neighbours, though I, trained
to my own different code, discerned it not
(mistaking other laws for lawlessness,
like raw and hasty travellers): and now
why should she, in a new world, all unapt
to judge its judgements, take so much on her
she did not in her old world, pick and choose
her pleasures and her tastes, her aims, her faiths,
breaking her smooth path with the thorny points
of upstart questions? She is just a bird
born in a wicker cage and brought away
into a gilded one: she does not pine
to make her nest in uncontrolled far woods,
but, unconceiving freedom, chirrups on,
content to see her prison bars so bright.

Yes, best for her; and, if not best for me,
I've my fault in it too: she's logical,
but what am I, who, having chosen her
for being all unlike the tutored type,
next try and mould her to it – chose indeed
my violet for being not a rose,
then bade it hold itself as roses do,
that passers by may note no difference?
The peasant ways must go, the homely burr,
the quaint strong English – ancient classic turns
mixed up with rustic blunders and misuse,
old grammar shot with daring grammarlessness;
the village belle's quick pertness, toss of head,
and shriek of saucy laughter – graces there,
and which a certain reckless gracefulness,
half hoydenish, half fawnlike, made in her
graces in even my eyes... there; the ease

of quick companionship; the unsoftened 'no's;
the ready quarrels, ready makings up;
all these must go, I would not have her mocked
among the other women who have learned
sweet level speech and quiet courtesies –
and then they jarred upon me like the noise
of music out of rule, which, heard at first,
took the fresh ear with novel melody,
but makes you restless, listened to too long,
with missing looked for rhythms. So I teach,
or let her learn, the way to speak, to look,
to walk, to sit, to dance, to sing, to laugh,
and then... the prized dissimilarity
was outer husk and not essential core:
my wife is just the wife my any friend
selects among my any friend's good girls
(a duplicate except that here and there
the rendering's faulty or touched in too strong);
my little rugged bit of gold I mined,
cleared from its quartz and dross and pieced for use
with recognised alloy, is minted down
one of a million stamped and current coins.

My poor dear Madge, it half seems treasonous
to let regret touch any thought of you,
loyal and loving to me as you are;
and you are very very dear to me,
I could not spare you, would not change your love
to have the rich ideal of my hope
in any other woman; as you are
I love you, being you. And for the rest,
if I, my theory's too eager fool,
mistook the freedom of blunt ignorance
for one with freedom of the instructed will,
and took yours for a nature made to keep
its hardiness in culture, gaining strength
to be itself more fully; if I looked
for some rare perfectness of natural gifts,
developing not changed, pruned and not dwarfed;
if I believed you would be that to me
so many men have sung by women's names
and known no woman for, where is your fault,
who did but give yourself as you were then,

and with so true a giving? Violet,
whose is the blame if, rooted from your place,
where you grew truly to your natural law,
set by my hand in artificial soil,
bound to unwonted props, whose blame if you
are not quite violet and not quite rose?

She's happy though, I think: she does not bear
the pain of my mistake, and shall not bear;
and she'll not ever guess of a mistake.

Mistake − 'tis a hard word. Well let it pass:
it shall not wrong her: for was it in her
or in myself I was mistaken most?
What, I, who have been bold to hurl revolt
at great Queen Bugaboo Society,
did I not teach her suit and service first,
wincing when she infringed some useless law?
do I not wince today beside the fire
at every word or gesture she shall use
not scheduled in the warrant what to do?
do I not bid her have the table thus,
assort such viands, use such furniture,
wear such a stuff at morning, such at night,
all to the warrant of Queen Bugaboo,
and feel a something missing when she fails,
a discord setting all my teeth on edge?
Why, what a score of small observances;
mere fashionable tricks, are to my life
the butter on the bread, without which salve
the bit's too coarse to swallow; what a score
of other small observances and tricks,
worn out of fashion or not yet come in,
reek worse than garlic to my pampered taste,
making the wholesomest food too difficult!
And that which in an ancient yesterday
was but some great man's humour is to me
duty by rote today. I had not felt
my own life that punctilious copy-book,
writ to stock patterns set to all a school,
I have called usual lives, but my poor Madge
has unawares informed me of myself.

We can no other; 'tis as natural
to men to take this artificial kind
as to the flowers, which, grown in neighbour ranks,
taste the same winds and feed on the same soil,
to take inoculation by the bees
of one another's dyes and be alike
in new unlikeness to their primal types.
Our gift is imitation and to share
the subtle current of all sympathies;
we breathe each other's thoughts, as in a crowd
we breathe each other's breaths, unconsciously;
and if there could be a mere human man
to singly be creator, make the thing
which none has hoped for near him, say the things
which none has thought beside him, were there one
to be the god we claim in our rash word
original, needs were he such a one
as we call savage, one apart in woods
and friendless deserts, planning by himself
some first instinctive art, or questioning
blank ignorance and wonder into thoughts.
And as for us, the men who live in days
when what the West has whispered finds the East
across an ocean in a breath of time;
when the old era's painful manuscripts,
too choice and rare for less than sage's needs,
reach the new era changed to daily showers
of schoolboys' textbooks raining from the press;
when we shake hands with our antipodes
for being neighbour to us; when, like streets
of the city where we are burghers, half the world
is our admitted home, the other half
our summer pleasure-grounds outside our walls;
we, who are scholars of all times and lands,
must be content, each several man, to feel
we are no sovereign units each to rule
the small world of himself, but knitted links,
one drawing on the other in a chain –
a bondage say, but have we not its worth,
help, movement, and the chain grows lengthening on
to span the universe? A braggart whim,
were it a possible, if any link,
breaking away from hundreds side by side,
would be a separate spangle.

        Yet, alack,
sometimes we links get drawn we know not where,
but think there's mud about us. Still the chain
lies in God's hands, though the sly devil comes
and gives a crooked tug or so at times.

Links in a chain – my metaphor goes well,
convinces me where first I was convinced –
links in a chain, drawing each other on:
but never yet material metaphor
would fit a mind's whole thought, and the hitch comes
where I bid mine goodbye. Links in a chain,
but what of hearts and wills that are in us,
hopes, aims, beliefs? Must we go measuring them
by 'the world says', 'so other people think',
dock our near tastes and natures to the shapes
in common wear, make lay figures of our lives,
as women of their bodies, to be decked
and draped or trimmed and swathed or let go bare
by strict indefinite despots out of sight?
Why, let us have that freedom we accord
inanimate things, to grow each to his kind
and to his best, cattle and servile beasts,
to grow each to his kind and to his best;
but we – oh, monstrous folly – we, designed
each man so much unlike to all men else
as one whole kind of beasts to other kinds,
must train and pattern our reluctant souls
into one liveried sameness!

        Oh, I am tired!
tired, tired, of this bland smiling slavery,
monotonous waste of life. And, while we fools
are making curtsies and brave compliments
to our rare century, and, courtierly,
swaddling our strength in trammels of soft silk,
the rotten depths grow rottener. Every day
more crime, more pain, more horror. We are good
no doubt, we 'better classes' – oh, we boast
our modern virtues in the dead men's teeth
that were our fathers – we are earnest now,
and charitable, and we wash ourselves,
and have a very fair morality;

most well brought up, in fine, of any men
that any age has nurtured, and besides
so equal in our manners and our coats:
and then the classes which, though bettering,
are not quite *better* yet, are the most shrewd,
most apt, most honest, most intelligent,
that ever the world saw yet. True all of it
for aught I know, some of it as I think,
but underneath – great God, how many souls
are born an hour as provender for hell!

Oh horrible days! Our goodness growing ripe,
a spreading scent of sweets, but with no power
to disinfect the spreading foulnesses;
and by mere birthrate vice made multiplex!
From the murk lanes, and from the fetid courts,
and from the shameful dens where poverty
hobnobs with wolfish crime, out of the reek
of lust and filth, out of the festering homes
of pestilence and famine, the hoarse cry
grows multitudinous, the cavernous cry
of shame and ignorance hunger and greed
become despair and devilishness... And we
gravely thank God for culture and new lights!

Most horrible days: and we who know the worst
(or dream it, sitting in our easy chairs,
sorry that all men have not easy chairs),
and would do somewhat, do it all amiss.
We pelt our broadcast gold into the mire,
then comes a scramble, foul grows fouler yet;
with a Samaritan hand we feed and feed
the daughters of the horseleech, drunkenness
and dissolute idleness, that cry 'give, give',
sucking the lifeblood from our people's heart;
we pension beggars, buy the burglar tools
and the sot gin, and pay the harlot's rent:
societies, committees, vestry rooms,
with fingers in our purses, lavish wealth,
past common counting, to keep up the tale
of pauper legions and bribe new recruits,
sow coin that, like the pestilent dragon's teeth,
bear us a poisonous crop of human harm:

OUT OF MY BORROWED BOOKS

all all endeavours go, like witches' prayers,
backwards against the meaning, and bring down
the counter-curse of blessings that were asked.

What should we do? I know not; but I think
there's moral in a hackneyed classic tale:
when the great gulf still yawned, after the gold
and treasures had been thrown, there came a man
and gave himself, and then the great gulf closed.

But how? How? And I know not; but I think
if the strong pith and freshness of our lives
were not so sucked and dried away, our span
not maimed and dwarfed, our sight not warped untrue,
by eating custom, petty disciplines,
footlight perspectives cramped to suit our stage,
if we were men, not types and portraitures
and imitative shadows, some of us
might learn –

          Learn, learn, and if we learned,
saw by what boldness, or what sacrifice,
or what endurance, or what vehemence,
the goal of our beginning might be reached,
the padded skeleton we call the world,
that mumming glib Duessa who usurps
the true world's rule and rights, would trip us up
with half a league of silken barriers
too soft for us to break and breaking us.
Oh, but I know it, I, who time by time,
fierce with the turbulent goodness of my youth,
rushed to the clamourous call of new crusades,
and time by time dropped baffled and worn weak
before a rampart as of dancing pumps,
a wind as if it blew from ladies' fans,
till now I sit a weary man growing old
among the ruins of his purposes,
hopeless of any good to be by him.

Oh, with how full a hope, when morning glowed,
I donned my armour, who at night ride back
foolish and broken! I have set myself
to fight with shadows stronger than a man,

being impalpable and everywhere,
and striking done no hurt but to myself;
and I have ridden at ranks in adamant
and fallen, strained and useless, under foot;
and I have sieged impenetrable walls
and waited day by day till I grew faint;
and never have I triumphed in my cause,
whether it were a great one, or a dream,
a pettish whim, or too divinely large:
for if I strove against contagious ills
cankering the core of us or but at spots
that fleck the smooth gloss of our drawingrooms,
and if I rose to claim some wide desire
of general good or but my own escape
from some small prickings of our social gyves,
always I was against the multitude,
against strong Custom's army plodding on,
unconquerable, calm, like a great stream
whose power is that its waters drift one way.

Tired, tired — grown sick of battle and defeat,
lying in harbour, like a man worn out
by storms, and yet not patient of my rest:
how if I went to some kind southern clime
where, as they say, lost in long summer dreams,
the mind grows careless with sun-drunkenness
and sleeps and wakens softly like a child?
Would Madge be over sorry to come out
into free loneliness with me a while?
Clear tints and sunshine, glowing seas and skies,
beauty of mountains and of girdled plains,
the strangeness of new peoples, change and rest,
would these atone to her for so much lost
which she counts precious? For she loves that round
of treadmill ceremonies, mimic tasks,
we make our women's lives — Good heavens what work
to set the creatures to, whom we declare
God purposed for companions to us men...
companions to each other only now,
their business but to waste each other's time.
So much to do among us, and we spend
so many human souls on only this!
in petty actress parts in the long game

(grave foolery like children playing school,
setting themselves hard tasks and punishments),
that lasts till death and is Society:
the sunlight working hours all chopped and chipped
in stray ten minutes by some score of friends
who, grieved their friend's not out, come rustling in
by ones and twos to say the weather's fine;
or paid away, poor soul, on pilgrimage
reciprocally due to tell them so:
each woman owing tax of half her life
as plaything for the others' careless hours,
each woman setting down her foot to hold
her sister tightly to the tethered round,
will she or nill she: all with rights on each
greater than hers... and I might say than God's,
since He made work the natural food of minds,
cheated of which they dwindle and go dead
like palsied limbs, and gives to each that sense
of beasts, who know their food, to know its work,
choosing the great or little.

      But myself,
have I befooled the instinct by warped use?
for is not the fruit rotten I have found
by all my labours; nothing to the world
and to me bitterness? And I forget
the strong joy of endeavour, and the fire
of hope is burned out in me; all grows dull,
rest is not rest and I am sick of toil:
I count the cost, and —

      Ready, love, at last?
Why, what a rosy June! A flush of bloom
sparkling with crystal dews — Ah silly one,
you love these muslin roses better far
than those that wear the natural dew of heaven.
I thought you prettier when, the other day,
the children crowned you with the meadow-sweets:
I like to hear you teach them wild flowers' names
and make them love them; but yourself —

      What's that?
'The wild flowers in a room's hot stifling glare

would die in half a minute.' True enough:
your muslin roses are the wiser wear.
Well, I must see you start. Draw your hood close:
and are you shawled against this east wind's chills?

from *A Book of Rhyme* (1881)

from *English Rispetti*

The Flowing Tide

The slow green wave comes curling from the bay
    And leaps in spray along the sunny marge,
And steals a little more and more away,
    And drowns the dulse, and lifts the stranded barge.
Leave me, strong tide, my smooth and yellow shore;
But the clear waters deepen more and more:
    Leave me my pathway of the sands, strong tide;
    Yet are the waves more fair than all they hide.

Late Roses

The swallows went last week, but 'twas too soon;
    For, look, the sunbeams streaming on their eaves;
And, look, my rose, a very child of June,
    Spreading its crimson coronet of leaves.
Was it too late, my rose, to bud and blow?
For when the summer wanes her roses go:
    Bloom, rose, there are more roses yet to wake,
    With hearts of sweetness for the summer's sake.

The Frozen River

Dead stream beneath the icy silent blocks
    That motionless stand soddening into grime,
Thy fretted falls hang numb, frost pens the locks;
    Dead river, when shall be thy waking time?
'Not dead'; the river spoke and answered me,
'My burdened current, hidden, finds the sea',
    'Not dead, not dead'; my heart replied at length,
    'The frozen river holds a hidden strength.'

from *Mother and Daughter*
An Uncompleted Sonnet Sequence (1895)

VII

Her father lessons me I at times am hard,
    Chiding a moment's fault as too grave ill,
    And let some little blot my vision fill,
Scanning her with a narrow near regard.
True. Love's unresting gaze is self-debarred
    From all sweet ignorance, and learns a skill,
    Not painless, of such signs as hurt love's will,
That would not have its prize one tittle marred.

Alas! Who rears and loves a dawning rose
    Starts at a speck upon one petal's rim:
Who sees a dusk creep in the shrined pearl's glows,
    Is ruined at once: 'My jewel growing dim!'
I watch one bud that on my bosom blows,
    I watch one treasured pearl for me and him.

VIII

A little child she, half defiant came
    Reasoning her case – 'twas not so long ago –
    'I cannot mind your scolding, for I know
However bad I were you'd love the same.'
And I, what countering answer could I frame?
    'Twas true, and true, and God's self told her so.
    One does but ask one's child to smile and grow,
And each rebuke has love for its right name.

And yet, methinks, sad mothers who for years,
    Watching the child pass forth that was their boast,
Have counted all the footsteps by new fears
Till even lost fears seem hopes whereof they're reft
And of all mother's good love sole is left –
    Is their Love, Love, or some remembered ghost?

IX

Oh weary hearts! Poor mothers that look back!
  So outcasts from the vale where they were born
  Turn on their road and, with a joy forlorn,
See the far roofs below their arid track:
So in chill buffets while the sea grows black
  And windy skies, once blue, are tost and torn,
  We are not yet forgetful of the morn,
And praise anew the sunshine that we lack.

Oh, sadder than pale sufferers by a tomb
  That say 'My dead is happier, and is more'
  Are they who dare no 'is' but tell what's o'er –
  Thus the frank childhood, those the lovable ways –
  Stirring the ashes of remembered days
For yet some sparks to warm the livelong gloom.

XII

She has made me wayside posies: here they stand,
  Bringing fresh memories of where they grew.
  As new-come travellers from a world we knew
Wake every while some image of their land,
So these whose buds our woodland breezes fanned
  Bring to my room the meadow where they blew,
  The brook-side cliff, the elms where wood-doves coo –
And every flower is dearer for her hand.

Oh blossoms of the paths she loves to tread,
  Some grace of her is in all thoughts you bear:
  For in my memories of your homes that were
The old sweet loneliness they kept is fled,
And would I think it back I find instead
  A presence of my darling mingling there.

XIII

My darling scarce thinks music sweet save mine:
  'Tis that she does but love me more than hear.
  She'll not believe my voice to stranger ear

Is merely measure to the note and line;
'Not so,' she says; 'Thou hast a secret thine:
    The others' singing's only rich, or clear,
    But something in thy tones brings music near;
As though thy song could search me and divine.'

Oh voice of mine that in some day not far
    Time, the strong creditor, will call his debt,
Will dull – and even to her – will rasp and mar,
    Sing Time asleep because of her regret,
Be twice thy life the thing her fancies are,
    Thou echo to the self she knows not yet.
                Caserta, April, 1882

XIV

To love her as today is so great bliss
    I needs must think of morrows almost loth,
    Morrows wherein the flower's unclosing growth
Shall make my darling other than she is.
The breathing rose excels the bud I wis,
    Yet bud that will be rose is sweet for both;
    And by-and-by seems like some later troth
Named in the moment of a lover's kiss.

Yes, I am jealous, as of one now strange
    That shall instead of her possess my thought,
Of her own self made new by any change,
    Of her to be by ripening morrows brought.
My rose of women under later skies!
Yet, ah! my child with the child's trustful eyes!
                Cernobbio

XV

That some day Death who has us all for jest
    Shall hide me in the dark and voiceless mould,
    And him whose living hand has mine in hold,
Where loving comes not nor the looks that rest,
Shall make us nought where we are known the best,
    Forgotten things that leave their track untold

As in the August night the sky's dropped gold –
This seems no strangeness, but Death's natural hest.

But looking on the dawn that is her face
        To know she too is Death's seems misbelief;
        She should not find decay, but, as the sun
Moves mightier from the veil that hides his place,
Keep ceaseless radiance. Life is Death begun:
        But Death and her! That's strangeness passing grief.

XVII

And how could I grow old while she's so young?
        Methinks her heart sets tune for mine to beat,
        We are so near; her new thoughts, incomplete,
Find their shaped wording happen on my tongue;
Like bloom on last year's winterings newly sprung
        My youth upflowers with hers, and must repeat
        Old joyaunces in me nigh obsolete.
Could I grow older while my child's so young?

And there are tales how youthful blood instilled
        Thawing frore Age's veins gave life new course,
And quavering limbs and eyes made indolent
        Grew freshly eager with beginning force:
She so breathes impulse. Were my years twice spent,
Not burdening Age, with her, could make me chilled.

XIX

Life on the wane: yes, sudden that news breaks.
        And yet I would 'twere suddenly and less soon;
        Since no forewarning makes loss opportune.
And now I watch that slow advance Time makes:
Watch as, while silent flow spreads broad the lakes
        Mid the land levels of a smooth lagoon,
        One waiting, pitiful, on a tidal dune,
Aware too long before it overtakes.

Ah! there's so quick a joy in hues and sun,
　　　　And will my eyes see dim? Will vacant sense
Forget the lark, the surges on the beach?
Shall I step wearily and wish 'twere done?
　　　　　Well, if it be love will not too go hence,
Love will have new glad secrets yet to teach.

XX

There's one I miss. A little questioning maid
　　　　That held my finger, trotting by my side,
　　　　And smiled out of her pleased eyes open wide,
Wondering and wiser at each word I said.
And I must help her frolics if she played,
　　　　And I must feel her trouble if she cried;
　　　　My lap was hers past right to be denied;
She did my bidding, but I more obeyed.

Dearer she is today, dearer and more;
　　　　Closer to me, since sister womanhoods meet;
Yet, like poor mothers some long while bereft,
I dwell on toward ways, quaint memories left,
　　　　I miss the approaching sound of pit–pat feet,
The eager baby voice outside my door.

XXIV

'You scarcely are a mother, at that rate.
　　　　Only one child!' The blithe soul pitied loud.
　　　　And doubtless she, amid her household crowd,
When one brings care in another's fortunate;
When one fares forth another's at her gate.
　　　　Yea, were her first-born folded in his shroud,
　　　　Not with a whole despair would she be bowed,
She has more sons to make her heart elate.

Many to love her singly, mother theirs,
　　　　To give her the dear love of being their need,
　　　　To storm her lap by turns and claim their kiss,
To kneel around her at their bed-time prayers;

Many to grow her comrades! Some have this.
Yet I, I do not envy them indeed.

Ramsgate, 1886

XXVII

Since first my little one lay on my breast
    I never needed such a second good,
    Nor felt a void left in my motherhood
She filled not always to the utterest.
The summer linnet, by glad yearnings pressed,
    Builds room enough to house a callow brood:
    I prayed not for another child – nor could;
My solitary bird had my heart's nest.

But she is cause that any baby thing
    If it but smile, is one of mine in truth,
    And every child becomes my natural joy:
And, if my heart gives all youth fostering,
    Her sister, brother, seems the girl or boy:
    My darling makes me mother to their youth.

Mathilde Blind
1841–96

The only collected edition of Mathilde Blind's poetry was compiled in 1900 by her literary executor, the poet and critic Arthur Symons (1865–1945). As he explains in his preface, he was scrupulous in respecting the texts; he was not scrupulous, though, in cutting and pasting, retitling and reordering her work into sections 'which seem to me to belong to the same sequence of moods'.[1] The result dismembers her work: in place of poetic development and the narrative expansiveness that Blind can command, Symons created a memorial. Richard Garnett's respectful memoir in the volume, although an essential source of information which draws on Blind's own notes for an autobiography, further silences her authentic voice.

Freed from the discreet possessiveness of her executors, Blind emerges as an original and intractable poet. Garnett's timid allusion to the difficulty of convincing her that 'social conventions or artistic refinements could count for anything' in comparison to the demands of the truth of art hints at the energy with which she did not so much defy as ignore the constraints of literary tradition. Webster explores how women live within the script that is written for them; Blind, for whom both English and social conventions were second languages, lived to a different script. She grew up with European revolutionaries; she was an atheist; if she was at home anywhere in a rootless life, it was in the unconventional, un-English circles of Pre-Raphaelite painters and Aesthetic writers; she wrote in impersonal genres on a large, narrative scale – translations, essays, biographies, epics of evolutionary science and politics. She wrote the first biography of George Eliot (1883); she shares Eliot's intellectual grasp of theory as a tool for defining the world, and her poetry has Eliot's scientific sense of how the dense texture of external reality can be understood as part of a larger pattern.

Only four years older than Webster (whom she knew), Blind is different in kind: European, unclassifiable within English society, her life marked by the chance forces of political upheaval. It was a freedom not to belong that she would live by. She was born Mathilde Cohen in Mannheim, Germany, in 1841. Her father died when she was a baby, and her mother subsequently married Karl Blind. Like Marx, he was of the German generation swept to England by the events of 1848, the year of revolutions in Europe. Karl Blind had already been expelled from university in 1846 and imprisoned in 1847 for publishing a seditious pamphlet; by 1849 the Blind family was in exile in Paris, where Blind was again imprisoned. In August 1849, Blind (along with Marx and others) was ejected from Paris. He travelled to England and was joined by the rest of his family a few months later. Thereafter, Mathilde Blind grew up in St John's Wood, among the disputatious intellects of revolutionary Europe in exile. Garibaldi drank German wine with the Blinds in the 1860s, and Giuseppe Mazzini, whom Mathilde Blind revered all her life, was a frequent visitor. Karl Blind – as the penurious Marx noted with some resentment – made a material success of life in England. He wrote for English newspapers and magazines, lectured and served on committees.[2] He established himself in literary circles beyond the expatriate community, counting the Rossettis and Swinburne as friends – it was through Karl Blind that Swinburne was able to meet his hero Mazzini in 1867. He was a friend, too, of John Chapman, who in 1869 invited Mathilde Blind to review William Rossetti's edition of Shelley in *The Westminster Review*. Her lengthy article[3] marks an important moment in establishing her intellectual credentials.

Whatever formal education she had seems to have been stimulatingly haphazard. At one school Blind, in her own words, 'turned Christian for a time' and then lost her faith entirely, influenced by an independent-minded schoolfriend who 'again and again came back to the strange discrepancies between the account of Creation in Genesis and the history of our globe as revealed to us by the rocks and stones'. In what was probably a satisfyingly dramatic outcome, Blind was asked by the school to give up her beliefs or leave, and duly left, an adolescent martyr to the cause of atheism.[4] (As with other German exiles of 1848, the Blinds, products of the European Enlightenment, appear to have been entirely secular and nominal Jews.) Garnett finds in the subsequent gap in her autobiography evidence of the 'intensity of her anguish'; she seems to have recovered by 1859, when she was staying at the house of her maternal uncle in Zurich and undertaking a walking tour alone through Switzerland, adopting an eighteen-year-old's stratagem of living on chocolate when she ran out of money. 'For once,' she wrote, 'I felt truly free.' Put on a train back to Zurich by a concerned English family (she had announced an intention to travel on alone to the Caucasus), she gained the sort of education among a 'group of brilliant revolutionists' that no English schoolroom could provide, studying philology, Latin and Old German. Back with her family in St John's Wood, she continued to live in a Europe of the mind, developing a knowledge of Goethe, Heine and Schiller. In 1866 her younger brother Ferdinand committed suicide in prison after a failed attempt to assassinate Bismarck, an affair that attracted widespread attention in England.

Mathilde's first collection of poems, dedicated to Mazzini, was published under the pseudonym 'Claude Lake' the following year.

In 1871, when she was thirty, Blind left the family home. For the rest of her life she lived in the precarious independence of a single woman, travelling and staying for long periods in friends' homes. She would have no secure income for another twenty years. She found companionship among the freethinking intellectual circles where Aestheticism intersected with radicalism. She was closely enough linked to Swinburne for it to have been supposed that they were lovers; she knew Whistler, the poet James Thomson, William Morris and the Marx family, was a friend of William Rossetti, and spent a part of each year living in the Ford Madox Brown household in London and in Manchester. She reviewed Swinburne and Morris, lectured on Morris's translation of the Volsunga Saga and contributed to *The Dark Blue*, a short-lived magazine that was an influential voice of the emergent Aesthetic movement for a few years in the 1870s, publishing work by, among others, Morris, Swinburne and Rossetti.[5]

More particularly, Blind was also part of a network of women writers whose lives create a dialogue that runs from mid-Victorian feminism to the early twentieth century: Augusta Webster, Vernon Lee, Amy Levy, Olive Schreiner, Eleanor Marx and the polemical feminist writer Mona Caird (1854–1932), with whom Blind was closely linked towards the end of her life. Like Eleanor Marx, Blind realigned her revolutionary inheritance towards a specifically feminist politics. In 1890 she published her translation from French of *The Journal of Marie Bashkirtseff* (1887), a work whose emotional account of frustrated artistic aspirations became, as *Blackwood's* described it, 'a kind of secret Bible' for 'tired and discontented women'. In her introduction, Blind calls the work 'the drama of a woman's soul'; an allusion to Elizabeth Barrett Browning makes explicit the particular significance of the *Journal* as the link in Blind's work between aestheticism and political engagement. Like Webster's 'Castaway' or Levy's 'Xantippe', the *Journal* is a drama in which the protagonist finds the language to write the book of herself. Behind each stands Barrett Browning's *Aurora Leigh* (1856), the poem that was a touchstone for Blind, as for so many Victorian women writers. Blind's poetry, like Levy's, shares the Aesthetic valuing of the fleeting moment, the imagery of the solitary, rootless artist:

> Lo, haply walking in some clattering street –
> Where throngs of men and women dumbly pass,
> Like shifting pictures seen within a glass
> Which leave no trace behind...[6]

But in her most ambitious poems, *The Heather on Fire* (1886) and *The Ascent of Man* (1889), she fuses that individualism with an aspiration that recalls Aurora Leigh's ambition, both hubristic and self-effacing, to claim the poet's traditional role as the singer of the age's myths, revealing the pattern of individual fates in the long perspectives of history. It is a dual inheritance that makes these awkward, unshapely poems such profoundly feminist narratives.

The Heather on Fire is an epic of the Highland Clearances. Blind had made a number of visits to Scotland during the 1870 and 1880s, and the landscape had moved her greatly, as wild and solitary places always did; but she could also read the politics of wilderness:

> The moors and valleys, whose blank silence is only broken by the rush of tumbling streams or the cry of some solitary bird, were once enlivened by the manifold sounds of human industry and made musical with children's voices... it was but yesterday that they were inhabited by a brave, moral and industrious peasantry, full of poetic instincts and ardent patriotism, ruthlessly expelled from their native land to make way for sporting grounds rented by merchant princes and American millionaires.[7]

In the poem, Blind brings a sociologist's marshalling of documentation to bear on her imaginative response to such solitude. The 1886 edition included eighteen pages of supporting material, including extracts from the 1884 Commissioners' report on the condition of Highland crofters, accounts of the economy of the Highlands and personal recollections of eviction. Among these, Blind printed a lengthy section from Alfred Russel Wallace's *Land Nationalisation: Its Necessity and Its Aims* (1882). Wallace (1823–1913), who later wrote an introduction to the second (1899) edition of her *Ascent of Man*, provided the intellectual framework for both *The Heather on Fire* and the vaster vision of *The Ascent of Man*. A biologist and evolutionist, he derived his interest in land reform, as well as his support for other radical causes, including that of women's education, from a fundamentally optimistic interpretation of evolution as a force for 'the true advancement of the race'.[8] He was a key figure to Blind and other feminist writers of the 1880s and 1890s such as Mona Caird, because his work provided both an analytical language and a mythology of limitless possibility for polemic and utopian fictions. A lecture on Shelley that she delivered in 1886 shows Blind's preoccupations at the time she was writing her two epic poems: had the poet had the opportunity of 'harmonising his views of Nature with those so luminously developed by Darwin, Alfred Russel Wallace, and other scientific thinkers', she argues, Shelley would have shown humanity emerging from barbarity and 'continually progressing to higher stages of moral and mental development'.[9] Her own *Ascent of Man* fulfils such a programme, opening with the 'electrical vapour' from which life is created and ending with mystical oneness with the universe.

Like the exiles of 1848 among whom she grew up, Blind creates new myths of human destiny – and as in the myths of revolution, the soaring potential is undercut by a vertiginous sense of individuals swept away in the vast cycles of history and certainties dissolving.[10] Constellations come into being and are extinguished as they spin through space. Blind struggles to find a language in which to express the invisible forces and limitless vistas of the scientific world: the poem begins to push into abstraction, until Blind seems on the verge of moving her poetry into a new and more radical place, where language is shaken into momentary patterns of sound and texture:

> Ever showering from their flaming fountains
> Light more light on each far-circling earth,
> Till life stirred crepuscular seas…

In 1892 Blind became the sole heir to her step-brother's fortune, giving her financial security and the means to travel more widely. In her later years, particularly after the death of Ford Madox Brown, this woman who had always been a little apart from English culture achieved even greater distance, in visits to Egypt. In the 'Orient' poems of her final collection, *Birds of Passage: Songs of the Orient and Occident* (1895), she fuses a *fin de siècle* aestheticism with a dislocated – disorientated – sense of freedom. A letter suggests how deeply felt was her response:

> The silence and solitude of the arid wilderness… suited my mind to perfection… I think with longing of its infinite vastness, of the air that blows over its leagues and leagues of lion coloured sand, of the luminous blue sky that turns the horror of it into something divine. Never shall I forget returning one evening in the after-glow… the arc of light spreading outwards from the horizon turned into the hues of an immense prism above the desolation it defied. Then, as the glow faded into lemon-colour, the little stars, faint and far between, looked down on the pitch-black sand. A few lights, shining here and there in the Bishareen camp, showed I was nearing Assouan. A tall woman with a pitcher on her head could be seen coming from the Nile.[11]

It is a profound encounter, not with an oriental 'other', but with a woman who becomes, for a moment, the mirror to Blind's own solitariness; both women at once at ease and alone in the landscape, although they have arrived at that moment from different places.

Notes

1 *The Poetical Works of Mathilde Blind*, ed. Arthur Symons, with a memoir by Richard Garnett, T. Fisher Unwin, London 1900, p. viii. The memoir, pp. 2–43, is the main source for the biographical details that follow.
2 See Rosemary Ashton, *Little Germany: German Refugees in Victorian Britain*, Oxford University Press, Oxford 1989, pp. 167–73.
3 *Westminster Review*, July 1870, pp. 75–97.
4 'Memoir', pp. 6, 7. Blind remained a freethinking secularist for the rest of her life.
5 See James Diedrick, ' "My love is a force that will force you to care": Subversive Sexuality in Mathilde Blind's Dramatic Monologues', *Victorian Poetry* 40, 2002, pp. 359–86.
6 From 'Haunted Streets'.
7 Preface to *The Heather on Fire*.
8 Alfred Russel Wallace, 'Darwinism in Sociology', *The Eagle and the Serpent* 1, September 1898, pp. 57–9.
9 'Shelley's View of Nature Contrasted with Darwin's', lecture privately printed London 1886, pp. 12, 19. Available at the Victorian Women Writers Project, www.indiana.edu/~letrs/vwwp/blind/shelley.html.
10 In a metaphor that echoes *The Ascent of Man*, Blind wrote to Richard Garnett after reading Ibsen's *Ghosts* that 'our ideals of moral conduct are really undergoing a process of disintegration... as if the earth were beginning to rock under one's feet' (quoted in Diedrick, p. 375).
11 'Memoir', p. 39.

from *Poems by Claude Lake* (1867)

from *Poems to J.M.*

I   The Torrent

Oh torrent, roaring in thy giant fall,
    And thund'ring grandly o'er th' opposing blocks,
Thy voice, far louder than the lion's call,
    Through trackless forests shakes the heart of rocks,
Runs through the marrow of the earth with shocks,
    Lashes the clouds with terror, for they fly
Along the high wide blue with streaming locks,
    And round thee foam white dazzling flashes high
And with forked water-flames half licks the central sky.

Oh, what a storm of waters! Oh, what chasms
    Of foam! what seething hills! what whirling rain!
Billows on billows press, though torn by spasms;
    Wounded and bleeding, yet defying pain!
They grappled with the stones, that gnash in vain
    Their cruel teeth, for smarting wounds they brave,
And toss in scorn their wildly flowing mane,
    When with exulting cries big wave on wave
Rolls with a mighty sweep o'er a slain foeman's grave.

Roll on, great torrent, with triumphal song,
    Through caverned cliff, through rock and mountain roll;
Force all the barriers that around thee throng,
    Thou know'st th' eternal ocean for thy goal.
Hence thine impetuous rush, and roar, and roll;
    Hence thy wild heavings as thou flow'st amain;
Hence thy far-reaching and tempestuous call
    For stream and river, brook and rill and rain,
    Thou on thy Titan breast would'st carry to the main.

Roll on! The heavens are with thee, for they fling
    Their lovely rainbows round thy gleaming brow;
Rainbows, that like the crown of heroes cling
    For ever round thee with their magic glow;
Or like the wondrous halo which will flow
    Around the martyr's head; for those sweet hues,
They hover round thee in thy weal and woe,

Like love, that with its tender tears bedews
And heals the bitter pain of ev'ry earthly bruise!

Roll on! with a white heat upon thy way!
    Lo yon, a little tiny woodland bird
Flits on wet wing through all the surf and spray,
    And settles on a jagged rock unscared,
Round whose grim base a billowy din is heard;
    A bright amazèd ray from its black eyes
It darts around, and listens not afeared –
    Then diamond-powdered to the woods it flies,
And sings to forest ears the mighty melodies.

E'en thus *thou* art! For that Titanic stream
    But a material symbol was of thee!
A dim reflection of thy being did seem
    Thou man, high-souled as son of man can be!
Into whose mind, vast, noble, pure, and free,
    Flash awful revelations light-like in:
Unveiling spiritual laws to thee;
    Great central truths, that glow all life within,
That move the nations on, and make the planets spin.

Thou hero! For through prejudice's walls,
    That lock up earth against the quick'ning floods,
And 'gainst the fresh regenerating falls
    Of young ideas, that in sprouting mood
Seethe like new wine, stirred by the grape's hot blood,
    In the old bottles; thou, oh, brave and bold!
Didst force thy way, crushing night's deathly brood,
    As George the sainted, in the days of old –
The dragon, who beneath his footstep writhing roll'd.

Dragons, alas! still darken the green earth,
    War with the good, the beautiful, the wise;
From gulfs of ancient night they've issued forth,
    And with their shadowy wings blot out the skies;
Old creeds that gasp forth curses, tyrannies
    All foul with feeding on their own decay,
Old cramping forms, and crippling social lies,
    Whose venomous breathing with corruption slay,
Like loathsome rattlesnakes that glut upon their prey.

But thou assail'st them, fearless, though they spurt
      Their reeking poison in thy smarting face;
And careless of thy bruises and thy hurt,
      Thou still press'st on with an undaunted pace;
A bold path-finder for the coming race,
      And in thy faith, strong as the morning star,
Piercing the welt'ring clouds with lucent rays;
      Thy voice, a light above time's din and war,
      Proclaimeth to mankind the rosy dawn afar!

Thou martyr! For the world it knows thee not,
      Scoffs at thee, scorns thee, rails and laughs and sneers;
With barbèd darts embitters thy hard lot,
      As oft of old to prophets and to seers;
With its bleared sight the veil it cannot pierce,
      And see the future rise upon the days!
Thus persecutes with hatred blind and fierce,
      And, 'stead of crowns plucked from the living bays,
      It binds thy brows with thorns – thorns that will turn to rays!

Still from thy heart's vast deeps the shouts arise,
      And swell along, a rushing lava stream –
A lava stream of burning melodies,
      Shaking thy brethren from a sluggish dream,
To strive and *be* the thing they fain would seem;
      With thee, false custom's cramping bounds to leap,
To trust the rising of the virgin beam,
      And at thy call through death and danger sweep
      Towards the free, the pure, the renovating deep.

And still around thee, thro' the battle's roar,
      Shimmers in splendour and unfading bloom,
Brighter than moonlight on the seething shore,
      Sweeter than roses clust'ring round the tomb,
Born of the struggle with the fatal gloom;
      A subtle gleam, fleeting 'mid tears and ruth,
A dewy prophecy of days to come,
      When *one* great rainbow, love, and light and truth,
Encircle will the world with an eternal youth!

But I, behold, like to the tiny thing,
      The forest bird; I feel a magic spell,
That draws me strongly on uncertain wing

MATHILDE BLIND

Away from all the violet woodland smell,
To hear the words that from thy spirit well:
    Enchained, entranced, oh! let me list, while flame
And dazzling light in billows round me swell;
    Then flying back to shades from whence I came
    I will heroic deeds, prophetic words, proclaim.

The Orange-Peel in the Gutter

Behold, unto myself I said,
This place how dull and desolate,
For lovely thoughts how all unmeet,
This drear and darksome London street.
Above, beneath, and all around,
Not one slight crumb is to be found;
Not one so slight poetic crumb
For sparrow-poet to feed upon.
For lo! above there is no sky!
No living blue to glad the eye!
No sun that shines, no flying cloud!
But fog, that in a huge dun shroud
Wraps all the London town about;
And with it comes the drizzling rain,
And dusky houses wets in vain –
It ne'er can wash them white again.
Those houses, yea, how cold and bare,
With self-same aspect stand they there,
With grimy windows two and two,
It makes me sick to look at you!
No tree, no shrub, to lend you grace,
With drooping branch to hide your face;
No solitary blossom e'en
To brighten you with flow'ry sheen;
Nor living things I here espy,
Save yon black cat, with sharp green eye,
Sliding along with stealthy pace:
The very spirit of the place.
And in the road hops here and there
A sparrow, searching scanty fare,
The pauper of the sons of air.
Nought! nought! but wall and iron spike,
Cold, cruel, as if fain 'twould like

To run some beggar through and through,
And guard the door from him and you.
And underfoot? – no flowers, no grass,
T' arrest the step before you pass,
To send up whispers low and sweet,
To smile, to beckon, and to greet;
No gurgling brook, no silent pool,
In whose pure waters, still and cool,
The flying bird, the flitting cloud,
The sunbeam peering in and out,
The star that slides through limpid air,
Are glassed in beauty wondrous fair.
None – none of these, but miry clay,
To cling tenaciously all day,
With heavy clutch to your poor heel,
And in the gutter you, the peel
Of some sweet golden orange fruit,
Though smothered now with dirt and soot
Still darting forth through dull decay,
The splendour of a bygone day,
The ling'ring of a dying ray.
Oh, wondrous strange! I feel the deep
Hush of Italian nights slow creep
Around me, see the fuller light
Of southern stars strike through the night,
And hear the sweeter breathèd sighs
Of southern breezes swell and rise;
Rise, swell I hear the balm-fed breeze,
Through the dark grove of orange trees,
Where silver gleams of creamy bloom,
In fragrance flash along the gloom;
And the gold fruit through dark doth shine
A star! A mystery divine!
I hear the sweeter sighs of love,
By southern hearts breathed through the grove,
Like to the cooing of a dove;
Like to the soft falls of summer rain,
On hoary wood and parched plain;
Like to the drops of pale moonlight,
That sink upon the sea at night;
Heart melts with heart, and kiss with kiss,
In holy night, in holy bliss,
As in the wondrous sunset skies

MATHILDE BLIND

III

Hues melt with hues, and dyes with dyes,
Till all in one vast glory lies.

But what a full and deep-set roar
Heaves, swells, and surges more and more,
Like billows on a stormy shore.
Yet here flows not the dark blue sea,
But street on street continually;
Here walls on walls press nigh and nigher,
And roofs on roofs rise high and higher,
And spire still greets the rising spire.
The clang, the clash, the row, the roar,
London, great London, 'tis once more,
With hurry, flurry, to and fro,
Time scarce to snarl a 'yes' or 'no';
Time scarce t' evade your neighbour's toe.
But here's the market fair to see,
An island green within that sea
Of streets, a little flow'ry spot,
Reminding him who's long forgot,
Of country fields and waving trees,
Of hedges, birds and flowers and bees.
The snowdrop stands in moist brown ground,
And purifies the air around;
The violet scatters woodland smells,
And hyacinths ring their honeyed bells.
This man sells grapes from sunny Spain;
Lombardian almonds this again;
Pears, peaches, with the morning down,
All in that worldwide lap are thrown,
By all the nations, and they vie
In fruits, nursed by a southern sky.
The chaff'ring crowd, the bart'ring maid,
Here buy and sell, and choose and trade.
There sits a woman lean and old,
She shivers in the east wind's cold;
She knits; how fast her fingers fly!
Her fingers, oh! how worn and dry.
But still she knits, because she knows
Her crying grandchild's icy toes.
Her basket stands close by her side,
With orange heaps in golden pride;
Surely imprisoned sunbeams throw

Around them such a flush and glow,
That seeing them we seem to see
A glimpse of sun-loved Italy.
Oh, may they all be bought, and give
The old woman wherewithal to live!

Here in the garret, 'neath the leads,
Slowly spin out life's weary threads;
Slowly and slowly ebbs away
The breath of one poor child of clay.
The throbbing pulse, the great'ning eye,
The parchèd lips, the impatient sigh,
The mother marks 'twixt hope and fright,
From weary noon to weary night,
From midnight round to noon again:
Each hour crammed full with aching pain,
And anxious fluttering of hope,
As both alternately find scope.
And as she breathless notes each sound,
He whispers, turning round and round,
'Oh! mother, mother, give me drink.'
She's up, she's back scarce in a wink,
And to her darling's burning lips,
The luscious fruit she holds, he sips
With breaths long drawn, still on and on,
Till all the cooling juice is gone,
And only left of fragrant meal,
Is that still golden orange-peel.

The orange-peel! Ah, where am I?
Beneath the deep Italian sky?
In Covent Garden's crowded fair?
Or 'neath the roof of pain and care?
Ah, still within the darksome street,
So all unlovely and unsweet!
The welt'ring fog, the drizzling rain,
The dirt, the dust upon each pane,
The iron rails so hard and bare,
The miry clay, they all are here!
What did befall? Then did I dream?
Was all but air? Did all but seem?
How caught I then this wondrous gleam?
Ah! here you bit of sunny gold,

Within the gutter I behold;
Across my mind its life it flashed,
The fragrance of the past it dashed,
Dying, it kindled life, and hurled
My soul through heights and depths of world.
In bud and blossom, fruit and tree,
Revealed life's perfect harmony!
Revealed the throbs of mutual love,
Ensphered by kindling stars above!
Revealed the stir of busy life,
The trade, the turmoil, and the strife!
Struggles of honest poverty;
A watching mother's agony!
Child-life that hangs upon a breath,
The tremblings betwixt life and death –
Revealed the mystic link, that thrills
Through joy and pain, through good and ills,
Wafts influences from afar,
Connects the worm still with the star,
And binds the earth, the skies, the main,
The worlds, with one electric chain!
Behold, unto myself I said,
There's nought on earth so desolate,
But if the eye is there to see
Will find a joy and mystery,
As under dark and mossy dells
The violet hides with spring-like smells!
No cell, no garret, and no tomb,
For which no flower of love doth bloom!
No place so waste, so dark, so drear,
But heavenly beauty lurketh there!
And from these two will ever spring,
As music from the harp's sweet string,
As from the nest the lark soars high,
As from the flame the live sparks fly,
The fountain of great poesy,
Will shine and flash, and flame and glow,
Like to the million coloured bow
Of hope and peace, a lovely sign,
Flinging around that world of thine
A glory that is all divine!

The Wanderer

On unknown paths I falter forth,
　　A homeless wand'rer in the world;
Doubtful I flit across the earth,
　　Whither by blowing fates I'm hurled.

I grope about the pathless wood;
　　I tread along the boundless plain;
And with the wind's capricious mood,
　　I sink and rise upon the main.

The lonely cloud within the sky,
　　That by conflicting gales is torn,
Sways to and fro no more than I,
　　Now eastward, and now westward borne.

The crested billow on the deep
　　Knows to which shore its current lies;
The blast – the realms which he must sweep;
　　The ant – the hill to which it hies.

The stork that seeks the tropic glows,
　　It knoweth whither it is bound;
And the revolving planet knows
　　The circle of its luminous round.

But I, confusèd, seek a way
　　In darkness here; I fall, I sigh,
Upon a broken wing I stray,
　　And all my help lies in a cry!

from *The Heather on Fire*
A Tale of the Highland Clearances (1886)

from *Duan Third*

And lo! once more it was the time of year
When berries crimson and green leaves grow sere;
When bluebells shelter numb, belated bees,
And on the outstretched arms of wayside trees
Dangle long wisps of oats, whose casual grain
The thievish sparrows plunder, as the wain

Creaks slowly, lurching sideways, to the croft,
Whose sheaves, by stout arms tossed, are stored in barn and loft;

That time of year when, smoke-like, from the deep
Atlantic ocean, fast ascending, sweep
Innumerably the rain-burthened clouds
Taking the sun by storm, and with dim crowds
Confusing heaven, as, flying from the gale,
They blur the lineaments of hill and dale,
Till, dashed on giddy peak and blasted scaur,
Their waters breaking loose, crash in one long downpour.

A drear autumnal night! The gusty rain
Drums on the thatch; the tousled birches strain,
Bending before the blast; and far and wide
The writhen pines roar like a roaring tide,
With which the tumult of the troubled stream
Mingles its rumbling flood: a night to dream
Of dire shipwrecks and sudden deaths at sea –
Yet here, 'neath lowly cot, all sleep most peacefully.

All sleep but Mary, hushing in her arm
The child whose moans now mingle with the storm
And now fall silent, as his curly head
Nestles against her breast, that burns to shed
The warmth of life into her ailing bairn,
O'er whom her eyes compassionately yearn
With love, such as some master genius fine
Limned in her namesake's eyes, bent o'er the child divine.

Yea, Mary watched alone, while round her lay
The nut-brown heads of children, and the grey
Deep-furrowed brows of age: now and again,
In the brief pauses of the hurricane,
She caught their rhythmic breathing through the thick
Laborious cough and panting of the sick
And feverish child, who now and then made moan –
'Oh, mother, mother dear! take off that heavy stone.'

'Aye, aye,' she crooned, stifling a heavy sigh;
'Aye, aye, my precious darlin', mother'll try.'
And all the night by the red peat-fire's glare,
As many a night before of carking care,

With healing warmth she eased the poor child's ache,
And with sweet cooling drinks his thirst did slake.
At last the racking, troublous cough did cease,
And dozing off towards dawn, he slumbered more at ease.

The tempest too lulled suddenly: a swound
As of spent forces hushed the wuthering sound
And tumult of the elements; wan and grey
In the eastern heavens broke the irresolute day
Still pale and tearful, as the close-veiled sun
Like one who fears to see the havoc done
Peered furtively; his first and faltering ray
Hailed by a lark's clear voice hymning the new-born day.

A poor caged lark! But as the exultant note
Burst from the little palpitating throat
Of the imprisoned songster, the dull yoke
Of care that seemed to stifle Mary broke
In a hot flood of tears; yea, hope once more,
Like a tall pillar of fire, shone before
Her groping steps – the bird's voice seemed to tell
Her listening, anxious heart all would be well, be well.

'Yea, all would yet be well,' she murmured; 'soon,
With this first quarter of the hunter's moon
Father would come back from the seas, and bring
His gains wherewith to buy so many a thing
Sore needed by the bairn!' Therewith she rose
More comforted at heart, and tucked the clothes
Warmly around the child, and softly kissed
The little sleeper's thin, brown, closely curled-up fist.

And lifting his moist curls, she faintly smiled,
Remembering how last June her ailing child,
As blithe and bonnie as the other twin,
His sister Mary, had come toddling in,
Ruffled and rosy, pressing to his breast
With chubby fingers, a forsaken nest,
From which the startled lark had fled in fear,
When 'mid the falling swathes the mowers' scythes rang near.

But he had rescued it from being crushed
By trampling feet, and eager-eyed and flushed

Had toddled to the cottage with its shy,
Poor half-fledged nestling, that did feebly cry
For food and warmth and mother's folding wing;
But lovingly he tended the wee thing –
And lo! it lived, ceasing to pine and fret:
In narrow cage it sang, sweet Michael's cherished pet.

The song aroused the household. One by one
They rose to do their taskwork with the sun;
All but the aged woman, now too sore
To leave her bed, or labour any more,
Save with her hands, which still found strength to knit
Warm stockings for her son. Old Rory lit
His pipe, and bending o'er the smouldering fire,
Piled on the well-dried peats and made the flame leap higher.

Fair Ranza hurried to her dear-loved cow,
Shobhrag, the primrose-hued, that with a low
Of deep content greeted the little maid,
Who bade her a good day, and fondly laid
A soft pale cheek against her shaggy side;
Then pressing the full udders, sat astride
On her small three-legged stool, and watched the white
Warm stream of milk filling her pail with keen delight:

Yet took great care not to take more than half,
Nor rob the little, cuddling, week-old calf
That stood near by – a glossy golden brown,
Most like a chestnut roughly tumbled down,
When its smooth burnished kernel seems to swell
And burst athwart the trebly-cloven shell –
Whose limpid eyes, pathetically meek,
From their mute depths unto the gentle child did speak.

And bare-legged ruddy Ion, whistling shrill,
Scampered across the grass all wet and chill,
And littered with brown leaves and berries red,
While as he brushed the hedge its brambles shed
Brief showers upon him, as with prying look
He keenly searched each ditch and hidden nook
For a scarce egg or two, which now and then
Was laid safe out of sight by some secretive hen.

And Mary, bending o'er the peat-fire's glare,
Its bright light dancing on her crispy hair
And white face worn with watching, yet so grand
Lit with those eyes of her, turned with one hand
The well-browned oat-cakes, while her other one
Had hold of little Maisie, whose bright fun
Was kept in check by whispers from her mother,
Not to disturb or wake the little sleeping brother.

At last they gathered round the humble fare,
The youngest child repeating the Lord's prayer
With broken baby tones and bended head:
'Give us,' she lisped, 'this day our daily bread,'
When a loud hurried knocking at the door
Startled the little circle; even before
They well knew how, into the room there broke
A hurried, flurried group of scared, distracted folk,

Wild, panic-stricken neighbours, blanched with dread.
How helpless looked the strong! Discomfited,
Like men from field-work driven by sudden foe
Who yet instinctive clutched their spade or hoe!
And unkempt wives anomalously dressed
With querulous infants huddled to the breast;
Showing, in quivering lip and quailing eye,
The inevitable stroke of swift calamity.

Yet ere one spoke, or could have said a word,
Mary had waved them back: 'Nay, by the Lord,
Not here, not here,' she whispered hoarse and low;
'My child is sick – the sleep he's sleeping now
Is worth a life'; then with a pleading sign
She to the old man's care seemed to resign
Her little ones, and softly closed the door,
Bracing each quivering nerve for some dire grief in store,

And walked slow-footed to the outer gate,
'Gainst which she leant her body like a weight;
And with dry lips, low querying, barely sighed –
'Michael? The tempest?' But a neighbour cried,
One of her kin, who grasped her round the waist –
'No, no, look yon!' And with bare arm upraised
She pointed up the glen, whence drifting came
Dark clouds of rolling smoke lit by red tongues of flame.

And through the rolling smoke a troop of men
Tramped swiftly nearer from the upper glen;
Fierce, sullen, black with soot, some carrying picks,
Axes, crowbars, others armed with sticks,
Or shouldering piles of faggots – to the fore.
A little limping man, who cursed and swore
Between each word, came on post-haste; his hand,
Stretched like a vulture's claw, seemed grabbing at the land.

'The deil a one of all the lot shall stay;
They've a' been warned – I'll grant no more delay;
So let them e'en be smoked out from their holes,
To which the stubborn beggars stick like moles,
Cumbering the ill-used soil they hack and scratch,
And call it tillage! Silly hens that'd hatch
Their addled eggs, whether they will or no,
Are beaten off, and sure these feckless fules maun go.'

So on from glen to glen, from hut to hut,
The hated factor came with arrogant strut
And harsh imperious voice, and at one stroke,
Of house and home bereft these hapless folk,
Biding all inmates to come forth in haste:
For now shall their poor dwellings be laid waste,
Their thatch be fired, walls levelled with the leas,
And they themselves be shipped far o'er the wide, wild seas.

★★★★★

from *Duan Fourth*

For many there with sobs and bitter moans
Were clinging round the thorn trees and the stones:
More desperate than any, Rory clave,
Frenzied in turn and fawning, to the grave
Of the Mackinnons. 'I shall stay,' he cried,
'With mine own people! Where my forebears died,
The good, God-fearing folk, years upon years,
There Rory too will die and mix his dust with theirs.'

And then with humbly supplicating mien
Begged and entreated like a frightened wean –

'No, no, ye won't begrudge a little span
Of ground wherein to bury an old man
Four score and over, who will not, for sure,
Long cumber earth that is not for the poor?'
And low he grovelled 'mid the tombstones there,
Brushing the long rank grass with his white floating hair

He might as well have pleaded with the sea
When, even as then, the surf rolls angrily,
Raging against its bourne. Deaf to his prayer,
They swore to hale him forward by the hair
If he demurred, who, fiercely struggling, shook
His old notched crutch; when Michael, with the look
Of a sick lion, groaned 'Come, father, come,
Our country casts us forth, banished from hearth and home.

'God may have given the land to dress and keep
Unto our hands, but then his lordship's sheep
Fetch more i' the market. So with all our roots,
Like ill-weeds choking up the corn's young shoots,
He plucks us from the soil. His sovereign word
Hath driven us hence. As with a flaming sword
Doth he not bar the entrance to our glen?
But, father, if we must, shall we not go like men?'

Then with his children Michael strode along,
His father followed through the elbowing throng
Of men and women, darting here and there
To snatch up children, or their household ware,
Splashing through sea pools, stumbling over blocks,
To where the boats banged sharply on the rocks,
Bobbing like corks, and bearing from the shore
Their freight of human souls towards the *Koh-i-noor*.

But as the shout of sailors, as the stroke
And dip of oars upon his senses broke,
The old man started back, and 'mid the loud
Din and confusion of the pushing crowd
He disappeared unnoticed, as the ship,
With many a lunge and shake and roll and dip,
Now weighed her anchors, and with bulging sail
Close-reefed, and creaking shrouds, drove on before the gale.

MATHILDE BLIND   121

And crowding on the decks, with hungry eyes
Straining towards the coast that flies and flies,
The crofters stand; and whether with tears or foam
The faces fastened on their dwindling home
Are wet, they know not, as they lean and yearn
Over the trickling bulwark by the stern
Toward each creek and headland of that shore,
The long-love lineaments they may see never more.

Therewith it seemed as if their Scottish land
Bled for its children, yea, as though some hand —
Stretching from where on the horizon's verge
The rayless sun hung on the reddening surge —
Incarnadined the sweep of perilous coast
And the embattled storm-clouds swarthy host,
With such wild hues of mingling blood and fire
As though the heavens themselves flashed in celestial ire.

And in the kindling of that wrathful light
Their huts, yet flaming up from vale and height,
Grew pale as watch-fires in the glare of day;
White constellated isles leagues far away,
Headlands and reefs and paps, whose fretted stone
Breasted the sucking whirlpool's clamorous moan,
Grew incandescent o'er the wind-flogged sea,
Scaled over with whitening scum as struck with leprosy.

For as the winds blew up to hurricane,
Like a mere spark quenched on the curdled main
The ship was swept beyond the old man's sight,
A dizzy watcher on that lonesome height,
Where, grappled to a fragment of the keep,
He hung and swung high o'er the raging deep
While sea-gulls buffeted about his locks,
Slipped shrieking into chinks and crannies of the rocks.

And now the waves that thundered on the shore
Him seemed the iron-throated cannon's roar;
And now his heart, upstarting as from sleep,
Shuddered for those that sailed upon the deep,
As in brief flashes of his clouded mind
He knew himself sole crofter left behind
Of all his clan — crying now and again,
'She's cleared the Sound of Sleat — safe on the open main.

'She's safe now with the treacherous reefs behind!'
He shouted, as in answer to the wind
That had swung round like some infuriate host,
With all its blasts set full upon the coast;
And hounded back, the ship, as if at bay,
Came reeling through the twilight, thick, and grey
With rags of solid foam and shock of breaking
Waters, beneath whose blows the very rocks were shaking.

Yea, near and nearer to the deadly shore
She pitches helpless 'mid the bellowing roar
Of confluent breakers, as with sidelong keel,
Dragging her anchors, she doth plunge and reel,
Dashed forwards, then recoiling from the rocks,
Whose flinty ribs ring to the Atlantic shocks –
On, on, and ever on, till hurled and battered
Sheer on the rock she springs, and falls back wrecked and shattered.

And through the smoke of waters and the clouds
Of driving foam, boats, rigging, masts, and shrouds
Whirled round and round; and then athwart the storm
The old man saw, or raving saw, the form
Of his own son, as with his children pressed
Close to his heart, borne on the giddy crest
Of a sheer wall of wave, he rose and rose,
Then with the refluent surge rolled whelmed beneath its snows.

And through the lurid dusk and mist of spray
That quenched the last spark of the smouldering day,
Faces of drowning men were seen to swim
Amid the vortex, or a hand or limb
To push through whelming waters, or the scream
Wrung from a swimmer's choking lips would seem
To be borne in upon the reeling brain
Of that old man, who swooned beneath the mortal strain.

Yea, thus once more upon the natal coast,
Which, living, those brave hearts had left and lost,
The pitying winds and waves drove back to land,
If but to drown them by the tempest's hand,
The banished Highlanders. Safe in the deep,
With their own seas to rock their hearts to sleep,
The crofters lay: but faithful Rory gave
His body to the land that had begrudged a grave.

from *The Ascent of Man* (1889)

from *Part I*

Chaunts of Life

I

Struck out of dim fluctuant forces and shock of electrical vapour,
Repelled and attracted the atoms flashed mingling in union primeval,
And over the face of the waters far heaving in limitless twilight
Auroral pulsations thrilled faintly, and, striking the blank heaving
                                                                surface,
The measureless speed of their motion now leaped into light on
                                                        the waters.
And lo, from the womb of the waters, upheaved in volcanic
                                                convulsion,
Ribbed and ravaged and rent there rose bald peaks and the rocky
Heights of confederate mountains compelling the fugitive vapours
To take a form as they passed them and float as clouds through the
                                                        azure.
Mountains, the broad-bosomed mothers of torrents and rivers
                                                perennial,
Feeding the rivers and plains with patient persistence, till slowly,
In the swift passage of æons recorded in stone by Time's graver,
There germ grey films of the lichen and mosses and palm-ferns
                                                gigantic,
And jungle of tropical forest fantastical branches entwining,
And limitless deserts of sand and wildernesses primeval.

II

Lo, moving o'er chaotic waters,
        Love dawned upon the seething waste,
Transformed in ever new avatars
        It moved without or pause or haste:
Like sap that moulds the leaves of May
It wrought within the ductile clay.

And vaguely in the pregnant deep,
        Clasped by the glowing arms of light
From and eternity of sleep
        Within unfathomed gulfs of night
A pulse stirred in the plastic slime
Responsive to the rhythm of Time.

Enkindled in the mystic dark
  Life built herself a myriad forms,
And, flashing its electric spark
  Through films and cells and pulps and worms,
Flew shuttlewise above, beneath,
Weaving the web of life and death.

And multiplying in the ocean,
  Amorphous, rude, colossal things
Lolled on the ooze in lazy motion,
  Armed with grim jaws or uncouth wings;
Helpless to lift their cumbering bulk
They lurch like some dismasted hulk.

And virgin forest, verdant plain,
  The briny sea, the balmy air,
Each blade of grass and globe of rain,
  And glimmering cave and gloomy lair
Began to swarm with beasts and birds,
With floating fish and fleet-foot herds.

The lust of life's delirious fires
  Burned like a fever in their blood,
Now pricked them on with fierce desires,
  Now drove them famishing for food,
To seize coy females in the fray,
Or hotly hunted for prey.

And amorously urged them on
  In wood or wild to court their mate,
Proudly displaying in the sun
  With antics strange and looks elate,
The vigour of their mighty thews
Or charm of million-coloured hues.

There crouching 'mid the scarlet bloom,
  Voluptuously the leopard lies,
And through the tropic forest gloom
  The flaming of his feline eyes
Stirs with intoxicating stress
The pulses of the leopardess.

MATHILDE BLIND

Or two swart bulls of self-same age
        Meet furiously with thunderous roar,
And lash together, blind with rage,
        And clanging horns that fain would gore
Their rival, and so win the prize
Of those impassive female eyes.

Or in the nuptial days of spring,
        When April kindles bush and brier,
Like rainbows that have taken wing,
        Or palpitating gems of fire,
Bright butterflies in one brief day
Live but to love and pass away.

And herds of horses scour the plains,
        The thickets scream with bird and beast
The love of life burns in their veins,
        And from the mightiest to the least
Each preys upon the other's life
In inextinguishable strife.

War rages on the teeming earth;
        The hot and sanguinary fight
Begins with each new creature's birth:
        A dreadful war where might is right;
Where still the strongest slay and win,
Where weakness is the only sin.

There is no truce to this drawn battle,
        Which ends but to begin again;
The drip of blood, the hoarse death-rattle,
        The roar of rage, the shriek of pain,
Are rife in fairest grove and dell,
Turning earth's flowery haunts to hell.

A hell of hunger, hatred, lust,
        Which goads all creatures here below,
Or blindworm wriggling in the dust,
        Or penguin in the Polar snow:
A hell where there is none to save,
Where life is life's insatiate grave.

And in the long portentous strife,
      Where types are tried even as by fire,
Where life is whetted upon life
      And step by panting step mounts higher,
Apes lifting hairy arms now stand
And free the wonder-working hand.

They raise a light aërial house
      On shafts of widely branching trees,
Where, harboured warily, each spouse
      May feed her little ape in peace,
Green cradled in his heaven-roofed bed,
Leaves rustling lullabies o'erhead.

And lo, 'mid reeking swarms of earth
      Grim struggling in the primal wood,
A new strange creature hath its birth:
      Wild – stammering – nameless – shameless – nude;
Spurred on by want, held in by fear,
He hides his head in caverns drear.

Most unprotected of earth's kin,
      His fight for life that seems so vain
Sharpens his senses, till within
      The twilight mazes of his brain,
Like embryos within the womb,
Thought pushes feelers through the gloom.

And slowly in the fateful race
      It grows unconscious, till at length
The helpless savage dares to face
      The cave-bear in his grisly strength;
For stronger than its bulky thews
He feels a force that grows with use.

From age to dumb unnumbered age,
      By dim gradations long and slow,
He reaches on from stage to stage,
      Through fear and famine, weal and woe
And, compassed round with danger, still
Prolongs his life by craft and skill.

MATHILDE BLIND

With cunning hand he shapes the flint,
     He carves the horn with strange device,
He splits the rebel block by dint
     Of effort – till one day there flies
A spark of fire from out the stone:
Fire which shall make the world his own.

★★★★★

from *Part III*

The Leading of Sorrow

Our spirits have climbed high
By reason of the passion of our grief,
And from the top of sense, looked over sense
To the significance and heart of things
Rather than things themselves.
               E.B. Browning

★★★★★

Fallen lies the fair old town, its houses
     Charred and ruined gape in smoking heaps;
Here with shouts a ruffian band carouses,
     There an outraged woman vainly weeps.
In the fields where the ripe corn lies mangled,
     Where the wounded groan beneath the dead,
Friend or foe, now helplessly entangled,
     Stain red poppies with a guiltier red.

There the dog howls o'er his perished master,
     There the crow comes circling from afar;
All vile things that batten on disaster
     Follow feasting in the wake of war.
Famine follows – what they ploughed and planted
     The unhappy peasants shall not reap;
Sickening of strange meats and fever haunted,
     To their graves they prematurely creep.

'Hence' – I cried in unavailing pity –
     'Let us flee these scenes of monstrous strife,
Seek the pale of some imperial city

Where the law rules starlike o'er man's life.'
Straightway floating o'er blue sea and river,
     We were plunged into a roaring cloud,
Wherethrough lamps in ague fits did shiver
     O'er the surging multitudinous crowd.

Piles of stone, their cliff-like walls uprearing,
     Flashed in luminous lines along the night;
Jets of flame, spasmodically flaring,
     Splashed black pavements with a sickly light;
Fabulous gems shone here, and glowing coral,
     Shimmering stuffs from many an Eastern loom,
And vast piles of tropic fruits and floral
     Marvels seemed to mock November's gloom.

But what prowls near princely mart and dwelling,
     Whence through many a thundering thoroughfare
Rich folk roll on cushions softly swelling
     To the week-day feast and Sunday prayer?
Yea, who prowl there, hunger-nipped and pallid,
     Breathing nightmares limned upon the gloom?
'Tis but human rubbish, gaunt and squalid,
     Whom their country spurns for lack of room.

In their devious track we mutely follow,
     Mutely climb dim flights of oozy stairs,
Where through the gap-toothed, mizzling roof the yellow
     Pestilent fog blends with the fetid air.
Through the unhinged door's discordant slamming
     Ring the gruesome sounds of savage strife –
Howls of babes, the drunken father's damning,
     Counter-cursing of the shrill-tongued wife.

Children feebly crying on their mother
     In a wailful chorus – 'Give us food!'
Man and woman glaring at each other
     Like two gaunt wolves with a famished brood.
Till he snatched a stick, and, madly staring,
     Struck her blow on blow upon the head;
And she, reeling back, gasped, hardly caring –
     'Ah, you've done it now, Jim' – and was dead.

Dead – dead – dead – the miserable creature –
     Never to feel hunger's cruel fang

Wring the bowels of rebellious nature
      That her infants might be spared the pang.
'Dead! Good luck to her!' The man's teeth chattered,
      Stone-still stared he with blank eyes and hard,
Then, his frame with one big sob nigh shattered,
      Fled – and cut his throat down in the yard.

Dark the night – the children wail forsaken,
      Crane their wrinkled necks and cry for food,
Drop off into fitful sleep, or waken
      Trembling like a sparrow's ravished brood.
Dark the night – the rain falls on the ashes,
      Feebly hissing on the feeble heat,
Filters through the ceiling, drops in splashes
      On the little children's naked feet.

Dark the night – the children wail forsaken –
      Is there none, ah, none, to heed their moan?
Yea, at dawn one little one is taken,
      Four poor souls are left, but one is gone.
Gone – escaped – flown from the shame and sorrow
      Waiting for them at life's sombre gate,
But the hand of merciless tomorrow
      Drags the others shuddering to their fate.

But one came – a girlish thing – a creature
      Flung by wanton hands 'mid lust and crime –
A poor outcast, yet by right of nature
      Sweet as odour of the upland thyme.
Scapegoat of a people's sins, and hunted,
      Howled at, hooted to the wilderness,
To that wilderness of deaf hearts, blunted
      To the depths of woman's dumb distress.

Jetsam, flotsam of the monster city,
      Spurned, defiled, reviled, that outcast came
To those babes that whined for love and pity,
      Gave them bread bought with the wage of shame.
Gave them bread, and gave them warm, maternal
      Kisses not on sale for any price:
Yea, a spark, a flash of some eternal
      Sympathy shone through those haunted eyes.

Ah, perchance through her dark life's confusion,
     Through the haste and taste of fevered hours,
Gusts of memory on her youth's pollution
     Blew forgotten scents of faded flowers.
And she saw the cottage near the wild wood,
     With its lichened and latticed panes,
Strayed once more through golden fields of childhood,
     Hyacinth dells and hawthorn-scented lanes.

★★★★★

But a rustic blossom! Love and duty
     Bound up in a child whom hunger slays!
Ah! but one thing still is left her – beauty
     Fresh, untainted yet – and beauty pays.
Beauty keeps her child alive a little,
     Then it dies – her woman's love with it –
Beauty's brilliant sceptre, ah, how brittle,
     Drags her daily deeper down the pit.

Ruin closes o'er her – hideous, nameless;
     Each fresh morning marks a deeper fall;
Till at twenty – callous, cankered, shameless,
     She lies dying at the hospital.
Drink, more drink, she calls for – her harsh laughter
     Grates upon the meekly praying nurse,
Eloquent about her soul's hereafter:
     'Souls be blowed!' she sings out with a curse.

And so dies, an unrepenting sinner –
     Pitched into her pauper's grave what time
That most noble lord rides by to dinner
     Who had wooed her in her innocent prime.
And in after-dinner talk he preaches
     Resignation – o'er his burgundy –
Till a grateful public dubs his speeches
     Oracles of true philanthropy.

Peace ye call this? Call this justice, meted
     Equally to rich and poor alike?
Better than this peace the battle's heated
     Cannon-balls that ask not whom they strike!
Better than this masquerade of culture

Hiding strange hyaena appetites,
         The frank ravening of the raw-necked vulture
    As its beak the senseless carrion smites.

What of men in bondage, toiling blunted
         In the roaring factory's lurid gloom?
What of cradled infants starved and stunted?
         What of woman's nameless martyrdom?
The all-seeing sun shines on unheeding,
         Shines by night the calm, unruffled moon,
Though the human myriads, preying, bleeding,
         Put creation harshly out of tune.

'Hence, ah, hence' – I sobbed in quivering passion –
         'From these fearful haunts of fiendish men!
Better far the plain, carnivorous fashion
         Which is practised in the lion's den.'
And I fled – yet staggering still did follow
         In the footprints of my shrouded guide –
To the sea-caves echoing with the hollow
         Immemorial moaning of the tide.

Sinking, swelling roared the wintry ocean,
         Pitch-black chasms struck with flying blaze,
As the cloud-winged storm-sky's sheer commotion
         Showed the blank moon's mute Medusa face
White o'er wastes of water – surges crashing
         Over surges in the formless gloom,
And a mastless hulk, with great seas washing
         Her scourged flanks, pitched toppling to her doom.

Through the crash of wave on wave gigantic,
         Through the thunder of the hurricane,
My wild heart in breaking shrilled with frantic
         Exultation – 'Chaos come again!
Yea, let earth be split and cloven asunder
         With man's still accumulating curse –
Life is but a momentary blunder
         In the cycle of the universe.

'Yea, let earth with forest-belted mountains,
         Hills and valleys, cataracts and plains,
With her clouds and storms and fires and fountains,

OUT OF MY BORROWED BOOKS

Pass with all her rolling sphere contains,
Melt, dissolve again into the ocean,
        Ocean fade into a nebulous haze!'
And I sank back without sense or motion
        'Neath the blank moon's mute Medusa face.

Moments, years, or ages passed, when, lifting
        Freezing lids, I felt the heavens on high,
And, innumerable as the sea-sands drifting,
        Stars unnumbered drifted through the sky.
Rhythmical in luminous rotation,
        In daedalian maze they reel and fly,
And their rushing light is Time's pulsation
        In his passage through Eternity.

Constellated suns, fresh lit, declining,
        Were ignited now, now quenched in space,
Rolling round each other, or inclining
        Orb to orb in multi-coloured rays.
Ever showering from their flaming fountains
        Light more light on each far-circling earth,
Till life stirred crepuscular seas, and mountains
        Heaved convulsive with the throes of birth.

And the noble brotherhood of planets,
        Knitted each to each by links of light,
Circled round their suns, nor knew a minute's
        Lapse or languor in their ceaseless flight.
And pale moons and rings and burning splinters
        Of wrecked worlds swept round their parent spheres,
Clothed with spring or sunk in polar winters
        As their sun draws nigh or disappears.

Still new vistas of new stars – far dwindling –
        Through the firmament like dewdrops roll,
Torches of the Cosmos which enkindling
        Flash their revelation on the soul.
Yea, One spake there – though nor form nor feature
        Shown – a Voice came from the peaks of time:
'Wilt thou judge me, wilt thou curse me, creature
        Whom I raised up from the ocean slime?

'Long I waited – ages rolled o'er ages –
       As I crystallised in granite rocks,
Struggled dumb through immemorial stages,
       Glacial aeons, fiery earthquake shocks.
In fierce throbs of flame or slow upheaval,
       Speck by tiny speck, I topped the seas,
Leaped from earth's dark womb, and in primeval
       Forests shot up shafts of mammoth trees.

'Through a myriad forms I yearned and panted,
       Putting forth quick shoots in endless swarms –
Giant-hoofed, sharp-tusked, or finned or planted
       Writhing on the reef with pinioned arms.
I have climbed from reek or sanguine revels
       In Cimmerian wood and thorny wild,
Slowly upwards to the dawnlit levels
       Where I bore thee, oh my youngest child!

'Oh, my heir and hope of my tomorrow,
       I – I draw thee on through fume and fret,
Croon to thee in pain and call through sorrow,
       Flowers and stars take for thy alphabet.
Through the eyes of animals appealing,
       Feel my fettered spirit yearn to thine,
Who, in storm of will and clash of feeling,
       Shape the life that shall be – the divine.

'Oh, redeem me from my tiger rages,
       Reptile greed, and foul hyaena lust;
With the hero's deeds, the thoughts of sages,
       Sow and fructify this passive dust;
Drop in dew and healing love of woman
       On the bloodstained hands of hungry strife,
Till there break from passion of the Human
       Morning-glory of transfigured life.

'I have cast my burden on thy shoulder;
       Unimagined potencies have given
That from formless Chaos thou shalt mould her
       And translate gross earth to luminous heaven.
Bear, oh, bear the terrible compulsion,
       Flinch not from the path thy fathers trod,
From Man's martyrdom in slow convulsion
       Will be born the infinite goodness – God.'

Ceased the Voice: and as it ceased it drifted
  Like the seashell's inarticulate moan;
From the Deep, on wings of flame uplifted,
  Rose the sun rejoicing and alone.
Laughed in light upon the living ocean,
  Danced and rocked itself upon the spray,
And its shivered beams in twinkling motion
  Gleamed like star-motes of the Milky Way.

And beside me in the golden morning
  I beheld my shrouded phantom-guide;
But no longer sorrow-veiled and mourning –
  It became transfigured by my side.
And I knew – as one escaped from prison
  Sees old things again with fresh surprise –
It was Love himself, Love re-arisen
  With the Eternal shining though his eyes.

Poems of the Open Air

The Sower

The winds had hushed at last as by command;
  The quiet sky above,
With its grey clouds spread o'er the fallow land,
  Sat brooding like a dove

There was no motion in the air, no sound
  Within the tree-tops stirred,
Save when some last leaf, fluttering to the ground,
  Dropped like a wounded bird:

Or when the swart rooks in a gathering crowd
  With clamorous noises wheeled,
Hovering awhile, then swooped with wranglings loud
  Down on the stubbly field.

For now the big-thewed horses, toiling slow
  In straining couples yoked,
Patiently dragged the ploughshare to and fro
  Till their wet haunches smoked.

Till the stiff acre, broken into clods,
　　Bruised by the harrow's tooth,
Lay lightly shaken, with its humid sods
　　Ranged into furrows smooth.

There looming lone, from rise to set of sun,
　　Without or pause or speed,
Solemnly striding by the furrows dun,
　　The sower sows the seed.

The sower sows the seed, which mouldering,
　　Deep coffined in the earth,
Is buried now, but with the future spring
　　Will quicken into birth.

Oh, poles of birth and death! Controlling Powers
　　Of human toil and need!
On this fair earth all men are surely sowers,
　　Surely all life is seed!

All life is seed, dropped in Time's yawning furrow,
　　Which with slow sprout and shoot,
In the revolving world's unfathomed morrow,
　　Will blossom and bear fruit.

The Teamster

With slow and slouching gait Sam leads the team;
　　He stoops i' the shoulders, worn with work not years;
One only passion has he, it would seem –
　　The passion for the horses which he rears:
He names them as one would some household pet,
　　May, Violet.

He thinks them quite as sensible as men;
　　As nice as women, but not near so skittish;
He fondles, cossets, scolds them now and then,
　　Nay, gravely talks as if they know good British:
You hear him call from dawn to set of sun,
　　'Goo back! Com on!'

Sam never seems depressed nor yet elate,
　　　Like Nature's self he goes his punctual round;
On Sundays, smoking by his garden gate,
　　　For hours he'll stand, with eyes upon the ground,
Like some tired cart-horse in a field alone,
　　　And still as stone.

Yet, howsoever stolid he may seem,
　　　Sam has his tragic background, weird and wild
Like some adventure in a drunkard's dream.
　　　Impossible, you'd swear, for one so mild:
Yet village gossips dawdling o'er their ale
　　　Still tell the tale.

In his young days Sam loved a servant-maid,
　　　A girl with happy eyes like hazel brooks
That dance i' the sun, cheeks as if newly made
　　　Of pouting roses coyly hid in nooks,
And warm brown hair that wantoned into curl:
　　　A fresh-blown girl.

Sam came a-courting while the year was blithe,
　　　When wet browed mowers, stepping out in tune,
With level stroke and rhythmic swing of scythe,
　　　Smote down the proud grass in the pomp of June,
And wagons, half-tipped over, seemed to sway
　　　With loads of hay.

The elder bush beside the orchard croft
　　　Brimmed over with its bloom like curds and cream;
From out grey nests high in the granary loft
　　　Black clusters of small heads with callow scream
Peered open-beaked, as swallows flashed along
　　　To feed their young.

Ripening towards the harvest swelled the wheat,
　　　Lust cherries dangled 'gainst the latticed panes;
The roads were baking in the windless heat,
　　　And dust had floured the glossy country lanes,
One sun-hushed, light-flushed Sunday afternoon
　　　The last of June.

MATHILDE BLIND

When, with his thumping heart all out joint,
      And pulses beating like a stroller's drum,
Sam screwed his courage to the sticking point
      And asked his blushing sweetheart if she'd come
To Titsey Fair; he meant to coax coy May
      To name the day.

But her rich master snapped his thumb and swore
      The girl was not for him! Should not go out!
And, whistling to his dogs, slammed-to the door
      Close in Sam's face, and left him dazed without
In the fierce sunshine, blazing in his path
      Like fire of wrath.

Unheeding, he went forth with hot wild eyes
      Past fields of feathery oats and wine-red clover;
Unheeded, larks soared singing to the skies,
      Or rang the plaintive cry of rising plover;
Unheeded, pheasants with a startled sound
      Whirred from the ground.

On, on he went by acres full of grain,
      By trees and meadows reeling past his sight,
As to a man whirled onwards in a train
      The land with spinning hedgerows seems in flight;
At last he stopped and leant a long, long while
      Against a stile.

Hours passed; the clock struck ten; a hush of night,
      In which even wind and water seemed at peace;
But here and there a glimmering cottage light
      Shone like a glowworm though the slumberous trees;
Or from some far-off homestead through the dark
      A watch-dog's bark.

But all at once Sam gave a stifled cry:
      'There's fire,' he muttered, 'fire upon the hills!'
No fire – but as the late moon rose on high
      Her light looked smoke-red as through belching mills:
No fire – but moonlight turning in his path
      To fire of wrath.

He looked abroad with eyes that gave the mist
  A lurid tinge above the breadths of grain
Owned by May's master. Then he shook his fist,
  Still muttering, 'Fire!' and measured o'er again
The road he'd come, where, lapped in moonlight, lay
  Huge ricks of hay.

There he paused glaring. Then he turned and waned
  Like mist into the misty, moon-soaked night,
Where the pale silvery fields were blotched and stained
  With strange fantastic shadows. But what light
Is that which leaps up, flickering lithe and long,
  With licking tongue!

Hungry it darts and hisses, twists and turns,
  And with each minute shoots up high and higher,
Till, wrapped in flames, the mighty hayrick burns
  And sends its sparks on to a neighbouring byre,
Where, frightened at the hot, tremendous glow,
  The cattle low.

And rick on rick takes fire; and next a stye,
  Whence through the smoke the little pigs rush out;
The house-dog barks; then, with a startled cry,
  The window is flung open, shout on shout
Wakes the hard-sleeping farm where man and maid
  Start up dismayed.

And with wild faces wavering in the glare,
  In nightcaps, bedgowns, clothes half huddled on
Some to the pump, some to the duck-pond tear
  In frantic haste, while others splashing run
With pails, or turn the hose with flame-scorched face
  Upon the blaze.

At last, when some wan streaks began to show
  In the chill darkness of the sky, the fire
Went out, subdued but for the sputtering glow
  Of sparks among wet ashes. Barn and byre
Were safe, but swallowed all the summer math
  By fire of wrath.

Still haggard from the night's wild work and pale,
        Farm-men and women stood in whispering knots,
Regaled with foaming mugs of nut-brown ale;
        Firing his oaths about like vicious shots,
The farmer hissed out now and then: 'Gad damn!
        It's that black Sam.'

They had him up and taxed him with the crime;
        Denying naught, he sulked and held his peace;
And so, a branded convict, in due time,
        Handcuffed and cropped, they shipped him overseas:
Seven years of shame sliced from his labourer's life
        As with a knife.

But through it all the image of a girl
        With hazel eyes like pebbled waters clear,
And warm brown hair that wantoned into curl,
        Kept his heart sweet through many a galling year,
Like to a bit of lavender long pressed
        In some black chest.

At last his time was up, and Sam returned
        To his dear village with its single street,
Where, in the sooty forge, the fire still burned,
        As, hammering on the anvil, red with heat,
The smith wrought at a shoe with tongues aglow,
        Blow upon blow.

There stood the church, with peals for death and birth,
        Its ancient spire o'ertopping ancient trees,
And there the graves and mounds of unknown earth,
        Gathered like little children round its knees;
There was the Bull, with sign above the door,
        And sanded floor.

Unrecognised Sam took his glass of beer,
        And picked up gossip which the men let fall:
How Farmer Clow had failed, and one named Steer
        Had taken on the land, repairs and all;
And how the Kimber girl was to be wed
        To Betsy's Ned.

Sam heard no more, flung down his pence, and took
　　　The way down to the well-remembered stile;
There, in the gloaming by the trysting brook,
　　　He came upon his May – with just that smile
For sheep-faced Ned, that light in happy eyes:
　　　Oh, sugared lies!

He came upon them with black-knitted brows
　　　And clenched brown hands, and muttered huskily:
'Oh, little May, are those your true love's vows
　　　You swore to keep while I was over-sea?'
Then crying, turned upon the other one,
　　　'Com on, com on.'

Then they fell to with faces set for fight,
　　　And hit each other hard with rustic pride;
But Sam, whose arm with iron force could smite,
　　　Knocked his cowed rival down, and won his bride.
May wept and smiled, swayed like a wild red rose
　　　As the wind blows.

She married Sam, who loved her with a wild
　　　Strong love he could not put to words – too deep
For her to gauge; but with her first-born child
　　　May dropped off, flower-like, into the long sleep,
And left him nothing but the memory of
　　　His little love.

Since then the silent teamster lives alone,
　　　The trusted headman of his master Steer;
One only passion seems he still to own –
　　　The passion for the foals he has to rear;
And still the prettiest, full of life and play,
　　　Is little May.

Reapers

Sun-tanned men and women, toiling there together;
  Seven I count in all, in yon field of wheat,
Where the rich ripe ears in the harvest weather
  Glow an orange gold though the sweltering heat.

Busy life is still, sunk in brooding leisure:
  Birds have hushed their singing in the hushed tree-tops;
Not a single cloud mars the flawless azure;
  Not a shadow moves o'er the moveless crops;

In the glassy shallow, that no breath is creasing,
  Chestnut-coloured cows in the rushes dank
Stand like cows of bronze, save when they flick the teasing
  Flies with switch of tail from each quivering flank.

Nature takes a rest – even her bees are sleeping,
  And the silent wood seems a church that's shut;
But these human creatures cease not from their reaping
  While the corn stands high, waiting to be cut.

Autumn Tints

 Coral-coloured yew-berries
   Strew the garden ways,
 Hollyhocks and sunflowers
   Make a dazzling blaze
   In these latter days.

 Marigolds by cottage doors
   Flaunt their golden pride,
 Crimson-punctured bramble leaves
   Dapple far and wide
   The green mountain-side.

 Far away, on hilly slopes
   Where fleet rivulets run,
 Miles on miles of tangled fern,
   Burnished by the sun,
   Glow a copper dun.

For the year that's on the wane,
Gathering all its fire,
Flares up through the kindling world
As, ere they expire,
Flames leap high and higher.

The Hunter's Moon

The Hunter's Moon rides high,
High o'er the close-cropped plain;
Across the desert sky
The herded clouds amain
Scamper tumultuously,
Chased by the hounding wind
That yelps behind.

The clamorous hunt is done,
Warm-housed the kennelled pack;
One huntsman rides alone
With dangling bridle slack;
He wakes a hollow tone,
Far echoing to his horn
In clefts forlorn.

The Hunter's Moon rides low,
Her course is nearly sped.
Where is the panting roe?
Where hath the wild deer fled?
Hunter and hunted now
Lie in oblivion deep:
Dead or asleep.

The Passing Year

No breath of wind stirs in the painted leaves,
    The meadows are as stirless as the sky,
    Like a saint's halo golden vapours lie
Above the restful valley's garnered sheaves.
The journeying Sun, like one who fondly grieves,
    Above the hills seems loitering with a sigh,
    As loth to bid the fruitful earth good-bye,
On these hushed hours of luminous autumn eves.

There is a pathos in his softening glow,
    Which like a benediction seems to hover
O'er the tranced earth, ere he must sink below
    And leave her widowed of her radiant Lover,
A frost-bound sleeper in a shroud of snow
    While winter winds howl a wild dirge above her.

The Red Sunsets, 1883

The twilight heavens are flushed with gathering light,
    And o'er wet roofs and huddling streets below
    Hand with a strange Apocalyptic glow
On the black fringes of the wintry night.
Such bursts of glory may have rapt the sight
    Of him to whom on Patmos long ago
    The visionary angel came to show
That heavenly city built of chrysolite.

And lo, three factory hands begrimed with soot,
    Aflame with the red splendour, marvelling stand,
And gaze with lifted faces awed and mute.
    Starved of earth's beauty by Man's grudging hand,
O toilers, robbed of labour's golden fruit,
    Ye, too, may feast in Nature's fairyland.

A Winter Landscape

All night, all day, in dizzy, downward flight,
    Fell the wild-whirling, vague, chaotic snow,
    Till every landmark of the earth below,
Trees, moorlands, roads, and each familiar sight
Were blotted out by the bewildering white.
    And winds, now shrieking loud, now whimpering low,
    Seemed lamentations for the world-old woe
That death must swallow life, and darkness light.

But all at once the rack was blown away,
    The snowstorm hushing ended in a sigh;
    Then like a flame the crescent moon on high
Leaped forth among the planets; pure as they,
Earth vied in whiteness with the Milky Way:
    Herself a star beneath the starry sky.

from *Dramas in Miniature* (1891)

The Russian Student's Tale

The midnight sun with phantom glare
Shone on the soundless thoroughfare
Whose shuttered houses, closed and still,
Seemed bodies without heart or will;
Yea, all the stony city lay
Impassive in that phantom day,
As amid livid wastes of sand
The sphinxes of the desert stand.

And we, we two, turned night to day,
As, whistling many a student's lay,
We sped along each ghostly street,
With girls whose lightly tripping feet
Well matched our longer, stronger stride,
In hurrying to the water-side.
We took a boat; each seized an oar,
Until on either hand the shore
Slipped backwards, as our voices woke
Far echoes, mingling like a dream
With swirl and tumult of the stream.

On – on – away, beneath the ray
Of midnight in the mask of day;
By great wharves where the masts at peace
Look like the ocean's barren trees;
Past palaces and glimmering towers,
And gardens fairy-like with flowers,
And parks of twilight green and closes,
The very Paradise of roses.
The waters flow; on, on we row,
Now laughing loud, now whispering low;
And through the splendour of the white
Electrically glowing night,
Wind-wafted from some perfumed dell,
Tumultuously there loudly rose
Above the Neva's surge and swell,
With amorous ecstasies and throes,
And lyric spasms of wildest wail,
The love-song of a nightingale.

I see her still beside me. Yea,
As if it were but yesterday,
I see her – see her as she smiled;
Her face that of a little child
For innocent sweetness undefiled;
And that pathetic flower-like blue
Of eyes which, as they look at you,
Seemed yet to stab your bosom through.
I rowed, she steered; oars dipped and flashed,
The broadening river roared and splashed,
So that we hardly seemed to hear
Our comrades' voices, though so near;
Their faces seeming far away,
As still beneath that phantom day
I looked at her, she smiled at me!
And then we landed – I and she.

There's an old café in the wood;
A students' haunt on summer eves,
Round which responsive poplar leaves
Quiver to each aeolian mood
Like some wild harp a poet smites
On visionary summer nights.
I ordered supper, took a room

Green-curtained by the tremulous gloom
Of those fraternal poplar trees
Shaking together in the breeze;
My pulse, too, like a poplar tree,
Shook wildly as she smiled at me.
Eye in eye, and hand in hand,
Awake amid the slumberous land,
I told her all my love that night —
How I had loved her at first sight;
How I was hers, and seemed to be
Her own to all eternity.
And through the splendour of the white
Electrically glowing night,
Wind-wafted from some perfumed dell,
Tumultuously there loudly rose
Above the Neva's surge and swell
With amorous ecstasies and throes,
And lyric spasms of wildest wail,
The love-song of the nightingale.

I see her still beside me. Yea,
As if it were but yesterday,
I hear her tell with cheek aflame
Her ineradicable shame —
So sweet flower in such vile hands!
Oh, loved and lost beyond recall!
Like one who hardly understands,
I heard the story of her fall.
The odious barter of her youth,
Of beauty, innocence and truth,
Of all that honest women hold
Most sacred — for the sake of gold.
A weary seamstress, half a child,
Left unprotected in the street,
Where, when so hungry, you would meet
All sorts of tempters that beguiled.
Oh, infamous and senseless clods,
Basely to taint so pure a heart,
And make a maid fit for the gods
A creature of the common mart!
She spoke quite simply of things vile —
Of devils with an angel's face;
It seemed the sunshine of her smile

Must purify the foulest place.
She told me all – she would be true –
Told me things too sad, too bad;
And, looking in her eyes' clear blue
My passion nearly drove me mad!
I tried to speak, but tried in vain;
A sob rose to my throat as dry
As ashes – for between us twain
A murdered virgin seemed to lie.
And through the splendour of the white
Electrically glowing night.
Wind-wafted from some perfumed dell,
Tumultuously there loudly rose
Above the Neva's surge and swell,
With amorous ecstasies and throes,
And lyric spasms of wildest wail,
The love-song of a nightingale.

Poor craven creature! What was I,
To sit in judgement on her life,
Who dared not make this child my wife,
And life her up to love's own sky?
This poor lost child we all – yes, all –
Had helped to hurry to her fall,
Making a social leper of
God's creature consecrate to love.
I looked at her – she smiled no more;
She understood it all before
A syllable had passed my lips;
And like a horrible eclipse,
Which blots the sunlight from the skies,
A blankness overspread her eyes –
The blankness as of one who dies.
I knew how much she loved me – knew
How pure and passionately true
Her love for me, which made her tell
What scorched her like the flames of hell.
And I, I loved her too, so much,
So dearly, that I dared not touch
Her lips that had been kissed in sin;
But with a reverential thrill
I took her work-worn hand and thin,
And kissed her fingers, showing still

Where needle-pricks had marred the skin.
And, ere I knew, a hot tear fell,
Scalding the place which I had kissed,
As between clenching teeth I hissed
Our irretrievable farewell.
And through the smouldering glow of night,
Mixed with the shining morning light
Wind-wafted from some perfumed dell,
Above the Neva's surge and swell,
With lyric spasms, as from a throat
Which dying breathes a faltering note,
There faded o'er the silent vale
The last sob of a nightingale.

The Message

From side to side the sufferer tossed
      With quick impatient sighs;
Her face was bitten as by frost,
The look as of one hunted crossed
      The fever of her eyes.

All seared she seemed with life and woe,
      Yet scarcely could have told
More than a score of springs or so;
Her hair had girlhood's morning glow,
      And yet her mouth looked old.

Not long for her the sun would rise,
      Nor that young slip of moon,
Wading through London's smoky skies,
Would dwindling meet those dwindling eyes,
      Ere May was merged in June.

May was it somewhere? Who, alas!
      Could fancy it was May?
For here, instead of meadow grass,
You saw, through naked panes of glass,
      Bare walls of whitish grey.

Instead of songs, where in the quick
        Leaves hide the blackbirds' nests,
You heard the moaning of the sick,
And tortured breathings harsh and thick
        Drawn from their labouring chests.

She muttered, 'What's the odds to me?'
        With an old cynic's sneer;
And looking up, cried mockingly,
'I hate you, nurse! Why, can't you see
        You'll make no convert here?'

And then she shook her fist at Heaven,
        And broke into a laugh!
Yes, though her sins were seven times seven,
Let others pray to be forgiven –
        She scorned such canting chaff.

Oh, it was dreadful, sir! Far worse
        In one so young and fair;
Sometimes she'd scoff and swear and curse;
Call me bad names, and vow each nurse
        A fool for being there.

And then she'd fall back on her bed,
        And many a weary hour
Would lie as rigid as one dead;
Her white throat with the golden head
        Like some torn lily flower.

We could do nothing, one and all
        How much we might beseech;
Her girlish blood had turned to gall:
Far lower than her body's fall
        Her soul had sunk from reach.

Her soul had sunk into a slough
        Of evil past repair.
The world had been against her; now
Nothing in heaven or earth should bow
        Her stubborn knees in prayer.

Yet I felt sorry all the same,
        And sometimes, when she slept,
With head and hands as hot as flame,
I watched beside her, half in shame,
        Smoothed her bright hair and wept.

To die like this – 'twas awful, sir!
        To know I prayed in vain;
And hear her mock me, and aver
That if her life came back to her
        She'd live her life again.

Was she a wicked girl? What then?
        She didn't care a pin!
She was not worse than all those men
Who looked so shocked in public, when
        They made and shared her sin.

'Shut up, nurse, do! Your sermons pall;
        Why can't you let me be?
Instead of worrying o'er my fall,
I wish, just wish, you sisters all
        Turned to the likes of me.'

I shuddered! I could bear no more,
        And left her to her fate;
She was too cankered at the core;
Her heart was like a bolted door,
        Where Love had knocked too late.

I left her in her savage spleen,
        And hoarsely heard her shout,
'What does the cursed sunlight mean
By shining in upon this scene?
        Oh, shut the sunlight out!'

Sighing, I went my round once more,
        Full heavy for her sin;
Just as Big Ben was striking four,
The sun streamed through the open door,
        As a young girl came in.

She held a basket full of flowers –
      Cowslip and columbine;
A lilac bunch from rustic bowers,
Strong-scented after morning showers,
      Smelt like some cordial wine.

There, too, peeped Robin-in-the-hedge,
      There daisies pearled with dew,
Wild parsley from the meadow's edge,
Sweet-william and the purple vetch,
      And hyacinth's heavenly blue.

But best of all the spring's array,
      Green boughs of milk-white thorn;
Their petals on each perfumed spray
Looked like the wedding gift of May
      On nature's marriage morn.

And she who bore those gifts of grace
      To our poor patients there,
Passed like a sunbeam through the place:
Dull eyes grew brighter for her face,
      Angelically fair.

She went the round with elf-like tread,
      And with kind words of cheer,
Soothing as balm of Gilead,
Laid wild flowers on each patient's bed,
      And made the flowers more dear.

At last she came where Nellie Dean
      Still moaned and tossed about –
'What does the cursed sunlight mean
By shining in upon this scene?
      Will no one shut it out?'

And then she swore with rage and pain,
      And moaning tried to rise;
It seemed her ugly words must stain
The child who stood with heart astrain,
      And large blue listening eyes.

Her fair face did not blush or bleach,
  She did not shrink away;
Alas! she was beyond the reach
Of sweet or bitter human speech –
  Deaf as the flowers of May.

Only her listening eyes could hear
  That hardening in despair,
Which made that other girl, so near
In age to her, a thing to fear
  Like fever-tainted air.

She took green boughs of milk-white thorn
  And laid them on the sheet,
Whispering appealingly, 'Don't scorn
My flowers! I think, when one's forlorn,
  They're like a message, Sweet.'

How heavenly fresh those blossoms smelt,
  Like showers on thirsty ground!
The sick girl frowned as if repelled,
And with hot hands began to pelt
  And fling them all around.

But then some influence seemed to stay
  Her hands with calm control;
Her stormy passion cleared away,
The perfume of the breath of May
  Had passed into her soul.

A nerve of memory had been thrilled,
  And, pushing back her hair,
She stretched out hungry arms half filled
With flower and leaf, and panting shrilled,
  'Where are you, mother, where?'

And then her eyes shone darkly bright
  Through childhood in a mist,
As if she suddenly caught sight
Of some one hidden in the light
  And waited to be kissed.

'Oh, mother dear!' we heard her moan,
       'Have you not gone away?
I dreamed, dear mother, you had gone,
And left me in the world alone,
       In the wild world astray.

'It was a dream; I'm home again!
       I hear the ivy-leaves
Tap-tapping on the leaded pane!
Oh, listen! how the laughing rain
       Runs from our cottage eaves!

'How very sweet the things do smell!
       How bright our pewter shines!
I am at home; I feel so well:
I think I hear the evening bell
       Above our nodding pines.

'The firelight glows upon the brick,
       And pales the rising moon;
And when your needles flash and click,
My heart, my heart, that felt so sick,
       Throbs like a hive in June.

'If only father would not stay
       And gossip o'er his brew;
Then, reeling homewards, lose his way,
Come staggering in at break of day
       And beat you black and blue!

'Yet he can be as good as gold,
       When mindful of the farm,
He tills the field and tends the fold:
But never fear; when I'm grown old
       I'll keep him out of harm.

'And then we'll be as happy here
       As kings upon their throne!
I dreamed you'd left me, mother dear;
That you lay dead this many a year
       Beneath the churchyard stone.

'Mother, I sought you far and wide,
    And ever in my dream,
Just out of reach you seemed to hide;
I ran along the streets and cried,
    "Where are you, mother, where?"

'Through never-ending streets in fear
    I ran and ran forlorn;
And through the twilight yellow-drear
I saw blurred masks of loafers leer,
    And point at me in scorn.

'How tired, how deadly tired, I got;
    I ached through all my bones!
The lamplight grew one quivering blot,
And like one rooted to the spot,
    I dropped upon the stones.

'A hard bed make the stones and cold,
    The mist a wet, wet sheet;
And in the mud, like molten gold,
The snaky lamplight blinking rolled
    Like guineas at my feet.

'Surely there were no mothers when
    A voice hissed in my ear,
"A sovereign! Quick! Come on!" – and then
A knowing leer! There were but men,
    And not a creature near.

'I went – I could not help it. Oh,
    I didn't want to die!
With now a kiss and now a blow,
Strange men would come, strange men would go;
    I didn't care – not I.

'Sometimes my life was like a tale
    Read in a story-book;
Our blazing nights turned daylight pale,
Champagne would fizz like ginger-ale,
    Red wine flow like a brook.

MATHILDE BLIND

'Then like a vane my dream would veer:
        I walked the street again;
And through the twilight yellow-drear
Blurred clouds of faces seemed to peer,
        And drift across the rain.'

She started with a piercing scream
        And wildly rolling eye:
'Ah me! it was no evil dream
To pass with the first market-team –
        That thing of shame am I.

'Where were you that you could not come?
        Were you so far above –
Far as the moon above a slum?
Yet, mother, you were all the sum
        I had of human love.

'Ah yes! you've sent this branch of May.
        A fair light from the past.
The town is dark – I went astray.
Forgive me, mother! Lead the way;
        I'm going home at last.'

In eager haste she tried to rise,
        And struggled up in bed,
With luminous, transfigured eyes,
As if they glassed the opening skies,
        Fell back, sir, and was dead.

A Carnival Episode

Nice, '87

We two there together alone in the night,
>   Where its shadow unconsciously bound us;
My beautiful lady all shrouded in white,
She and I looking down from the balcony's height
On the maskers below in the flickering light,
>   As they revelled and rioted round us.

Such a rush, such a rage, and a rapture of life
>   Such shouts of delight and of laughter,
On the quays that I watched with the General's wife;
Such a merry-go-reeling of figures was rife,
Turning round to the tune of gay fiddle and fife,
>   As if never a morning came after.

The houses had emptied themselves in the streets,
>   Where the maskers bombarded each other
With a shower of confetti and hailstorm of sweets.
Till the pavements were turning the colour of sheets;
Where a prince will crack jokes with a pauper he meets,
>   For the time like a man and a brother.

The Carnival frolic was now at its height;
>   The whole population in motion
Stood watching the swift constellations of light
That crackling flashed up on their arrowy flight,
Then spreading their fairy-like fires on the night,
>   Fell in luminous rain on the ocean.

And now and again the quick dazzle would flare,
>   Glowing red on black masks and white dresses.
We two there together drew back from the glare;
Drew in to the room, and her hood unaware
Fell back from the plaits of her opulent hair,
>   That uncoiled the brown snakes of its tresses.

How fatally fair was my lady, my queen,
>   As that wild light fell round her in flashes;
How fatally fair with that mutinous mien,
And those velvety hands all alive with the sheen
Of her rings, and her eyes that were narrowed between
>   Heavy lids darkly laced with long lashes!

MATHILDE BLIND
157

Almost I hated her beauty! The air
      I was breathing seemed steeped in her presence.
How maddening that waltz was! Ah, how came I there
Alone with that woman so fatally fair,
With the scent of her garments, the smell of her hair,
      Passing in to my blood like an essence?

Her eyes seemed to pluck at the roots of my heart,
      And to put all my blood in a fever;
My soul was on fire, my veins seemed to start,
To hold her, to fold her but once to my heart,
I'd have willingly bared broad chest to the dart,
      And been killed, ay, and damned too for ever.

I forgot, I forgot! – oh, disloyal, abhorred,
      With the spell of her eyes on my eyes –
That her husband, the man of all men I adored,
Might be fighting for us at the point of the sword;
Might be killing or killed by an African horde,
      Afar beneath African skies.

I forgot – nay, I cared not! What cared I tonight
      For aught but my lady, my love,
As she toyed with her mask in the flickering light,
Then suddenly dropped it, perchance, at the sight
Of my passion now reaching its uttermost height,
      As a tide with the full moon above!

Yet I knew, though I loved her so madly, I knew
      She was only just playing her game.
She would toy with my heart all the Carnival through;
She would turn to a traitor a man who was true;
She would drain him of love and then break him in two,
      And wash her white hands of his shame.

Yet beware, O my beautiful lady, beware!
      You must cure me of love or else kill.
That fire burns longest that's slowest to flare:
My love is a force that will force you to care;
Nay, I'll strangle us both in the ropes of your hair
      Should you dream you can drop me at will.

And then – how I know not – delirious delight!
     Her lips were pressed close upon mine;
My arms clung about her as when in affright
Wrecked men cling to spars in a tempest at night;
So madly I clung to her, crushed her with might
     To my heart which her heart made divine.

Oh, merciful Heavens! What drove us apart
     With a shudder of sundering lives?
Oh, was it the throb of my passionate heart
That made the doors tremble, the windows to start;
Or was it my lady just playing her part,
     Most indignant, most outraged of wives?

She was white as the chalk in the streets – was she fain
     To turn on me now with a sneer?
All the blood in my body surged up to my brain,
And my heart seemed half bursting with passion and pain,
As I seized her slim hands – but I dropped them again!
     Ah! treason is mother to fear.

Had it come upon us at that magical hour,
     The judgement of God the Most High?
The floor 'gan to heave and the ceiling to lower,
The dead walls to start with malevolent power,
Till your hair seemed to rise and your spirit to cower,
     As the very stones shook with a sigh.

'With you in my arms let the world crack asunder;
     Let us die, love, together!' I cried.
Then, with a clatter and boom as of thunder,
A beam crashed between us and drove us asunder,
And all things rocked round us, above us and under,
     Like a boat that is rocked on a tide.

She sprang like a greyhound – no greyhound more fleet –
     And ran down the staircase in motion;
And blindly I followed her into the street,
All choked up with people in panic retreat
From the houses that scattered their plaster like sleet
     On the crowd in bewildered commotion.

Black masks and white dominoes, hale men and dying,
      Scared women that shook as with fever
Poor babes in their bedgowns all piteously crying,
Tiles hurled from the housetops – all flying, all flying,
As I, wild with passion, implored her with sighing
      To fly with me now and for ever.

'Go, go!' and she waved me away as she spoke,
      Carried on by the crowd like a feather;
'You forget that it was but a Carnival joke.
Now blest be the terrible earthquake that broke
In between you and me, and has saved at a stroke
      Us two in the night there together.'

A Parting

The year is on the wing, my love,
      With tearful days and nights;
The clouds are on the wing above
      With gathering swallow-flights.

The year is on the wing, my sweet,
      And in the ghostly race,
With patter of unnumbered feet,
      The dead leaves fly apace.

The year is on the wing, and shakes
      The last rose from its tree;
And I, whose heart in parting breaks,
      Must bid adieu to thee.

from *Songs and Sonnets* (1893)

from *Love in Exile*

II

Winding all my life about thee,
    Let me lay my lips on thine;
What is all the world without thee,
    Mine – oh mine!

Let me press my heart out on thee,
    Grape of life's most fiery vine,
Spilling sacramental on thee
    Love's red wine.

Let thy strong eyes yearning o'er me
    Draw me with their force divine;
All my soul has gone before me
    Clasping thine.

Irresistibly I follow,
    As whenever we may run
Runs our shadow, as the swallow
    Seeks the sun.

Yea, I tremble, swoon, surrender
    All my spirit to thy sway,
As a star is drowned in splendour
    Of the day.

X

The woods shake in an ague-fit,
    The mad wind rocks the pine,
From sea to sea the white gulls flit
    Into the roaring brine.

The moon as if in panic grief
    Darts through the clouds on high,
Blown like a wild autumnal leaf
    Across the wilder sky.

MATHILDE BLIND

The gusty rain is driving fast,
> And through the rain we hear,
Above the equinoctial blast,
> The thunder of the weir.

The voices of the wind and rain
> Wail echoing through my heart —
That love is ever dogged by pain
> And fondest souls must part.

You made heart's summer, O my friend,
> But now we bid adieu,
There will be winter without end
> And tears for ever new.

XII

Like some wild sleeper who alone at night
Walks with unseeing eyes along a height,
> With death below and only stars above;
I, in broad daylight, walk as if in sleep,
Along the edges of life's perilous steep,
> The lost somnambulist of love.

I, in broad day, go walking in a dream,
Led on in safety by the starry gleam
> Of thy blue eyes that hold my heart in thrall;
Let no one wake me rudely, lest one day,
Startled to find how far I've gone astray,
> I dash my life out in my fall.

XV

Why will you haunt me unawares,
> And walk into my sleep,
> Pacing its shadowy thoroughfares,
Where long-dried perfume scents the airs,
> While ghosts of sorrow creep,
Where on Hope's ruined altar-stairs,
> With ineffectual beams,
The Moon of Memory coldly glares
> Upon the land of dreams?

My yearning eyes were fain to look
Upon your hidden face;
Their love, alas! you could not brook,
But in your own you mutely took
My hand, and for a space
You wrung it till I throbbed and shook,
And woke with wildest moan
And wet face channelled like a brook
With your tears or my own.

The Songs of Summer

The songs of summer are over and past!
The swallow's forsaken the dripping eaves;
Ruined and black 'mid the sodden leaves
The nests are rudely swung in the blast:
And ever the wind like a soul in pain
Knocks and knocks at the window-pane.

The songs of summer are over and past!
Woe's me for a music sweeter than theirs –
The quick, light bound of a step on the stairs,
The greeting of lovers too sweet to last:
And ever the wind like a soul in pain
Knocks and knocks at the window-pane.

On and On

By long leagues of wood and meadow
On and on we drive apace;
In the dreamy light and shadow
Veiling earth's autumnal face.

Rosy clouds are drifting o'er us,
Rooks rise parleying from their tryst,
And the road lies far before us,
Fading into amethyst.

On and on, through leagues of heather,
Deeps of scarlet beaded lane,
Like a pheasant's golden feather
Golden leaves around us rain.

On and on, where woodlands hoary,
       In October's lavish fire,
Flame up with unearthly glory,
       Beauteous summer's funeral pyre.

On and on, where casements blinking
       Lighten into transient gules,
As the dying day in sinking
       Splashes all the wayside pools.

On and on; the land grows dimmer,
       And our road recedes afar;
While on either hand there glimmer
       Setting sun and rising star.

Would I knew what thoughts steal o'er you,
       As the long road lengthens yet:
Ah, like hope it winds before you,
       And behind me like regret.

Lassitude

I laid me down beside the sea,
Endless in blue monotony;
The clouds were anchored in the sky,
Sometimes a sail went idling by.

Upon the shingles on the beach
Grey linen was spread out to bleach,
And gently with a gentle swell
The languid ripples rose and fell.

A fisher-boy, in level line,
Cast stone by stone into the brine:
Methought I too might do as he,
And cast my sorrows on the sea.

The old, old sorrows in a heap
Dropped heavily into the deep;
But with its sorrow on that day
My heart itself was cast away.

Haunted Streets

Lo, haply walking in some clattering street –
Where throngs of men and women dumbly pass,
Like shifting pictures seen within a glass
Which leave no trace behind – one seems to meet,
In roads once trodden by our mutual feet,
A face projected from that shadowy mass
Of faces, quite familiar as it was,
Which beaming on us stands out clear and sweet.

The face of faces we again behold
That lit our life when life was very fair,
And leaps our heart toward eyes and mouth and hair:
Oblivious of the undying love grown cold,
Or body sheeted in the churchyard mould,
We stretch out yearning hands and grasp – the air.

The After-Glow

It is a solemn evening, golden-clear –
        The Alpine summits flame with rose-lit snow
        And headlands purpling on wide seas below,
And clouds and woods and arid rocks appear
Dissolving in the sun's own atmosphere
        And vast circumference of light, whose slow
        Transfiguration – glow and after-glow –
Turns twilight earth to a more luminous sphere.

Oh heart, I ask, seeing that the orb of day
Has sunk below, yet left to sky and sea
        His glory's spiritual after-shine:
I ask if Love, whose sun hath set for thee,
May not touch grief with his memorial ray,
        And lend to loss itself a joy divine?

Manchester by Night

O'er this huge town, rife with intestine wars,
Whence as from monstrous sacrificial shrines
Pillars of smoke climb heavenward, Night inclines
Black brows majestical with glimmering stars.
Her dewy silence soothes life's angry jars:
And like a mother's wan white face, who pines
Above her children's turbulent ways, so shines
The moon athwart the narrow cloudy bars.

Now toiling multitudes that hustling crush
Each other in the fateful strife for breath,
And, hounded on by diverse hungers, rush
Across the prostrate ones that groan beneath,
Are swathed within the universal hush,
As life exchanges semblances with death.

from *Birds of Passage*
Songs of the Orient and Occident (1895)

Sphinx-Money

Where Pyramids and temple-wrecks are piled
    Confusedly on camel-coloured sands,
     And the mute Arab motionlessly stands,
Like some swart god who never wept or smiled,
I picked up mummy relics of the wild
    (And sea-shells once with clutching baby hands),
     And felt a wafture from old Motherlands,
And all the morning wonder of a child

To find Sphinx-money. So the Beduin calls
    Small fossils of the waste. Nay, poet's gold;
     'Twill give thee entrance to those rites of old,
When hundred-gated Thebes, with storied walls,
    Gleamed o'er her plain, and vast processions rolled
To Amon-Ra through Karnak's pillared halls.

The Desert

Uncircumscribed, unmeasured, vast,
Eternal as the Sea;
What lacks the tidal sea thou hast —
Profound stability.

Beneath the sun that burns and brands
In hushed noon's halting breath,
Calm as the Sphinx upon thy sands
Thou art — nay, calm as death.

The desert foxes hide in holes,
The jackal seeks his lair;
The sombre rocks, like reddening coals,
Glow lurid in the glare.

Only some vulture far away,
Bald-headed, harpy-eyed,
Flaps down on lazy wing to prey
On what has lately died.

No palm tree lifts a lonely shade,
No dove is on the wing;
It seems a land which Nature made
Without a living thing,

Or wreckage of some older world,
Ere children grew, or flowers,
When rocks and hissing stones were hurled
In hot, volcanic showers.

The solemn Blue bends over all;
Far as winged thought may flee
Roll ridges of black mountain wall,
And flat sands like the sea.

No trace of footsteps to be seen,
No tent, no smoking roof;
Nay, even the vagrant Beeshareen
Keeps warily aloof.

But yon, mid tumbled hillocks prone,
　　Some human form I scan –
A human form, indeed, but stone:
　　A cold, colossal Man!

How came he here mid piling sands,
　　Like some huge cliff enisled,
Osiris-wise, with folded hands,
　　Mute spirit of the wild?

Ages ago the hands that hewed,
　　And in the living rock
Carved this Colossus, granite-thewed
　　And curled each crispy lock:

Ages ago have dropped to rest
　　And left him passive, prone,
Forgotten on earth's barren breast,
　　Half statue and half stone.

And Persia ruled and Palestine;
　　And o'er her violet seas
Arose, with marble gods divine,
　　The grace of god-like Greece.

And Rome, the Mistress of the World,
　　Amid her diadem
Of Eastern Empires set impearled
　　The scarab's mystic gem.

Perchance he has been lying here
　　Since first the world began,
Poor Titan of some earlier sphere
　　Of prehistoric Man!

To whom we are as idle flies,
　　That fuss and buzz their day;
While still immutable he lies,
　　As long ago he lay.

Empurpled in the afterglow,
　　Thou, with the sun alone,
Of all the stormy waste below,
　　Art King, but king of stone!

Uncircumscribed, unmeasured, vast,
Eternal as the sea,
The present here becomes the past,
For all futurity.

Internal Firesides

Bewilderingly, from wildly shaken cloud,
Invisible hands, deft moving everywhere,
Have woven a winding sheet of velvet air,
And laid the dead earth in her downy shroud.
And more and more, in white confusion, crowd
Wan, whirling flakes, while o'er the icy glare
Blue heaven that was glooms blackening o'er the bare
Tree skeletons, to ruthless tempest bowed.

Nay, let the outer world be winter-locked;
Beside the hearth of glowing memories
I warm my life. Once more our boat is rocked,
As on a cradle by the palm-fringed Nile;
And, sharp-cut silhouettes, in single file,
Lank camels lounge against transparent skies.

A Parable

Between the sandhills and the sea
A narrow strip of silver sand,
Whereon a little maid doth stand,
Who picks up shells continually
Between the sandhills and the sea.

Far as her wondering eyes can reach
A Vastness, heaving grey in grey
To the frayed edges where the day
Furls his red standard on the breach,
Between the skyline and the beach.

The waters of the flowing tide
Cast up the sea-pink shells and weed;
She toys with shells, and doth not heed
The ocean, which on every side
Is closing round her vast and wide.

MATHILDE BLIND

It creeps her way as if in play,
      Pink shells at her pink feet to cast;
      But now the wild waves hold her fast,
And bear her off and melt away
A Vastness heaving grey in grey.

Rest

We are so tired, my heart and I.
Of all things here beneath the sky
One only thing would please us best –
Endless, unfathomable rest.

We are so tired; we ask no more
Than just to slip out by Life's door;
And leave behind the noisy rout
And everlasting turn about.

Once it seemed well to run on too
With her importunate, fevered crew,
And snatch amid the frantic strife
Some morsel from the board of life.

But we are tired. At Life's crude hands
We ask no gift she understands;
But kneel to him she hates to crave
The absolution of the grave.

AMY LEVY

1861–89

After her suicide in 1889, images of Levy were constructed in the terms of the time – Levy with her melancholy Jewish beauty, Levy as victim of the pressures of emancipation or the fear of hereditary insanity, Levy working among the poor of Whitechapel.[1] Modern discussions of Levy have used a different vocabulary, but have tended to be no less rigid in assigning her to an area reserved for outsiders, as a woman, a Jew and a lesbian. And yet Levy's life was as much shaped by membership of institutions and social groupings as by exclusion from them: family and Jewish culture, girls' school and Cambridge college, women's clubs, the literary milieu of journalism, friendships with activist, working women such as Clementina Black, Olive Schreiner, Beatrice Potter (the social scientist Beatrice Webb) and Eleanor Marx, and with writers such as Violet Paget (Vernon Lee) and her circle. To underrate the importance of such overlapping affiliations is both ahistorical and reductive of the complexity of Levy's own stance as a poet.

A generation younger than Augusta Webster, Levy belongs to a very particular moment in the changing relationship between women and the world outside the home. The institutions that had been the goals of the earlier pioneers were largely in existence: girls' schools and colleges, the beginnings of formalised career structures. It is, though, a tentative and fragile space; not only were the institutions themselves still in the process of taking shape, there were few patterns for the lives of single, educated, independent women, or by which others could interpret them. Levy was not so much doomed by her triple inheritance to be an outsider, as struggling to build a sense of self between the communities to which she belonged.

She was born into an Anglo-Jewish, middle-class London family. The Levys did not live in the East End; they were not poor; they were not immigrants. Her father was a stockbroker; both her parents' families had been established in England since the eighteenth century, when they had been ship-owners in Falmouth. Levy was neither the exotic oriental of the nineteenth-century imagination nor its modern equivalent, the alienated outsider. The kind of community to which the Levys belonged was defined as much by English culture and values as by Judaism; the increase in immigration from traditional communities of Eastern Europe in the 1880s if anything sharpened Anglo-Jewry's sense of national identity. Most legal barriers to Jews taking part in public life were giving way by 1858 when legislation enabled the first Jewish MP to take his seat in the House of Commons; religion 'among thinking people of all races', as the modern Jew Reuben Sachs remarks in Levy's novel of that title, has become 'a matter of personal idiosyncrasy'. In an article she published in the *Jewish Chronicle* in 1886, Levy would write of how 'the assertion of even comparative freedom on the part of a Jewess often means the severance of the closest ties, both of family and of race'. But the terms of her polemic are commonplaces of feminist argument of the mid-1880s, when widening opportunities challenged family and social conventions; the article is not based in any personal experience of a rift with her own family, with whom she lived while working as an independent woman in London.[2] The Levys gave all three of their daughters a modern, academic education in new girls' schools, and they apparently had no problem with one of Amy's first published pieces of writing appearing in a feminist journal, *The Pelican*, when she was thirteen, nor with her letter to the *Jewish Chronicle* on women's rights when she was seventeen.

From 1876 Levy attended the newly founded Brighton High School for Girls as a boarder. The school's headmistress was a dynamic young woman who had been one of the original five students of Newnham College in 1871; while running the school she was herself studying for a London University degree.[3] In permitting or encouraging Levy to go on to study at Newnham College in 1879, her parents were enabling her to take a further step into new territory. For a woman – a Jewish woman – to study at Cambridge was to gain a foothold at the centre of English culture; at the same time, it was to become part of another minority, still feeling its way to a sense of identity and purpose.

Levy left Newnham in 1881 at the end of her second year, either as a result of stress, or because she did not wish to follow the full, formal degree course which was being introduced for women, or because the publication in that year of her first book, *Xantippe and Other Verse*, gave her the confidence to strike out on her own path. The title poem was probably written before Levy went to university, but even so it is a 'Cambridge' poem, and it is unsurprising that a poetry society at Newnham was inaugurated with a reading of 'Xantippe'.[4] At many levels, the poem articulates the transitional moment in which Levy and her fellow students had to map out their lives. Like so many of her poems, it speaks of incompleteness, hesitancies, 'ling'ring on the threshold / half concealed'. Levy had almost certainly read Augusta Webster's dramatic monologues; she too was an initiate into classical culture, 'grinding' at Greek in her college room, as she records in letters home. Like Webster, she makes her

uneasy privilege into the content of the poem. Levy's Xantippe, belit-
tled for her 'high thoughts', her yearning 'for knowledge, for a tongue
/ That should proclaim the stately mysteries / Of this fair world, and
of the holy Gods', makes a weapon out of her silencing:

> A huge despair was stealing on my soul,
> A sort of fierce acceptance of my fate –
> He wished a household vessel – well! 'twas good,
> For he should have it!

After Cambridge, Levy spent much of the following three years trav-
elling in Germany and Switzerland, studying, occasionally teaching
English, and writing. Many of the poems in her second collection, *A
Minor Poet and Other Verse* (1884), were written in Dresden. They are
works in which Levy's sensibility of shadow and loss finds a voice in
the German Romantic lyrics to which she was always responsive. If
it were not for the writing, it would seem to have been a totally
conventional way of filling time. She mixed largely with other young
English people, and her letters are full of gossip about picnics and
boating parties, flirtations and hiking expeditions. There is sense of
holiday, but in the background is always an inescapable seriousness
of purpose that belongs to working life in London: 'I have been
working, but O the novel is so bad – it's no go. I have been wasting
my substance in riotous living – had a coffee party, and breakfast party,
the same day… My own melancholy is too large for words – O if I
needn't go home and begin the old struggle for existence!'[5]

In London, Levy moved among women whose identities were
both freed and constrained by an awareness of being outside the main-
stream. They claimed a freedom of movement and intellectual
exploration, crossing boundaries between the domestic, female world
and the male world of professions and scholarship, between the class
into which they were born and educated and the class among whom
some of them found their vocation, between the respectable London
of family homes and the places in which they could afford to live as
single women. They chose to remain single, or they formed marriages
and liaisons that ignored convention. They created alliances and
communities both formal and informal. Levy belonged to the
University Women's Club and a discussion club which was occa-
sionally hosted by the Levys at the family home (and to which she
introduced Bernard Shaw in 1885).[6] Although she was not particu-
larly politically active, in the late 1880s she sometimes worked in the
office of the Women's Provident and Protective League, supporting
Clementina Black's campaigns.

As writers, journalists and social investigators, Levy's London circle recorded their own newly invented lives. The hard choices of the 'struggle for existence' run through much of their writing, alongside their new freedoms. Beatrice Potter's diaries for the 1880s constitute a long coming to terms with 'the loneliness, the patient endurance needful to make even a little headway in work',[7] much as Levy's writing reiterates exhausted renunciation and fruitless effort:

> ... in the table drawer
> Large schemes of undone work. Poems half-writ;
> Wild drafts of symphonies; big plans of fugues;
> Some scraps of writing in a woman's hand: .
> No more – the scattered pages of a tale,
> A sorry tale that no man cared to read.[8]

After Levy's suicide in 1889, Beatrice Potter interpreted her as a casualty of 'a battle for an unknown cause': an incongruous but startlingly intuitive fellow-feeling, even if Potter's cause had never been Levy's.

Levy continued to make trips abroad throughout the 1880s, sustained by contact with European culture and by the sociability that was the counterbalance to life in London, where she repeatedly became exhausted and depressed, not least by her increasing deafness. On a long visit to Florence with Clementina Black in 1886, she met the art critic and novelist Violet Paget, who wrote under the name of Vernon Lee. Lee, who lived for part of each year in a villa in Florence, drew Levy into a different kind of circle. She counted among her friends Browning, Walter Pater, Henry James, William Morris and the Rossettis, as well as women writers such as the poets Agnes Mary Robinson and Dorothy Blomfield, and Bertha Thomas the novelist, who also became Levy's friends.

Levy fell in love with Lee (probably without being aware of Lee's relationships with the other women who were her romantic and intellectual devotees): Lee was friendly, and eventually indifferent. 'I don't love her, but she's a poor little person and clever and can talk poetry', she wrote in 1889; a month later, after Levy's suicide, she wrote as if Levy had been no more than an acquaintance: 'Poor Miss Levy!... She killed herself with charcoal.'[9] The contrast with the undisguised longing of Levy's love poems and the naïve appeals in her letters to Lee is painful ('I am almost afraid to go to Florence; it was so nice last year; and nice things never come over again...', 'I hope you sometimes think of me'[10]), but Lee, for all her ruthlessness, energised Levy as much as she made her unhappy. She gave her friends with whom she found emotional and intellectual companionship: Levy's letters are full of chat about Blomfield and Thomas. Dorothy Blomfield, she wrote in 1887, was 'the only person I have ever met with whom it gives me any real satisfaction to talk about verse and verse-making – a very isolating sort of industry'.[11] Above all, Lee gave Levy a model of a successful, confident, intellectual life for a woman writer on her own terms.

The community of writing and publishing was important to Levy. She wrote as a professional: journalism, novels, translation and poetry, recording what she earned from each, she made connections in literary London, with Wilde, with Yeats and Shaw; but her creativity draws on her sense of distance from the centre – a 'minor poet'. Two writers in particular redefine marginality for Levy. In the first, James Thomson, Levy found a dark affinity. The author of 'The City of Dreadful Night', who died in June 1882 after a life of spectacular misery, encompassing destitution, depression, prison and alcoholism, Thomson is the subject of her poem 'To a Dead Poet'; he is present in 'A Minor Poet'; in 1883 she published a sympathetic essay on him. Her understanding of the self-destructiveness that both fuelled and killed Thomson's creativity is unsettling:

> *The City of Dreadful Night...* stands forth as the very sign and symbol of that attitude of mind we call Weltschmerz, Pessimism, what you will, i.e., the almost perfect expression of a form of mental suffering which I can convey by no other means than by the use of a very awkward figure – by calling it 'grey pain'.[12]

His doomed, precarious life as a journalist and poet, living in boarding houses, working (like Levy) in the British Museum Reading Room, must have been recognisable to her, too, as a life that might have claimed her had she not had the security of a daughter living conventionally in the family home: 'when we consider the dark and narrow circumstances of his lonely life we can only stand aghast'.

In the second key figure, Heinrich Heine, Levy found a voice for the sense of separation that is the defining mode of her later poems. If she read Thomson with an empathy for a poet on the social margins, she responded to Heine with the understanding of shared culture.[13] Heine, for Levy, is not flawed by identity, George Eliot's 'half a Hebrew', Arnold's failed universal symbol who has in him both 'the spirit of Greece and of Judaea' and achieves only a 'half-result'. What she valued in him was not attempted universality but particularity – he is at his greatest when he is most a Jewish poet:

Heine, in truth, has given perfect expression to the very spirit of

Jewish humour; has cracked the communal joke, as it were, in the language of culture, for all to enjoy and understand… let us then be grateful to the man who has proved so triumphantly the worth, who has brought out so successfully the peculiar and delicate quality of the tribal humour.[14]

Her essay on Heine was one of a series of articles on Jewish heritage, culture and family that she wrote for the *Jewish Chronicle* in 1886. She engages combatively with Jewishness, but she writes with the complex, critical intimacy of the insider, for whom the core of identity is irreducible.

Levy was born into a community of culture, family, religion, was among the first generation to be educated in female communities of school and college, and among the first generation of women whose work followed a recognisable professional pattern. Each identity bound her into a community whose condition was to be a minority within the mainstream. Her life was shaped by communities, and her writing attempts to exist outside them. While her poetry looks to Augusta Webster and Barrett Browning, it increasingly withdraws from the social world that their writing inhabits: Levy's 'Magdalen' is allusive and hauntingly unplaced, in contrast to the novelistic texture of Webster's 'Castaway'. The unseen, observant obscurity of the minor poet becomes a form of expressiveness. In the lyrical poems of her last months, Levy creates a music of vanishing; it fades as soon as established:

> The sorrow of their souls to them did seem
> As real as mine to me, as permanent.
> Today, it is the shadow of a dream,
> The half-forgotten breath of breezes spent.[15]

She becomes a ghostly watcher, the sad double of Clementina Black's determined colleagues recording social conditions.

The reasons for Levy's suicide at the family home on 10 September 1889 are unknowable. She had suffered periods of depression from adolescence; 1889 was a stressful year of illness, the end of a relationship with Dorothy Blomfield, and the hostile reception in the Jewish press of her novel of Jewish life, *Reuben Sachs*. To Olive Schreiner, who had taken her on holiday that summer, she wrote, 'philosophy can't help me. I am too much shut in with the personal'.[16] Finally cutting loose from the multiple complexities of community, she writes herself into silence:

I thought my spirit and my heart were tamed
　　　To deadness; dead the pangs that agonise.
The old grief springs to choke me — I am shamed
　　　Before that little ghost with eager eyes.

O turn away, let her not see, not know!
　　　How should she bear it, how should understand?
O hasten down the stairway, haste and go,
And leave her dreaming in the silent land.[17]

Notes

1　A few weeks after Levy's death, her close friend Clementina Black attempted to deal with misinformed fascination in a deliberately calm letter to *The Athenaeum*: 'It is not true that she suffered from failing eyesight, nor from the loss of her sense of humour; nor that she devoted herself to work in the East End. She did suffer for several years from a slight deafness and from fits of extreme depression, the result not of unhappy circumstances or of unkind treatment, but... of the exhaustion produced by strenuous brain work. Most emphatically, it is not true that her family or her personal friends among the Jewish community treated her coldly on account of the publication of [her controversial novel] *Reuben Sachs*, and thus indirectly hastened her death. Her parents were justly proud of her; it was impossible to be more uniformly indulgent, more anxious to anticipate her every wish than they were' (5 October 1889, p. 457).

2　'Middle-Class Jewish Women of Today', *Jewish Chronicle*, 17 September 1886, p. 7, in *The Complete Novels and Selected Writings of Amy Levy*, ed. Melvyn New, University Press of Florida, Gainesville FL 1993, pp. 525–7. Levy is bringing home the discussion of the 'woman question' at a time of heightened tension within the community, when the *Jewish Chronicle*'s pages were full of anxieties about the impact of immigration from Europe and middle-class Jewish values were at their most defensive. As a piece of journalism, rather than confessional, its publication in the *Jewish Chronicle* appears as part of a debate within a community in the process of redefining itself under the pressures of social change, evidence of openness to cross-currents of thought rather than isolation from them.

3　Women could not at the time be awarded Cambridge degrees, and in the early days of the women's colleges, not all students even followed degree courses, as their schooling had not equipped them with an adequate level of knowledge.

4　Linda Hunt Beckman, *Amy Levy: Her Life and Letters*, Ohio University Press, Athens OH 2000, p. 91. Most biographical details that follow are drawn from Hunt Beckman's book.

5　Letter, 1884, from Germany, to her sister Katie, in Hunt Beckman p. 250.

6　Her article 'Women and Club Life' in *The Woman's World* (1, 1888, pp. 364–7, in New, pp. 532–8) shows Levy's awareness of the significance of such supportive groups, which provided 'a haven of refuge' away from the family circle, 'which can never bring itself to regard feminine leisure and feminine solitude as things to be accepted' (New, p. 533).

7　*The Diary of Beatrice Webb*, Vol. 1, ed. Norman and Jeanne MacKenzie, Virago

Press in association with the London School of Economics, London 1982, 21 August 1888, p. 258.

8 From 'A Minor Poet'.
9 Hunt Beckman, p. 208.
10 Hunt Beckman, pp. 256, 261.
11 Hunt Beckman, p. 265.
12 'James Thomson: A Minor Poet', *The Cambridge Review*, 21 and 28 February 1883, pp. 240–1, 257–8, in New, pp. 502–9.
13 Eleanor Marx recognised Levy's empathy with Heine: 'There are a good many English writers who have tried their hand at translating Heine's *Lieder*. Amy was the best of them' (Hunt Beckman, p. 82).
14 'Jewish Humour', *Jewish Chronicle*, 20 August 1886, in New, pp. 521–4.
15 From 'London Poets'.
16 *Olive Schreiner's Letters*, Vol. I, ed. Richard Rive, Oxford University Press, Oxford 1988, p. 157.
17 From 'The Old House'.

from *Xantippe and Other Verse* (1881)

Aus meinen grossen Schmerzen
Mach' ich die kleinen Lieder
Heine

Xantippe

A fragment

What, have I waked again? I never thought
To see the rosy dawn, or ev'n this grey,
Dull, solemn stillness, ere the dawn has come.
The lamp burns low; low burns the lamp of life:
The still morn stays expectant, and my soul,
All weighted with a passive wonderment,
Waiteth and watcheth, waiteth for the dawn.
Come hither, maids; too soundly have ye slept
That should have watched me; nay, I would not chide –
Oft have I chidden, yet I would not chide
In this last hour – now all should be at peace.
I have been dreaming in a troubled sleep
Of weary days I thought not to recall;
Of stormy days, whose storms are hushed long since;
Of gladsome days, of sunny days; alas!
In dreaming, all their sunshine seem'd so sad,
As though the current of the dark To-Be
Had flow'd, prophetic, through the happy hours.
And yet, full well, I know it was not thus;
I mind me sweetly of the summer days,
When, leaning from the lattice, I have caught
The fair, far glimpses of a shining sea;
And, nearer, of tall ships which thronged the bay,
And stood out blackly from a tender sky
All flecked with sulphur, azure, and bright gold;
And in the still, clear air have heard the hum
Of distant voices; and methinks there rose
No darker fount to mar or stain the joy
Which sprang ecstatic in my maiden breast
Than just those vague desires, those hopes and fears,
Those eager longings, strong, though undefined,
Whose very sadness makes them seem so sweet.
What cared I for the merry mockeries
Of other maidens sitting at the loom?

Or for sharp voices, bidding me return
To maiden labour? Were we not apart,
I and my high thoughts, and my golden dreams,
My soul which yearned for knowledge, for a tongue
That should proclaim the stately mysteries
Of this fair world, and of the holy gods?
Then followed days of sadness, as I grew
To learn my woman-mind had gone astray,
And I was sinning in those very thoughts –
For maidens, mark, such are not woman's thoughts –
(And yet, 'tis strange, the gods who fashion us
Have given us such promptings)...
       Fled the years,
Till seventeen had found me tall and strong,
And fairer, runs it, than Athenian maids
Are wont to seem; I had not learnt it well –
My lesson of dumb patience – and I stood
At Life's great threshold with a beating heart,
And soul resolved to conquer and attain...
Once, walking 'thwart the crowded market place,
With other maidens, bearing in the twigs
White doves for Aphrodite's sacrifice,
I saw him, all ungainly and uncouth,
Yet many gathered round to hear his words,
Tall youths and stranger-maidens – Sokrates –
I saw his face and marked it, half with awe,
Half with a quick repulsion at the shape...
The richest gem lies hidden furthest down,
And is the dearer for the weary search;
We grasp the shining shells which strew the shore,
Yet swift we fling them from us; but the gem
We keep for aye and cherish. So a soul,
Found after weary searching in the flesh
Which half repelled our senses, is more dear,
For that same seeking, than the sunny mind
Which lavish Nature marks with thousand hints
Upon a brow of beauty. We are prone
To overweigh such subtle hints, then deem,
In after disappointment, we are fooled...
And when, at length, my father told me all,
That I should wed me with great Sokrates,
I, foolish, wept to see at once cast down
The maiden image of a future love,

Where perfect body matched the perfect soul.
But slowly, softly did I cease to weep;
Slowly I 'gan to mark the magic flash
Leap to the eyes, to watch the sudden smile
Break round the mouth, and linger in the eyes;
To listen for the voice's lightest tone –
Great voice, whose cunning modulations seemed
Like to the notes of some sweet instrument.
So did I reach and strain, until at last
I caught the soul athwart the grosser flesh.
Again of thee, sweet Hope, my spirit dreamed!
I, guided by his wisdom and his love,
Led by his words, and counselled by his care,
Should lift the shrouding veil from things which be,
And at the flowing fountain of his soul
Refresh my thirsting spirit...
      And indeed,
In those long days which followed that strange day
When rites and song, and sacrifice and flow'rs,
Proclaimed that we were wedded, did I learn,
In sooth, a-many lessons; bitter ones
Which sorrow taught me, and not love inspired,
Which deeper knowledge of my kind impressed
With dark insistence on reluctant brain –
But that great wisdom, deeper, which dispels
Narrowed conclusions of a half-grown mind,
And sees athwart the littleness of life
Nature's divineness and her harmony,
Was never poor Xantippe's...
      I would pause
And would recall no more, no more of life,
Than just the incomplete, imperfect dream
Of early summers, with their light and shade,
Their blossom-hopes, whose fruit was never ripe;
But something strong within me, some sad chord
Which loudly echoes to the later life,
Me to unfold the after-misery
Urges with plaintive wailing in my heart.
Yet, maidens, mark; I would not that ye thought
I blame my lord departed, for he meant
No evil, so I take it, to his wife.
'Twas only that the high philosopher,
Pregnant with noble theories and great thoughts,

Deigned not to stoop to touch so slight a thing
As the fine fabric of a woman's brain –
So subtle as a passionate woman's soul.
I think, if he had stooped a little, and cared,
I might have risen nearer to his height,
And not lain shattered, neither fit for use
As goodly household vessel, nor for that
Far finer thing which I had hoped to be...
Death, holding high his retrospective lamp,
Shows me those first, far years of wedded life,
Ere I had learnt to grasp the barren shape
Of what the Fates had destined for my life.
Then, as all youthful spirits are, was I
Wholly incredulous that Nature meant
So little, who had promised me so much.
At first I fought my fate with gentle words,
With high endeavours after greater things;
Striving to win the soul of Sokrates,
Like some slight bird, who sings her burning love
To human master, till at length she finds
Her tender language wholly misconceived,
And that same hand whose kind caress she sought,
With fingers flippant flings the careless corn...
I do remember how, one summer's eve,
He, seated in an arbour's leafy shade,
Had bade me bring fresh wine-skins...
      As I stood
Ling'ring upon the threshold, half concealed
By tender foliage, and my spirit light
With draughts of sunny weather, did I mark
An instant, the gay group before mine eyes.
Deepest in shade, and facing where I stood,
Sat Plato, with his calm face and low brows
Which met above the narrow Grecian eyes,
The pale, thin lips just parted to the smile,
Which dimpled that smooth olive of his cheek.
His head a little bent, sat Sokrates,
With one swart finger raised admonishing,
And on the air were borne his changing tones.
Low lounging at his feet, one fair arm thrown
Around his knee (the other, high in air
Brandish'd a brazen amphor, which yet rained
Bright drops of ruby on the golden locks

And temples with their fillets of the vine),
Lay Alkibiades the beautiful.
And thus, with solemn tone, spake Sokrates:
'This fair Aspasia, which our Perikles
Hath brought from realms afar, and set on high
In our Athenian city, hath a mind,
I doubt not, of a strength beyond her race;
And makes employ of it, beyond the way
Of women nobly gifted: woman's frail —
Her body rarely stands the test of soul;
She grows intoxicate with knowledge; throws
The laws of custom, order, 'neath her feet,
Feasting at life's great banquet with wide throat.'
Then sudden, stepping from my leafy screen,
Holding the swelling wine-skin o'er my head,
With breast that heaved, and eyes and cheeks aflame,
Lit by a fury and a thought, I spake:
'By all great powers around us! Can it be
That we poor women are empirical?
That gods who fashioned us did strive to make
Beings too fine, too subtly delicate,
With sense that thrilled response to ev'ry touch
Of nature's and their task is not complete?
That they have sent their half-completed work
To bleed and quiver here upon the earth?
To bleed and quiver, and to weep and weep,
To beat its soul against the marble walls
Of men's cold hearts, and then at last to sin!'
I ceased, the first hot passion stayed and stemmed
And frighted by the silence: I could see,
Framed by the arbour foliage, which the sun
In setting softly gilded with rich gold,
Those upturned faces, and those placid limbs;
Saw Plato's narrow eyes and niggard mouth,
Which half did smile and half did criticise,
One hand held up, the shapely fingers framed
To gesture of entreaty — 'Hush, I pray,
Do not disturb her; let us hear the rest;
Follow her mood, for here's another phase
Of your black-browed Xantippe...'
   Then I saw
Young Alkibiades, with laughing lips
And half-shut eyes, contemptuous shrugging up

Soft, snowy shoulders, till he brought the gold
Of flowing ringlets round about his breasts.
But Sokrates, all slow and solemnly,
Raised, calm, his face to mine, and sudden spake:
'I thank thee for the wisdom which thy lips
Have thus let fall among us: prythee tell
From what high source, from what philosophies
Didst cull the sapient notion of thy words?'
Then stood I straight and silent for a breath,
Dumb, crushed with all that weight of cold contempt;
But swiftly in my bosom there uprose
A sudden flame, a merciful fury sent
To save me; with both angry hands I flung
The skin upon the marble, where it lay
Spouting red rills and fountains on the white;
Then, all unheeding faces, voices, eyes,
I fled across the threshold, hair unbound –
White garment stained to redness – beating heart
Flooded with all the flowing tide of hopes
Which once had gushed out golden, now sent back
Swift to their sources, never more to rise...
I think I could have borne the weary life,
The narrow life within the narrow walls,
If he had loved me; but he kept his love
For this Athenian city and her sons;
And, haply, for some stranger-woman, bold
With freedom, thought, and glib philosophy...
Ah me! the long, long weeping through the nights,
The weary watching for the pale-eyed dawn
Which only brought fresh grieving: then I grew
Fiercer, and cursed from out my inmost heart
The Fates which marked me an Athenian maid.
Then faded that vain fury; hope died out;
A huge despair was stealing on my soul,
A sort of fierce acceptance of my fate –
He wished a household vessel – well! 'twas good,
For he should have it! He should have no more
The yearning treasure of a woman's love,
But just the baser treasure which he sought.
I called my maidens, ordered out the loom,
And spun unceasing from the morn till eve;
Watching all keenly over warp and woof,
Weighing the white wool with a jealous hand.

I spun until, methinks, I spun away
The soul from out my body, the high thoughts
From out my spirit; till at last I grew
As ye have known me – eye exact to mark
The texture of the spinning; ear all keen
For aimless talking when the moon is up,
And ye should be a-sleeping; tongue to cut
With quick incision, 'thwart the merry words
Of idle maidens...
      Only yesterday
My hands did cease from spinning; I have wrought
My dreary duties, patient till the last.
The gods reward me! Nay, I will not tell
The after years of sorrow; wretched strife
With grimmest foes – sad Want and Poverty –
Nor yet the time of horror, when they bore
My husband from the threshold; nay, nor when
The subtle weed had wrought its deadly work.
Alas! alas! I was not there to soothe
The last great moment; never any thought
Of her that loved him – save at least the charge,
All earthly, that her body should not starve...
You weep, you weep; I would not that ye wept;
Such tears are idle; with the young, such grief
Soon grows to gratulation, as, 'her love
Was withered by misfortune; mine shall grow
All nurtured by the loving', or, 'her life
Was wrecked and shattered – mine shall smoothly sail'.
Enough, enough. In vain, in vain, in vain!
The gods forgive me! Sorely have I sinned
In all my life. A fairer fate befall
You all that stand there...
      Ha! the dawn has come;
I see a rosy glimmer – nay! it grows dark;
Why stand ye so in silence? Throw it wide,
The casement, quick; why tarry? – give me air –
O fling it wide, I say, and give me light!

A Prayer

Since that I may not have
Love on this side the grave,
     Let me imagine Love.
Since not mine is the bliss
Of 'claspt hands and lips that kiss',
     Let me in dreams it prove.
What tho' as the years roll
No soul shall melt to my soul,
     Let me conceive such thing;
Tho' never shall entwine
Loving arms around mine
     Let dreams caresses bring.
To live – it is my doom –
Lonely as in a tomb,
     This cross on me was laid;
My God, I know not why;
Here in the dark I lie,
     Lonely, yet not afraid.
It has seemed good to Thee
Still to withhold the key
     Which opes the way to men;
I am shut in alone,
I make not any moan,
     Thy ways are past my ken.
Yet grant me this, to find
The sweetness in my mind
     Which I must still forego;
Great God which art above,
Grant me to image Love –
     The bliss without the woe.

Ralph to Mary

Love, you have led me to the strand,
     Here, where the stilly, sunset sea,
     Ever receding silently,
Lays bare a shining stretch of sand;

Which, as we tread, in waving line,
     Sinks softly 'neath our moving feet;

And looking down our glances meet,
Two mirrored figures – yours and mine.

Tonight you found me sad, alone,
    Amid the noisy, empty books
    And drew me forth with those sweet looks,
And gentle ways which are your own.

The glory of the setting sun
    Has sway'd and softened all my mood;
    This wayward heart you understood,
Dear love, as you have always done.

Have you forgot the poet wild,
    Who sang rebellious songs and hurl'd
    His fierce anathemas at 'the world',
Which shrugg'd its shoulders, pass'd and smil'd?

Who fled in wrath to distant lands,
    And sitting, thron'd upon a steep,
    Made music to the mighty deep,
And thought, 'Perhaps *it* understands.'

Who back return'd, a wanderer drear,
    Urged by the spirit's restless pain,
    Sang his wild melodies in vain –
Sang them to ears that would not hear...

A weary, lonely thing he flies,
    His soul's fire with soul's hunger quell'd,
    Till, sudden turning, he beheld
His meaning–mirrored in your eyes!...

Ah, Love, since then have passed away
    Long years; some things are chang'd on earth;
    Men say that poet had his worth,
And twine for him the tardy bay.

What care I, so that hand in hand,
    And heart in heart we pace the shore?
    My heart desireth nothing more,
We understand – we understand.

Sonnet

Most wonderful and strange it seems, that I
Who but a little time ago was tost
High on the waves of passion and of pain,
With aching heat and wildly throbbing brain,
Who peered into the darkness, deeming vain
All things there found if but One thing were lost,
Thus calm and still and silent here should lie,
Watching and waiting – waiting passively.

The dark has faded, and before mine eyes
Have long, grey flats expanded, dim and bare;
And through the changing guises all things wear
Inevitable Law I recognise:
Yet in my heart a hint of feeling lies
Which half a hope and half a despair.

Run to Death

A true incident of pre-Revolutionary French history

Now the lovely autumn morning breathes its freshness in earth's face,
In the crowned castle courtyard the blithe horn proclaims the chase;
And the ladies on the terrace smile adieux with rosy lips
To the huntsmen disappearing down the cedar-shaded groves,
Wafting delicate aromas from their scented finger tips,
And the gallants wave in answer, with their gold-embroidered gloves.
On they rode, past bush and bramble, on they rode, past elm and oak;
And the hounds, with anxious nostril, sniffed the heather-scented air,
Till at last, within his stirrups, up Lord Gaston rose, and spoke –
He, the boldest and the bravest of the wealthy nobles there:
'Friends,' quoth he, 'the time hangs heavy, for it is not as we thought,
And these woods, tho' fair and shady, will afford, I fear, no sport.
Shall we hence, then, worthy kinsmen, and desert the hunter's track
For the chateau, where the wine cup and the dice cup tempt us back?'
'Ay,' the nobles shout in chorus; 'Ay,' the powder'd lacquey cries;
Then they stop with eager movement, reining in quite suddenly;
Peering down with half contemptuous, half with wonder-opened
                                                            eyes
At a 'something' which is crawling, with slow step, from tree to tree.
Is't some shadow phantom ghastly? No, a woman and a child,
Swarthy woman, with the 'gipsy' written clear upon her face;

Gazing round her with her wide eyes dark, and shadow-fringed,
                                                        and wild,
With the cowed suspicious glances of a persecuted race.
Then they all, with unasked question, in each other's faces peer,
For a common thought has struck them, one their lips dare scarcely
                                                        say —
Till Lord Gaston cries, impatient, 'Why regret the stately deer
When such sport as yonder offers? Quick! unleash the dogs – away!'
Then they breath'd a shout of cheering, grey-haired man and
                                                        stripling boy,
And the gipsy, roused to terror, stayed her step, and turned her
                                                        head —
Saw the faces of those huntsmen, lit with keenest cruel joy —
Sent a cry of grief to Heaven, closer clasped her child, and fled!

★

O ye nobles of the palace! O ye gallant-hearted lords!
Who would stoop for Leila's kerchief, or for Clementina's gloves,
Who would rise up all indignant, with your shining sheathless swords,
At the breathing of dishonour to your languid lady loves!
O, I tell you, daring nobles, with your beauty-loving stare,
Who ne'er long the coy coquetting of the courtly dames withstood,
Tho' a woman be the lowest, and the basest, and least fair,
In your manliness forget not to respect her womanhood,
And thou, gipsy, that hast often the pursuer fled before,
That hast felt ere this the shadow of dark death upon thy brow,
That hast hid among the mountains, that hast roamed the forest o'er,
Bred to hiding, watching, fleeing, may thy speed avail thee now!

★

Still she flees, and ever fiercer tear the hungry hounds behind,
Still she flees, and ever faster follow there the huntsmen on,
Still she flees, her black hair streaming in a fury to the wind,
Still she flees, tho' all the glimmer of a happy hope is gone.
'Eh? what? baffled by a woman! Ah, *sapristi*! she can run!
Should she 'scape us, it would crown us with dishonour and disgrace;
It is time' (Lord Gaston shouted) 'such a paltry chase were done!'
And the fleeter grew her footsteps, so the hotter grew the chase —
Ha! at last! The dogs are on her! Will she struggle ere she dies?
See! she holds her child above her, all forgetful of *her* pain,
While a hundred thousand curses shoot out darkly from her eyes,

AMY LEVY

And a hundred thousand glances of the bitterest disdain.
Ha! the dogs are pressing closer! They have flung her to the ground;
Yet her proud lips never open with the dying sinner's cry –
Till at last, unto the Heavens, just two fearful shrieks resound,
When the soul is all forgotten in the body's agony!
Let them rest there, child and mother, in the shadow of the oak,
On the tender mother-bosom of that earth from which they came.
As they slow rode back those huntsmen neither laughed, nor sang,
                                         nor spoke,
Hap, there lurked unowned within them throbbings of a secret
                                         shame.

But before the flow'ry terrace, where the ladies smiling sat,
With their graceful nothings trifling all the weary time away,
Low Lord Gaston bowed, and raising high his richly 'broider'd hat,
'Fairest ladies, give us welcome! 'Twas a famous hunt today.'

A Ballad of Last Seeing (1883)

It is so very long ago
      A little thing, I am aware;
I heard the music's ebb and flow,
      I raised my head and saw you there.
Cold was your face, as cold as fair,
      You did not stay to smile or greet;
Sunshine and music filled the air
      The last time that I saw you, sweet.

Beneath the arching portico
      Carved round about with carvings rare
You passed a space, then turned to go,
      I watched you down the sculptured stair.
I did not hear the organ's blare
      Sole heard I your departing feet;
I cared so much, you did not care,
The last time that I saw you, sweet.

Envoy

Friend, if indeed it must be so,
      And we no more on earth may meet,
One time was dear to me I know –
The last time that I saw you, sweet.

from *A Minor Poet and Other Verse* (1884)

To a Dead Poet

I knew not if to laugh or weep;
    They sat and talked of you –
"Twas here he sat; 'twas this he said!
    'Twas that he used to do.

'Here is the book wherein he read,
    The room wherein he dwelt;
And he' (they said) 'was such a man,
    Such things he thought and felt.'

I sat and sat, I did not stir;
    They talked and talked away.
I was as mute as any stone,
    I had no word to say.

They talked and talked; like to a stone
    My heart grew in my breast –
I, who had never seen your face
    Perhaps I knew you best.

A Minor Poet

What should such fellows as I do,
    Crawling between earth and heaven?

Here is the phial; here I turn the key
Sharp in the lock. Click! – there's no doubt it turned.
This is the third time; there is luck in threes –
Queen Luck, that rules the world, befriend me now
And freely I'll forgive you many wrongs!
Just as the draught began to work, first time,
Tom Leigh, my friend (as friends go in the world),
Burst in, and drew the phial from my hand,
(Ah, Tom! ah, Tom! that was a sorry turn!)
And lectured me a lecture, all compact
Of neatest, newest phrases, freshly culled
From works of newest culture: 'common good';
'The world's great harmonies'; 'must be content
With knowing God works all things for the best,

And Nature never stumbles.' Then again,
'The common good', and still, 'the common, good';
And what a small thing was our joy or grief
When weigh'd with that of thousands. Gentle Tom,
But you might wag your philosophic tongue
From morn till eve, and still the thing's the same:
I am myself, as each man is himself –
Feels his own pain, joys his own joy, and loves
With his own love, no other's. Friend, the world
Is but one man; one man is but the world.
And I am I, and you are Tom, that bleeds
When needles prick your flesh (mark, yours, not mine).
I must confess it; I can feel the pulse
A-beating at my heart, yet never knew
The throb of cosmic pulses. I lament
The death of youth's ideal in my heart;
And, to be honest, never yet rejoiced
In the world's progress – scarce, indeed, discerned;
(For still it seems that God's a Sisyphus
With the world for stone).
   You shake your head. I'm base,
Ignoble? Who is noble – you or I?
I was not once thus? Ah, my friend, we are
As the Fates make us.
   This time is the third;
The second time the flask fell from my hand,
Its drowsy juices spilt upon the board;
And there my face fell flat, and all the life
Crept from my limbs, and hand and foot were bound
With mighty chains, subtle, intangible;
While still the mind held to its wonted use,
Or rather grew intense and keen with dread,
An awful dread – I thought I was in Hell.
In Hell, in Hell! Was ever Hell conceived
By mortal brain, by brain Divine devised,
Darker, more fraught with torment, than the world
For such as I? A creature maimed and marr'd
From very birth. A blot, a blur, a note
All out of tune in this world's instrument.
A base thing, yet not knowing to fulfil
Base functions. A high thing, yet all unmeet
For work that's high. A dweller on the earth,
Yet not content to dig with other men

Because of certain sudden sights and sounds
(Bars of broke music; furtive, fleeting glimpse
Of angel faces 'thwart the grating seen)
Perceived in Heaven. Yet when I approach
To catch the sound's completeness, to absorb
The faces' full perfection, Heaven's gate,
Which then had stood ajar, sudden falls to,
And I, a-shiver in the dark and cold,
Scarce hear afar the mocking tones of men:
'He would not dig, forsooth; but he must strive
For higher fruits than what our tillage yields;
Behold what comes, my brothers, of vain pride!'
Why play with figures? trifle prettily
With this my grief which very simply's said,
'There is no place for me in all the world'?
The world's a rock, and I will beat no more
A breast of flesh and blood against a rock...
A stride across the planks for old time's sake.
Ah, bare, small room that I have sorrowed in;
Ay, and on sunny days, haply, rejoiced;
We know some things together, you and I!
Hold there, you rangèd row of books! In vain
You beckon from your shelf. You've stood my friends
Where all things else were foes; yet now I'll turn
My back upon you, even as the world
Turns it on me. And yet – farewell, farewell!
You, lofty Shakespere, with the tattered leaves
And fathomless great heart, your binding's bruised
Yet did I love you less? Goethe, farewell;
Farewell, triumphant smile and tragic eyes,
And pitiless world-wisdom!
                    For all men
These two. And 'tis farewell with you, my friends,
More dear because more near: Theokritus;
Heine that stings and smiles; Prometheus' bard;
(I've grown too coarse for Shelley latterly:)
And one wild singer of today, whose song
Is all aflame with passionate bard's blood
Lash'd into foam by pain and the world's wrong.
At least, he has a voice to cry his pain;
For him, no silent writhing in the dark,
No muttering of mute lips, no straining out
Of a weak throat a-choke with pent-up sound,

A-throb with pent-up passion...
        Ah, my sun!
That's you, then, at the window, looking in
To beam farewell on one who's loved you long
And very truly. Up, you creaking thing,
You squinting, cobwebbed casement!
        So, at last,
I can drink in the sunlight. How it falls.
Across that endless sea of London roofs,
Weaving such golden wonders on the grey,
That almost, for the moment, we forget
The world of woe beneath them.
        Underneath,
For all the sunset glory, Pain is king.
Yet, the sun's there, and very sweet withal;
And I'll not grumble that it's only sun,
But open wide my lips – thus – drink it in;
Turn up my face to the sweet evening sky
(What royal wealth of scarlet on the blue
So tender toned, you'd almost think it green)
And stretch my hands out – so – to grasp it tight.
Ha, ha! 'tis sweet awhile to cheat the Fates,
And be as happy as another man.
The sun works in my veins like wine, like wine!
'Tis a fair world: if dark, indeed, with woe,
Yet having hope and hint of such a joy,
That a man, winning, well might turn aside,
Careless of Heaven...
        O enough; I turn
From the sun's light, or haply I shall hope.
I have hoped enough; I would not hope again:
'Tis hope that is most cruel.
        Tom, my friend,
You very sorry philosophic fool;
'Tis you, I think, that bid me be resign'd,
Trust, and be thankful.
        Out on you! Resign'd?
I'm not resign'd, not patient, not school'd in
To take my starveling's portion and pretend
I'm grateful for it. I want all, all, all;
I've appetite for all. I want the best:
Love, beauty, sunlight, nameless joy of life.
There's too much patience in the world, I think.

We have grown base with crooking of the knee.
Mankind – say – God has bidden to a feast;
The board is spread, and groans with cates and drinks;
In troop the guests; each man with appetite
Keen-whetted with expectance.

       In they troop,
Struggle for seats, jostle and push and seize.
What's this? What's this? There are not seats for all!
Some men must stand without the gates; and some
Must linger by the table, ill-supplied
With broken meats. One man gets meat for two,
The while another hungers. If I stand
Without the portals, seeing others eat
Where I had thought to satiate the pangs
Of mine own hunger; shall I then come forth
When all is done, and drink my Lord's good health
In my Lord's water? Shall I not rather turn
And curse him, curse him for a niggard host?
O, I have hungered, hungered, through the years,
Till appetite grows craving, then disease;
I am starved, wither'd, shrivelled.

       Peace, O peace!
This rage is idle; what avails to curse
The nameless forces, the vast silences
That work in all things.

       This time is the third,
I wrought before in heat, stung mad with pain,
Blind, scarcely understanding; now I know
What thing I do.

       There was a woman once;
Deep eyes she had, white hands, a subtle smile,
Soft speaking tones: she did not break my heart,
Yet haply had her heart been otherwise
Mine had not now been broken. Yet, who knows?
My life was jarring discord from the first:
Tho' here and there brief hints of melody,
Of melody unutterable, clove the air.
From this bleak world, into the heart of night,
The dim, deep bosom of the universe,
I cast myself. I only crave for rest;
Too heavy is the load. I fling it down.

Epilogue

We knocked and knocked; at last, burst in the door,
And found him as you know — the outstretched arms
Propping the hidden face. The sun had set,
And all the place was dim with lurking shade.
There was no written word to say farewell,
Or make more clear the deed.
          I search'd and search'd;
The room held little: just a row of books
Much scrawl'd and noted; sketches on the wall,
Done rough in charcoal; the old instrument
(A violin, no Stradivarius)
He played so ill on; in the table drawer
Large schemes of undone work. Poems half-writ;
Wild drafts of symphonies; big plans of fugues;
Some scraps of writing in a woman's hand:
No more — the scattered pages of a tale,
A sorry tale that no man cared to read.
Alas, my friend, I lov'd him well, tho' he
Held me a cold and stagnant-blooded fool,
Because I am content to watch, and wait
With a calm mind the issue of all things.
Certain it is my blood's no turbid stream;
Yet, for all that, haply I understood
More than he ever deem'd; nor held so light
The poet in him. Nay, I sometimes doubt
If they have not, indeed, the better part —
These poets, who get drunk with sun, and weep
Because the night or a woman's face is fair.
Meantime there is much talk about my friend.
The women say, of course, he died for love;
The men, for lack of gold, or cavilling
Of carping critics. I, Tom Leigh, his friend
I have no word at all to say of this.
Nay, I had deem'd him more philosopher;
For did he think by this one paltry deed
To cut the knot of circumstance, and snap
The chain which binds all being?

OUT OF MY BORROWED BOOKS

Medea

A fragment in drama form, after Euripides

Persons
Medea
Jason
Citizens of Corinth: Aegeus, Nikias

Scene: Before Medea's house
(Enter Medea)

MEDEA Today, today, I know not why it is,
I do bethink me of my Colchian home.
Today, that I am lone and weary and sad,
I fain would call back days of pride and hope;
Of pride in strength, when strength was all unprov'd,
Of hope too high, too sweet, to be confined
In limits of conception.
      I am sad
Here in this gracious city, whose white walls
Gleam snow-like in the sunlight; whose fair shrines
Are filled with wondrous images of gods;
Upon whose harbour's bosom ride tall ships,
Black-masted, fraught with fragrant merchandise;
Whose straight-limbed people, in fair stuffs arrayed,
Do throng from morn till eve the sunny streets.
For what avail fair shrines and images?
What, cunning workmanship and purple robes?
Light of sweet sunlight, play and spray of waves?
When all around the air is charged and chill,
And all the place is drear and dark with hate?
Alas, alas, this people loves me not!
This strong, fair people, marble-cold and smooth
As modelled marble. I, an alien here,
That well can speak the language of their lips,
The language of their souls may never learn.
And in their hands, I, that did know myself
Ere now, a creature in whose veins ran blood
Redder, more rapid, than flows round most hearts,
Do seem a creature reft of life and soul.
If they would only teach the subtle trick
By which their hearts are melted into love,
I'd strive to learn it. I am very meek.

They think me proud, but I am very meek,
Ready to do their bidding. Hear me, friends!
Friends, I am very hungry, give me love!
'Tis all I ask! is it so hard to give?
You stand and front me with your hostile eyes;
You only give me hatred?
       Yet I know
Ye are not all unloving. Oft I see
The men and women walking in the ways,
Hand within hand, and tender-bated breath,
On summer evenings when the sky is fair.
O men and women, are ye then so hard?
Will ye not give a little of your love
To me that am so hungry?

(Enter Aegeus and Nikias, on the opposite side. Medea steps back on the threshold and pauses.)

      Ha, that word!
'Tis Jason's name they bandy to and fro.
I know not why, whene'er his name is spoke,
Once name of joy and ever name of love,
I wax white and do tremble; sudden seized
With shadowy apprehension. May't forbode
No evil unto him I hold so dear;
And ever dearer with the waxing years –
For this indeed is woman's chiefest curse,
That still her constant heart clings to its love
Through all time and all chances; while the man
Is caught with newness; coldly calculates,
And measures pain and pleasure, loss and gain;
And ever grows to look with the world's eye
Upon a woman, tho' his, body and soul. *(She goes within.)*

(The two citizens come forward.)

NIKIAS   I, in this thing, do hold our Jason wise;
Kreon is mighty; Glaukê very fair.

AEGEUS   An 'twere for that – the Colchian's fair enough.

NIKIAS   I like not your swart skins and purple hair;
Your black, fierce eyes where the brows meet across.

By all the gods! when yonder Colchian
Fixes me with her strange and sudden gaze,
Each hair upon my body stands erect!
Zeus, 'tis a very tiger, and as mute!

AEGEUS   'Tis certain that the woman's something strange.

NIKIAS   Gods, spare me your strange women, so say I.
Give me gold hair, lithe limbs and gracious smiles,
And spare the strangeness.

AEGEUS   I do marvel much
How she will bear the tidings.

NIKIAS   Lo, behold!
Here comes our Jason striding 'thwart the streets.
Gods! what a gracious presence!

AEGEUS   I perceive
The Colchian on the threshold. By her looks,
Our idle talk has reached her listening ears.

(Enter Jason. Medea reappears on the threshold.)

NIKIAS   Let's draw aside and mark them; lo, they meet.

(The two citizens withdraw, unperceived, to a further corner of the stage.)

MEDEA   'Tis false, 'tis false. O Jason, they speak false!

JASON   Your looks are wild, Medea; you bring shame
Upon this house, that stand with hair unbound
Beyond the threshold. Get you in the house.

MEDEA   But not till you have answered me this thing.

JASON   What is this thing that you would know of me?

MEDEA   O I have heard strange rumours – horrible!

JASON   Oft lies the horror of a tale in the ear
Of him that hears it. What is't you have heard?

MEDEA   Almost, for fear, I dare not give it tongue.
But tell me this? Love, you have not forgot
The long years passed in this Corinthian home?
The great love I have borne you through the years?
Nor that far time when, in your mighty craft,
You came, a stranger, to the Colchian shore?
O strong you were; but not of such a strength
To have escaped the doom of horrid death,
Had not I, counting neither loss nor gain,
Shown you the way to triumph and renown.

JASON   And better had I then, a thousand times,
Have fought with my good sword and fall'n or stood
As the high Fates directed; than been caught
In the close meshes of the magic web
Wrought by your hand, dark-thoughted sorceress.

NIKIAS   Did you mark that? Jason speaks low and smooth;
Yet there is that within his level tones,
And in the icy drooping of his lids
(More than his words, tho' they are harsh enough),
Tells me he hates her.

AEGEUS   Hush! Medea speaks.

MEDEA   O gods, gods; ye have cursed me in this gift!
Is it for this, for this that I have striven?
Have wrestled in the darkness? wept my tears?
Have fought with sweet desires and hopes and thoughts?
Have watched when men were sleeping? For long days
Have shunned the sunlight and the breaths of Heaven?
Is it for this, for this that I have prayed
Long prayers, poured out with blood and cries and tears?
Lo, I who strove for strength have grown more weak
Than is the weakest. I have poured the sap
Of all my being, my life's very life,
Before a thankless godhead; and am grown
No woman, but a monster. What avail
Charms, spells and potions, all my hard-won arts,
My mystic workings, seeing they cannot win
One little common spark of human love?
O gods, gods, ye have cursed me in this gift!
More should ye have withheld or more have giv'n;

Have fashioned me more weak or else more strong.
Behold me now, your work, a thing of fear –
From natural human fellowship cut off,
And yet a woman – sick and sore with pain;
Hungry for love and music of men's praise,
But walled about as with a mighty wall,
Far from men's reach and sight, alone, alone.

NIKIAS   Behold her, how she waves about her arms
And casts her eyes to Heaven.

AEGEUS   Ay, 'tis strange –
Not as our women do, yet scarce unmeet.

NIKIAS   Unmeet, unmeet? But Jason holds it so!
Mark you his white cheeks and his knitted brows,
What wrath and hate and scorn upon his face!

JASON   Hear me, Medea, if you still can hear
That seem so strangely lifted from yourself:
But I, that know you long, do know you well,
A thing of moods and passions; so I bear
Once more with your wild words and savage gests,
Ay, and for all your fury speak you fair.
You say you love me. Can I deem it so,
When what does most advantage me and mine
You shrink to hear of? For I make no doubt,
Fleet-footed rumour did anticipate
The tidings I was hastening to bear,
When you, wide-eyed, unveiled, unfilleted,
Rushed out upon me.
                Know then this once more:
That I have sworn to take as wedded wife
Glaukê, the daughter of our mighty king,
In this, in nowise hurting you and yours.
For you all fair provisions I have made,
So but you get beyond the city walls
Before the night comes on. Our little ones –
They too shall journey with you. I have said.
And had I found you in a mood more mild,
Less swayed by savage passion, I had told
How this thing, which mayhap seems a thing hard,
Is but a blessing, wrapped and cloaked about

In harsh disguisements. For tho' Kreon rule
Today within the city; Kreon dead,
Who else shall rule there saving I alone,
The king's son loved of him and other men?
And in those days Medea's sons and mine
Shall stand at my right hand, grown great in power.
Medea, too, if she do but control
Her fiery spirit, may yet reign a queen
Above this land of Corinth. I have said.

NIKIAS   Well said.

AEGEUS   But none the better that 'twas false.

NIKIAS   I'd sooner speak, for my part, fair than true.
Mark Jason there; how firm his lithe, straight limbs;
How high his gold-curled head, crisped like a girl's.
And yet for all his curled locks and smooth tones
Jason is very strong. I never knew
A man of such a strange and subtle strength.

AEGEUS   The Colchian speaks no word; and her swart hands,
Which waved, a moment since, and beat the air
In mad entreaty, are together clasped
Before her white robe in an iron clasp.
And her wild eyes, which erst did seek the heav'ns,
And now her lord and now again the earth,
Are set on space and move not. The tall shape
Stands there erect and still. This calm, I think,
Is filled with strangest portent.

NIKIAS   O ye gods,
She is a pregnant horror as she stands.

AEGEUS   She speaks; her voice sounds as a sound far off.

MEDEA   As you have said, O Jason, let it be.
I for my part am nothing loth to break
A compact never in fair justice framed,
Seeing how much one gave and one how much.
For you, you thought: This maid has served me well,
And yet may serve me. When I touch her palm
The blood is set a-tingle in my veins;

For these things I will make her body mine.
And I, I stood before you, clean and straight,
A woman some deemed fair and all deemed wise;
A woman, yet no simple thing nor slight,
By nature fashioned in no niggard mould;
And looked into your eyes with eyes that spake:
Lo, utterly, for ever, I am yours.
And since that you, this gift I lavish laid
Low at your feet, have lightly held and spurned –
I in my two arms, thus, shall gather it up
So that your feet may not encounter it
Which is not worthy for your feet to tread!
Yet pause a moment, Jason. Haply now
In some such wise as this your thoughts run on:
I loved this woman for a little space;
Alas, poor soul, she loved me but too well –
It is the way with women! Some, I think,
Did deem her fierce; gods! she was meek enough,
Content with what I gave; when I gave not
Nothing importunate.
      Ah, Jason, pause.
You never knew Medea. You forget,
Because so long she bends the knee to you,
She was not born to serfdom.
      I have knelt
Too long before you. I have stood too long
Suppliant before this people. You forget
A redder stream flows in my Colchian veins
Than the slow flood which courses round your hearts,
O cold Corinthians, with whom I long have dwelt
And never ere this day have known myself.
Nor have ye known me. Now behold me free,
Ungyved by any chains of this man wrought;
Nothing desiring at your hands nor his.
Free, freer than the air or wingèd birds;
Strong, stronger than the blast of wintry storms;
And lifted up into an awful realm
Where is nor love, nor pity, nor remorse,
Nor dread, but only purpose.
      There shall be
A horror and a horror in this land;
Woe upon woe, red blood and biting flame;
Most horrid death and anguish worse than death;

Deeds that shall make the shores of Hades sound
With murmured terror; with an awful dread
Shall move the generations yet unborn;
A horror and a horror in the land.

JASON   Shrew, triple-linked with Hell, get you within.
Shame not my house! 'Tis your own harm you work.

(Medea goes within. Jason moves off slowly. Aegeus and Nikias go off conferring in whispers.)

Scene II
(Time: after an interval; the evening of the same day. Scene: street. A crowd of people running to and fro.)

NIKIAS   O horror, horror, have ye heard the tale?

AEGEUS   Alas, a bloody rumour reached mine ears
Of awful purport: that the king lies dead –

NIKIAS   And by his side, his daughter; both caught up
In sudden toils of torment. With his grief
Jason is all distraught; behold her deed,
The swift and subtle tigress!

AEGEUS   Woe! Alas!
Woe for the state, woe for our Kreon slain,
For hapless Glaukê, for our Jason, woe!
But three times woe for her that did the deed –
Her womanhood sham'd; her children basely wrong'd.

NIKIAS   Hold back our pity till the tale be told,
For never was there horror like to this.
Ere now in Corinth, haply, you have heard
How she did use for her crime's instruments
The tender boys sprung from great Jason's loins;
Bidding them bear the garments wrought in Hell
As bridal gifts to grace the marriage morn
Of gold-hair'd Glaukê. Serpent! Sorceress!

AEGEUS   Alas, consider; so the tigress springs
When that her cubs are menaced. 'Twas her love
That wrought the deed – evil, yet wrought for love.

NIKIAS   Spare me such love. I never yet could deem,
Ev'n ere the horror, that Medea held
The love of human mothers in her breast.
For I have seen her, when her children played
Their innocent, aimless sports about her knees,
Or held her gown across the market-place,
Move all unheeding with her swart brows knit
And fierce eyes fixed; not, as is mothers' wont,
Eager to note the winning infant ways,
A-strain to catch the babbling treble tones
Of soft lips clamouring for a kiss or smile.
And once I marked her ('twas a summer's morn)
Turn suddenly and, stooping, catch and strain
One tender infant to her breast. She held
Her lips to his and looked into his eyes,
Not gladly, as a mother with her child,
But stirred by some strange passion; then the boy
Cried out with terror, and Medea wept.

AEGEUS   Your tale is strange.

NIKIAS   Stranger is yet to come.
How that the Colchian did send forth her sons,
Innocent doers of most deadly deed,
Has reached your knowledge. When the deed was done,
And the dead king lay stretched upon the floor
Clutching his daughter in a last embrace,
Arose great clamour in the palace halls;
Wailing and cries of terror; women's screams;
A rush of flying feet from hall to hall;
The clanging fall of brazen instruments
Upon the marble.
            The two tender boys,
Half apprehending what thing had befallen,
Fled forth unmarked, and all affrighted reached
The house of Jason, where Medea stood
Erect upon the threshold. From afar
Sounded and surged the fiercely frighted roar
Of the roused city, and, like waves of the sea,
Grew nearer ev'ry beating of the pulse.
Forth from the inmost chambers fled the slaves,
Made fleet with sudden fear; the little ones
With arms outspread rushed to the Colchian,

And clung about her limbs and caught her robe,
Hiding their faces.
                    And Medea stood
Calm as a carven image. As the sound
Of wrath and lamentation drew more near,
The pale lips seemed to smile. But when she saw
Her children clinging round her, she stretched forth
One strong, swart hand and put the twain away,
And gathered up the trailing of her robe.
I saw the deed, I, Nikias, with these eyes!
Then spake she (Zeus! grant that I may not hear
Such tones once more from human lips!). She spake:
'I will not have ye, for I love ye not!'
Then all her face grew alien. Those around
Stood still, not knowing what she planned.
          Then she
Forth from her gathered garment swiftly drew
A thing that gleamed and glinted; in the air
She held it poised an instant; then – O gods!
How shall I speak it? – on the marble floor
Was blood that streamed and spurted; blood that flow'd
From two slain, innocent babes!

AEGEUS   O woeful day!

NIKIAS   Then brake a cry from all about: a wail
Of lamentation. But above the sound
A fierce long shriek, that froze the blood i' the veins,
Rang out and rose, cleaving the topmost cloud.

AEGEUS   O evil deed! O essence of all evil
Stealing the shape of woman!

NIKIAS   After that
All is confusion; from all sides surged up
The people, cursing, weeping. 'Thwart the din
Each other moment the strained ear might catch
Medea's name, or Jason's, or the King's;
And women wailed out 'Glaukê' through their tears.
Then sudden came a pause; the angry roar
Died down into a murmur; and the throng
Grew still, and rolled aside like a clov'n sea.
And Jason strode between them till he reached

His own home's threshold where the twain lay dead,
Long gazed he on their faces; then he turned
To the hush'd people; turned to them and spake:
(His face was whiter than the dead's, his eyes
Like to a creature's that has looked on Hell)
'Where is the woman?' Lo, and when they sought
Medea, no eye beheld her. And no man
Had looked upon her since that moment's space
When steel had flashed and blood foamed in the air.
Then Jason stood erect and spake again:
'Let no man seek this woman; blood enough
Has stained our city. Let the furies rend
Her guilty soul; nor we pollute our hands
With her accursèd body...'

AEGEUS   Cease, my friend;
It is enough. You judged this thing aright;
This woman was dark and evil in her soul;
Black to her fiend-heart's root; a festering plague
In our fair city's midst.

NIKIAS   Spake I not true?

(Night; outside the city. Medea leaning against a rock.)

MEDEA   Here let me rest; beyond men's eyes, beyond
The city's hissing hate. Why am I here?
Why have I fled from death? There's sun on the earth,
And in the shades no sun – thus much I know;
And sunlight's good.
                    Wake I, or do I sleep?
I'm weary, weary; once I dream'd a dream
Of one that strove and wept and yearned for love
In a fair city. She was blind indeed.
They say the woman had a fiend at heart,
And afterwards – Hush, hush, I dream'd a dream.
How cold the air blows; how the night grows dark,
Wrapping me round in blackness. Darker too
Grows the deep night within. I cannot see;
I grope with weary hands; my hands are sore
With fruitless striving. I have fought with the Fates
And I am vanquished utterly. The Fates
Yield not to strife; nay, nor to many prayers.

Their ways are dark.
> One climbs the tree and grasps
A handful of dead leaves; another walks,
Heedless, beneath the branches, and the fruit
Falls mellow at his feet.
> This is the end:
I have dash'd my heart against a rock; the blood
Is drain'd and flows no more; and all my breast
Is emptied of its tears.
> Thus go I forth
Into the deep, dense heart of the night – alone.

Sinfonia Eroica

To Sylvia

My Love, my Love, it was a day in June,
A mellow, drowsy, golden afternoon;
And all the eager people thronging came
To that great hall, drawn by the magic name
Of one, a high magician, who can raise
The spirits of the past and future days,
And draw the dreams from out the secret breast,
Giving them life and shape.
> I, with the rest,
Sat there athirst, atremble for the sound;
And as my aimless glances wandered round,
Far off, across the hush'd, expectant throng,
I saw your face that fac'd mine.
> Clear and strong
Rush'd forth the sound, a mighty mountain stream;
Across the clust'ring heads mine eyes did seem
By subtle forces drawn, your eyes to meet.
Then you, the melody, the summer heat,
Mingled in all my blood and made it wine.
Straight I forgot the world's great woe and mine;
My spirit's murky lead grew molten fire;
Despair itself was rapture.
> Ever higher,
Stronger and clearer rose the mighty strain;
Then sudden fell; then all was still again,
And I sank back, quivering as one in pain.
Brief was the pause; then, 'mid a hush profound,

Slow on the waiting air swell'd forth a sound
So wondrous sweet that each man held his breath;
A measur'd, mystic melody of death.
Then back you lean'd your head, and I could note
The upward outline of your perfect throat;
And ever, as the music smote the air,
Mine eyes from far held fast your body fair.
And in that wondrous moment seem'd to fade
My life's great woe, and grow an empty shade
Which had not been, nor was not.
        And I knew
Not which was sound, and which, O Love, was you.

To Sylvia

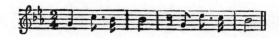

'O Love, lean thou thy cheek to mine,
And let the tears together flow' –
Such was the song you sang to me
      Once, long ago.

Such was the song you sang; and yet
(O be not wroth!) I scarcely knew
What sounds flow'd forth; I only felt
      That you were you.

I scarcely knew your hair was gold,
Nor of the heavens' own blue your eyes.
Sylvia and song, divinely mixt,
      Made Paradise.

These things I scarcely knew; today,
When love is lost and hope is fled,
The song you sang so long ago
      Rings in my head.

Clear comes each note and true; today,
As in a picture I behold
Your turn'd-up chin, and small, sweet head
      Misty with gold.

I see how your dear eyes grew deep,
How your lithe body thrilled and swayed,
And how were whiter than the keys
    Your hands that played...

Ah, sweetest! Cruel have you been,
And robbed my life of many things.
I will not chide; ere this I knew
    That Love had wings.

You've robbed my life of many things —
Of love and hope, of fame and pow'r.
So be it, sweet. You cannot steal
    One golden hour.

Magdalen

All things I can endure, save one.
The bare, blank room where is no sun;
The parcelled hours; the pallet hard;
The dreary faces here within;
The outer women's cold regard;
The Pastor's iterated 'sin' —
These things could I endure, and count
No overstrain'd, unjust amount;
No undue payment for such bliss —
Yea, all things bear, save only this:
That you, who knew what thing would be,
Have wrought this evil unto me.
It is so strange to think on still —
That you, that *you* should do me ill!
Not as one ignorant or blind,
But seeing clearly in your mind
How this must be which now has been,
Nothing aghast at what was seen.
Now that the tale is told and done,
It is so strange to think upon.
You were so tender with me, too!
One summer's night a cold blast blew,
Closer about my throat you drew
The half-slipt shawl of dusky blue.
And once my hand, on a summer's morn,

I stretched to pluck a rose; a thorn
Struck through the flesh and made it bleed
(A little drop of blood indeed!)
Pale grew your cheek; you stoopt and bound
Your handkerchief about the wound;
Your voice came with a broken sound;
With the deep breath your breast was riven;
I wonder, did God laugh in Heaven?

How strange, that *you* should work my woe!
How strange! I wonder, do you know
How gladly, gladly I had died
(And life was very sweet that tide)
To save you from the least, light ill?
How gladly I had borne your pain.
With one great pulse we seem'd to thrill –
Nay, but we thrill'd with pulses twain.

Even if one had told me this,
'A poison lurks within your kiss,
Gall that shall turn to night his day':
Thereon I straight had turned away –
Ay, tho' my heart had crack'd with pain –
And never kiss'd your lips again.

At night, or when the daylight nears,
I hear the other women weep;
My own heart's anguish lies too deep
For the soft rain and pain of tears.
I think my heart has turn'd to stone,
A dull, dead weight that hurts my breast;
Here, on my pallet-bed alone,
I keep apart from all the rest.
Wide-eyed I lie upon my bed,
I often cannot sleep all night;
The future and the past are dead,
There is no thought can bring delight.
All night I lie and think and think;
If my heart were not made of stone,
But flesh and blood, it needs must shrink
Before such thoughts. Was ever known
A woman with a heart of stone?

The doctor says that I shall die.
It may be so, yet what care I?
Endless reposing from the strife?
Death do I trust no more than life.
For one thing is like one arrayed,
And there is neither false nor true;
But in a hideous masquerade
All things dance on, the ages through.
And good is evil, evil good;
Nothing is known or understood
Save only Pain. I have no faith
In God or Devil, Life or Death.

The doctor says that I shall die.
You, that I knew in days gone by,
I fain would see your face once more,
Con well its features o'er and o'er;
And touch your hand and feel your kiss,
Look in your eyes and tell you this:
That all is done, that I am free;
That you, through all eternity,
Have neither part nor lot in me.

Christopher Found

I

At last; so this is you, my dear!
How should I guess to find you here?
So long, so long, I sought in vain
In many cities, many lands,
With straining eyes and groping hands;
The people marvelled at my pain.
They said: 'But sure, the woman's mad;
What ails her, we should like to know,
That she should be so wan and sad,
And silent through the revels go?'
They clacked with such a sorry stir!
Was I to tell? Were they to know
That I had lost you, Christopher?
Will you forgive me for one thing?
Whiles, when a stranger came my way,

My heart would beat and I would say:
'Here's Christopher!' — then lingering
With longer gaze, would turn away
Cold, sick at heart. My dear, I know
You will forgive me for this thing.
It is so very long ago
Since I have seen your face — till now;
Now that I see it — lip and brow,
Eyes, nostril, chin, alive and clear;
Last time was long ago; I know
This thing you will forgive me, dear.

II

There is no Heaven — this is the best;
O hold me closer to your breast;
Let your face lean upon my face,
That there no longer shall be space
Between our lips, between our eyes.
I feel your bosom's fall and rise.
O hold me near and yet more near;
Ah sweet; I wonder do you know
How lone and cold, how sad and drear,
Was I a little while ago;
Sick of the stress, the strife, the stir;
But I have found you, Christopher.

III

If only you had come before!
(This is the thing I most deplore)
A seemlier woman you had found,
More calm, by courtesies more bound,
Less quick to greet you, more subdued
Of appetite; of slower mood.
But ah! you come so late, so late!
This time of day I can't pretend
With slight, sweet things to satiate
The hunger-cravings. Nay, my friend,
I cannot blush and turn and tremble,
Wax loth as younger maidens do.
Ah, Christopher, with you, with you,
You would not wish me to dissemble?

IV

So long have all the days been meagre,
With empty platter, empty cup,
No meats nor sweets to do me pleasure,
That if I crave – is it over-eager,
The deepest draught, the fullest measure,
The beaker to the brim poured up?

V

Shelley, that sprite from the spheres above,
Says, and would make the matter clear,
That love divided is larger love –
We'll leave those things to the bards, my dear.

For you never wrote a verse, you see;
And I – my verse is not fair nor new.
Till the world be dead, you shall love but me,
Till the stars have ceased, I shall love but you.

Epilogue

Thus ran the words; or rather, thus did run
Their purport. Idly seeking in the chest
(You see it yonder), I had found them there:
Some blotted sheets of paper in a case,
With a woman's name writ on it: 'Adelaide'.
Twice on the writing there was scored the date
Of ten years back; and where the words had end
Was left a space, a dash, a half-writ word,
As tho' the writer minded, presently
The matter to pursue.
                    I questioned her,
That worthy, worthy soul, my châtelaine,
Who, nothing loth, made answer.
                        There had been
Another lodger ere I had the rooms,
Three months gone by – a woman.
                    'Young, sir? No.
Must have seen forty if she'd seen a day!
A lonesome woman; hadn't many friends;
Wrote books, I think, and things for newspapers.
Short in her temper – eyes would flash and flame

At times, till I was frightened. Paid her rent
Most regular, like a lady.
      Ten years back,
They say (at least Ann Brown says), ten years back
The lady had a lover. Even then
She must have been no chicken.
      Three months since
She died. Well, well, the Lord is kind and just.
I did my best to tend her, yet indeed
It's bad for trade to have a lodger die.
Her brother came, a week before she died:
Buried her, took her things, threw in the fire
The littered heaps of paper.
      Yes, the sheets,
They must have been forgotten in the chest –
I never knew her name was Adelaide.'

A Dirge

*Mein Herz, mein Herz ist traurig
Doch lustig leuchtet der Mai*

There's May amid the meadows,
      There's May amid the trees;
Her May-time note the cuckoo
      Sends forth upon the breeze.

Above the rippling river
      May swallows skim and dart;
November and December
      Keep watch within my heart.

The spring breathes in the breezes,
      The woods with wood-notes ring,
And all the budding hedgerows
      Are fragrant of the spring.

In secret, silent places
      The live green things upstart;
Ice-bound, ice-crown'd dwells winter
      For ever in my heart.

Upon the bridge I linger,
Near where the lime-trees grow;
Above, swart birds are circling,
Beneath, the stream runs slow.

A stripling and a maiden
Come wand'ring up the way;
His eyes are glad with springtime,
Her face is fair with May.

Of warmth the sun and sweetness
All nature takes a part;
The ice of all the ages
Weighs down upon my heart.

The Sick Man and the Nightingale

From Lenau

So late, and yet a nightingale?
Long since have dropp'd the blossoms pale,
The summer fields are ripening,
And yet a sound of spring?

O tell me, didst thou come to hear,
Sweet Spring, that I should die this year;
And call'st across from the far shore
To me one greeting more?

A June-Tide Echo

After a Richter concert

In the long, sad time, when the sky was grey,
    And the keen blast blew through the city drear,
When delight had fled from the night and the day,
    My chill heart whispered, 'June will be here!

'June with its roses a-sway in the sun,
    Its glory of green on mead and tree.'
Lo, now the sweet June-tide is nearly done,
    June-tide, and never a joy for me

Is it so much of the gods that I pray?
    Sure craved man never so slight a boon!
To be glad and glad in my heart one day –
    One perfect day of the perfect June.

Sweet sounds tonight rose up, wave upon wave;
    Sweet dreams were afloat in the balmy air.
This is the boon of the gods that I crave –
    To be glad, as the music and night were fair.

For once, for one fleeting hour, to hold
    The fair shape the music that rose and fell
Revealed and concealed like a veiling fold;
    To catch for an instant the sweet June spell.

For once, for one hour, to catch and keep
    The sweet June secret that mocks my heart;
Now lurking calm, like a thing asleep,
    Now hither and thither with start and dart.

Then the sick, slow grief of the weary years,
    The slow, sick grief and the sudden pain;
The long days of labour, the nights of tears –
    No more these things would I hold in vain.

I would hold my life as a thing of worth;
    Pour praise to the gods for a precious thing.
Lo, June in her fairness is on earth,
    And never a joy does the niggard bring.

AMY LEVY

To Lallie

Outside the British Museum

Up those Museum steps you came,
And straightway all my blood was flame,
        O Lallie, Lallie!

The world (I had been feeling low)
In one short moment's space did grow
        A happy valley.

There was a friend, my friend, with you;
A meagre dame, in peacock blue
        Apparelled quaintly;

This poet-heart went pit-a-pat;
I bowed and smiled and raised my hat;
        You nodded – faintly.

My heart was full as full could be;
You had not got a word for me,
        Not one short greeting;

That nonchalant small nod you gave
(The tyrant's motion to the slave)
        Sole mark'd our meeting.

Is it so long? Do you forget
That first and last time that we met?
        The time was summer;

The trees were green; the sky was blue;
Our host presented me to you –
        A tardy comer.

You look'd demure, but when you spoke
You made a little, funny joke,
        Yet half pathetic.

Your gown was grey, I recollect,
I think you patronised the sect
        They call 'Aesthetic'.

I brought you strawberries and cream,
I plied you long about a stream
            With duckweed laden;

We solemnly discussed the heat.
I found you shy and very sweet,
            A rosebud maiden.

Ah me, today! You passed inside
To where the marble gods abide:
            Hermes, Apollo,

Sweet Aphrodite, Pan; and where,
For aye reclined, a headless fair
            Beats all fairs hollow.

And I, I went upon my way,
Well – rather sadder, let us say;
            The world looked flatter.

I had been sad enough before,
A little less, a little more,
            What *does* it matter?

In a Minor Key

An echo from a larger lyre

That was love that I had before
            Years ago, when my heart was young;
Ev'ry smile was a gem you wore;
            Ev'ry word was a sweet song sung.

You came – all my pulses burn'd and beat.
            (O sweet wild throbs of an early day!)
You went – with the last dear sound of your feet
            The light wax'd dim and the place grew grey.

And I us'd to pace with a stealthy tread
            By a certain house which is under a hill;
A cottage stands near, wall'd white, roof'd red –
            Tall trees grow thick – I can see it still!

How I us'd to watch with a hope that was fear
      For the least swift glimpse of your gown's dear fold!
(You wore blue gowns in those days, my dear –
      One light for summer, one dark for cold.)

Tears and verses I shed for you in show'rs;
      I would have staked my soul for a kiss;
Tribute daily I brought you of flow'rs,
      Rose, lily, your favourite eucharis.

There came a day we were doomed to part;
      There's a queer, small gate at the foot of a slope:
We parted there – and I thought my heart
      Had parted for ever from love and hope.

★

Is it love that I have today?
      Love, that bloom'd early, has it bloom'd late
For me, that, clothed in my spirit's grey,
      Sit in the stillness and stare at Fate?

Song nor sonnet for you I've penned,
      Nor passionate paced by your home's wide wall
I have brought you never a flow'r, my friend,
      Never a tear for your sake let fall.

And yet – and yet – ah, who understands?
      We men and women are complex things!
A hundred tunes Fate's inexorable hands
      May play on the sensitive soul-strings.

Webs of strange patterns we weave (each owns)
      From colour and sound; and like unto these,
Soul has its tones and its semitones,
      Mind has its major and minor keys.

Your face (men pass it without a word)
      It haunts my dreams like an odd, sweet strain;
When your name is spoken my soul is stirr'd
      In its deepest depths with a dull, dim pain.

I paced, in the damp grey mist, last night
            In the streets (an hour) to see you pass:
Yet I do not think that I love you – quite;
            What's felt so finely 'twere coarse to class.

And yet – and yet – I scarce can tell why
            (As I said, we are riddles and hard to read),
If the world went ill with you, and I
            Could help with a hidden hand your need;

But, ere I could reach you where you lay,
            Must strength and substance and honour spend;
Journey long journeys by night and day –
            Somehow, I think I should come, my friend!

A Farewell

After Heine

The sad rain falls from Heaven,
            A sad bird pipes and sings;
I am sitting here at my window
            And watching the spires of King's.

O fairest of all fair places,
            Sweetest of all sweet towns!
With the birds, and the greyness and greenness,
            And the men in caps and gowns.

All they that dwell within thee,
            To leave are ever loth,
For one man gets friends, and another
            Gets honour, and one gets both.

The sad rain falls from Heaven;
            My heart is great with woe –
I have neither a friend nor honour,
            Yet I am sorry to go.

from *A London Plane Tree and Other Verse* (1889)

Mine is an urban Muse, and bound
By some strange law to paven ground.
Austin Dobson

To Clementina Black

More blest than was of old Diogenes,
I have not held my lantern up in vain.
Not mine, at least, this evil – to complain:
'There is none honest among all of these.'

Our hopes go down that sailed before the breeze;
Our creeds upon the rock are rent in twain;
Something it is, if at the last remain
One floating spar cast up by hungry seas.

The secret of our being, who can tell?
To praise the gods and Fate is not my part;
Evil I see, and pain; within my heart
There is no voice that whispers: 'All is well.'

Yet fair are days in summer; and more fair
The growths of human goodness here and there.

A London Plane-Tree

Green is the plane-tree in the square,
The other trees are brown;
They droop and pine for country air;
The plane-tree loves the town.

Here from my garret-pane, I mark
The plane-tree bud and blow,
Shed her recuperative bark,
And spread her shade below.

Among her branches, in and out,
The city breezes play;
The dun fog wraps her round about;
Above, the smoke curls grey.

Others the country take for choice,
       And hold the town in scorn;
But she has listened to the voice
       On city breezes borne.

London in July

What ails my senses thus to cheat?
       What is it ails the place,
That all the people in the street
       Should wear one woman's face?

The London trees are dusty-brown
       Beneath the summer sky;
My love, she dwells in London town,
       Nor leaves it in July.

O various and intricate maze,
       Wide waste of square and street;
Where, missing through unnumbered days,
       We twain at last may meet!

And who cries out on crowd and mart?
       Who prates of stream and sea?
The summer in the city's heart –
       That is enough for me.

A March Day in London

The east wind blows in the street today;
The sky is blue, yet the town looks grey.
'Tis the wind of ice, the wind of fire,
Of cold despair and of hot desire,
Which chills the flesh to aches and pains,
And sends a fever through all the veins.

From end to end, with aimless feet,
All day long have I paced the street.
My limbs are weary, but in my breast
Stirs the goad of a mad unrest.
I would give anything to stay

The little wheel that turns in my brain;
The little wheel that turns all day,
That turns all night with might and main.

What is the thing I fear, and why?
Nay, but the world is all awry –
The wind's in the east, the sun's in the sky.
The gas-lamps gleam in a golden line;
The ruby lights of the hansoms shine,
Glance, and flicker like fire-flies bright;
The wind has fallen with the night,
And once again the town seems fair
Thwart the mist that hangs i' the air.

And o'er, at last, my spirit steals
A weary peace; peace that conceals
Within its inner depths the grain
Of hopes that yet shall flower again.

Ballade of an Omnibus

To see my love suffices me.
Ballades in Blue China

Some men to carriages aspire;
On some the costly hansoms wait;
Some seek a fly, on job or hire;
Some mount the trotting steed, elate.
I envy not the rich and great,
A wandering minstrel, poor and free,
I am contented with my fate –
An omnibus suffices me.

In winter days of rain and mire
I find within a corner strait;
The 'busmen know me and my lyre
From Brompton to the Bull-and-Gate.
When summer comes, I mount in state
The topmost summit, whence I see
Croesus look up, compassionate –
An omnibus suffices me.

I mark, untroubled by desire,
Lucullus' phaeton and its freight.
The scene whereof I cannot tire,
The human tale of love and hate,
The city pageant, early and late
Unfolds itself, rolls by, to be
A pleasure deep and delicate.
An omnibus suffices me.

Princess, your splendour you require,
I, my simplicity; agree
Neither to rate lower nor higher.
An omnibus suffices me.

Ballade of a Special Edition

He comes; I hear him up the street –
    Bird of ill omen, flapping wide
The pinion of a printed sheet,
    His hoarse note scares the eventide.
Of slaughter, theft, and suicide
    He is the herald and the friend;
Now he vociferates with pride –
    A double murder in Mile End!

A hanging to his soul is sweet;
    His gloating fancy's fain to bide
Where human-freighted vessels meet,
    And misdirected trains collide.
With Shocking Accidents supplied,
    He tramps the town from end to end.
How often have we heard it cried –
    A double murder in Mile End.

War loves he; victory or defeat,
    So there be loss on either side.
His tale of horrors incomplete,
    Imagination's aid is tried.
Since no distinguished man has died,
    And since the Fates, relenting, send
No great catastrophe, he's spied
    This double murder in Mile End.

Fiend, get thee gone! No more repeat
     Those sounds which do mine ears offend.
It is apocryphal, you cheat,
     Your double murder in Mile End.

Straw in the Street

Straw in the street where I pass today
Dulls the sound of the wheels and feet.
'Tis for a failing life they lay
     Straw in the street.

Here, where the pulses of London beat,
Someone strives with the Presence grey;
Ah, is it victory or defeat?

The hurrying people go their way,
Pause and jostle and pass and greet;
For life, for death, are they treading, say
     Straw in the street?

Between the Showers

Between the showers I went my way,
     The glistening street was bright with flowers;
It seemed that March had turned to May
     Between the showers.

Above the shining roofs and towers
     The blue broke forth athwart the grey;
Birds carolled in their leafless bowers.

Hither and tither, swift and gay,
     The people chased the changeful hours;
And you, you passed and smiled that day,
     Between the showers.

Out of Town

Out of town the sky was bright and blue,
  Never fog-cloud, lowering, thick, was seen to frown;
Nature dons a garb of gayer hue,
  Out of town.

Spotless lay the snow on field and down,
  Pure and keen the air above it blew;
All wore peace and beauty for a crown.

London sky, marred by smoke, veiled from view,
  London snow, trodden thin, dingy brown,
Whence that strange unrest at thoughts of you
  Out of town?

The Piano-Organ

My student-lamp is lighted,
  The books and papers are spread;
A sound comes floating upwards,
  Chasing the thoughts from my head.

I open the garret window,
  Let the music in and the moon;
See the woman grin for coppers,
  While the man grinds out the tune.

Grind me a dirge or a requiem,
  Or a funeral-march sad and slow,
But not, O not, that waltz tune
  I heard so long ago.

I stand upright by the window,
  The moonlight streams in wan –
O God! with its changeless rise and fall
  The tune twirls on and on.

London Poets

In memoriam

They trod the streets and squares where now I tread,
With weary hearts, a little while ago;
When, thin and grey, the melancholy snow
Clung to the leafless branches overhead;
Or when the smoke-veiled sky grew stormy-red
In autumn; with a re-arisen woe
Wrestled, what time the passionate spring winds blow;
And paced scorched stones in summer – they are dead.

The sorrow of their souls to them did seem
As real as mine to me, as permanent.
Today, it is the shadow of a dream,
The half-forgotten breath of breezes spent.
So shall another soothe his woe supreme –
'No more he comes, who this way came and went.'

The Village Garden

To E.M.S.

Here, where your garden fenced about and still is,
    Here, where the unmoved summer air is sweet
With mixed delight of lavender and lilies,
    Dreaming I linger in the noontide heat.

Of many summers are the trees recorders,
    The turf a carpet many summers wove;
Old-fashioned blossoms cluster in the borders,
    Love-in-a-mist and crimson-hearted clove.

All breathes of peace and sunshine in the present,
    All tells of bygone peace and bygone sun,
Of fruitful years accomplished, budding, crescent,
    Of gentle seasons passing one by one.

Fain would I bide, but ever in the distance
    A ceaseless voice is sounding clear and low –
The city calls me with her old persistence,
    The city calls me – I arise and go.

Of gentler souls this fragrant peace is guerdon;
    For me, the roar and hurry of the town,
Wherein more lightly seems to press the burden
    Of individual life that weighs me down.

I leave your garden to the happier comers
    For whom its silent sweets are anodyne.
Shall I return? Who knows, in other summers
    The peace my spirit longs for may be mine?

New Love, New Life

I

She, who so long has lain
    Stone-stiff with folded wings,
Within my heart again
    The brown bird wakes and sings.

Brown nightingale, whose strain
    Is heard by day, by night,
She sings of joy and pain,
    Of sorrow and delight.

II

'Tis true – in other days
    Have I unbarred the door;
He knows the walks and ways –
    Love has been here before.

Love blest and love accurst
    Was here in days long past;
This time is not the first,
    But this time is the last.

Impotens

If I were a woman of old,
    What prayers I would pray for you, dear;
My pitiful tribute behold –
    Not a prayer, but a tear.

The pitiless order of things,
    Whose laws we may change not nor break,
Alone I could face it – it wrings
    My heart for your sake.

The Dream

Believe me, this was true last night,
Tho' it is false today.
                A.M.F. Robinson

A fair dream to my chamber flew:
Such a crowd of folk that stirred,
Jested, fluttered; only you,
You alone of all that band,
Calm and silent, spake no word.
Only once you neared my place,
And your hand one moment's space
Sought the fingers of my hand;
Your eyes flashed to mine; I knew
All was well between us two.

★

On from dream to dream I past,
But the first sweet vision cast
Mystic radiance o'er the last.

★

When I woke the pale night lay
Still, expectant of the day;
All about the chamber hung
Tender shade of twilight gloom;
The fair dream hovered round me, clung
To my thought like faint perfume –

Like sweet odours, such as cling
To the void flask, which erst encloses
Attar of rose; or the pale string
Of amber which has lain with roses.

On the Threshold

O God, my dream! I dreamed that you were dead;
Your mother hung above the couch and wept
Whereon you lay all white, and garlanded
With blooms of waxen whiteness. I had crept
Up to your chamber-door, which stood ajar,
And in the doorway watched you from afar,
Nor dared advance to kiss your lips and brow.
I had no part nor lot in you, as now;
Death had not broken between us the old bar;
Nor torn from out my heart the old, cold sense
Of your misprision and my impotence.

The Birch-Tree at Loschwitz

At Loschwitz above the city
          The air is sunny and chill;
The birch-trees and the pine-trees
          Grow thick upon the hill.

Lone and tall, with silver stem,
          A birch-tree stands apart;
The passionate wind of spring-time
          Stirs in its leafy heart.

I lean against the birch-tree,
          My arms around it twine;
It pulses, and leaps, and quivers,
          Like a human heart to mine.

One moment I stand, then sudden
          Let loose mine arms that cling:
O God! the lonely hillside,
          The passionate wind of spring!

In the Night

Cruel? I think there never was a cheating
    More cruel, thro' all the weary days than this!
This is no dream, my heart kept on repeating,
    But sober certainty of waking bliss.

Dreams? O, I know their faces – goodly seeming,
    Vaporous, whirled on many-coloured wings;
I have had dreams before, this is no dreaming,
    But daylight gladness that the daylight brings.

What ails my love; what ails her? She is paling;
    Faint grows her face, and slowly seems to fade!
I cannot clasp her – stretch out unavailing
    My arms across the silence and the shade.

Borderland

Am I waking, am I sleeping?
As the first faint dawn comes creeping
Thro' the pane, I am aware
Of an unseen presence hovering,
Round, above, in the dusky air:
A downy bird, with an odorous wing,
That fans my forehead, and sheds perfume,
As sweet as love, as soft as death,
Drowsy-slow through the summer-gloom.
My heart in some dream-rapture saith,
It is she. Half in a swoon,
I spread my arms in slow delight.
O prolong, prolong the night,
For the nights are short in June!

At Dawn

In the night I dreamed of you;
All the place was filled
With your presence; in my heart
The strife was stilled.

All night I have dreamed of you;
Now the morn is grey.
How shall I arise and face
The empty day?

Last Words

Dead! all's done with!
R. Browning

These blossoms that I bring,
This song that here I sing,
These tears that now I shed,
I give unto the dead.

There is no more to be done,
Nothing beneath the sun,
All the long ages through,
Nothing – by me for you.

The tale is told to the end;
This, ev'n, I may not know –
If we were friend and friend,
If we were foe and foe.

All's done with utterly,
All's done with. Death to me
Was ever Death indeed;
To me no kindly creed

Consolatory was given.
You were of earth, not Heaven...
This dreary day, things seem
Vain shadows in a dream,

Or some strange, pictured show;
And mine own tears that flow,
My hidden tears that fall,
The vainest of them all.

June

Last June I saw your face three times;
    Three times I touched your hand;
Now, as before, May month is o'er,
    And June is in the land.

O many Junes shall come and go,
    Flow'r-footed o'er the mead;
O many Junes for me, to whom
    Is length of days decreed.

There shall be sunlight, scent of rose;
    Warm mist of summer rain;
Only this change – I shall not look
    Upon your face again.

A Reminiscence

It is so long gone by, and yet
    How clearly now I see it all!
The glimmer of your cigarette,
    The little chamber, narrow and tall.

Perseus; your picture in its frame;
    (How near they seem and yet how far!)
The blaze of kindled logs; the flame
    Of tulips in a mighty jar.

Florence and spring-time: surely each
    Glad things unto the spirit saith.
Why did you lead me in your speech
    To these dark mysteries of death?

OUT OF MY BORROWED BOOKS

The Sequel to 'A Reminiscence'

Not in the street and not in the square,
    The street and square where you went and came;
With shuttered casement your house stands bare,
    Men hush their voice when they speak your name.

I, too, can play at the vain pretence,
    Can feign you dead; while a voice sounds clear
In the inmost depths of my heart: Go hence,
    Go, find your friend who is far from here.

Not here, but somewhere where I can reach!
    Can a man with motion, hearing and sight,
And a thought that answered my thought and speech,
    Be utterly lost and vanished quite?

Whose hand was warm in my hand last week? ...
    My heart beat fast as I neared the gate –
Was it this I had come to seek,
    'A stone that stared with your name and date';

A hideous, turfless, fresh-made mound;
    A silence more cold than the wind that blew?
What had I lost, and what had I found?
    My flowers that mocked me fell to the ground –
Then, and then only, my spirit knew.

In the Mile End Road

How like her! But 'tis she herself,
    Comes up the crowded street,
How little did I think, the morn,
    My only love to meet!

Whose else that motion and that mien?
    Whose else that airy tread?
For one strange moment I forgot
    My only love was dead.

AMY LEVY

Contradictions

Now, even, I cannot think it true,
My friend, that there is no more you.
Almost as soon were no more I,
Which were, of course, absurdity!
Your place is bare, you are not seen,
Your grave, I'm told, is growing green;
And both for you and me, you know,
There's no Above and no Below.
That you are dead must be inferred,
And yet my thought rejects the word.

In September

The sky is silver-grey; the long
    Slow waves caress the shore.
On such a day as this I have been glad,
    Who shall be glad no more.

The Old House

In through the porch and up the silent stair;
    Little is changed, I know so well the ways;
Here, the dead came to meet me; it was there
    The dream was dreamed in unforgotten days.

But who is this that hurries on before,
    A flitting shade the brooding shades among?
She turned – I saw her face – O God, it wore
    The face I used to wear when I was young!

I thought my spirit and my heart were tamed
    To deadness; dead the pangs that agonise.
The old grief springs to choke me – I am shamed
    Before that little ghost with eager eyes.

O turn away, let her not see, not know!
    How should she bear it, how should understand?
O hasten down the stairway, haste and go,
    And leave her dreaming in the silent land.

OUT OF MY BORROWED BOOKS

Alma Mater

A haunted town thou art to me.
Andrew Lang

Today in Florence all the air
Is soft with spring, with sunlight fair;
In the tall street gay folks are met;
Duomo and Tower gleam overhead,
Like jewels in the city set,
Fair-hued and many-faceted.
Against the old grey stones are piled
February violets, pale and sweet,
Whose scent of earth in woodland wild
Is wafted up and down the street.
The city's heart is glad; my own
Sits lightly on its bosom's throne.

⋆

Why is it that I see today,
Imaged as clear as in a dream,
A little city far away,
A churlish sky, a sluggish stream,
Tall clust'ring trees and gardens fair,
Dark birds that circle in the air,
Grey towers and fanes; on either hand,
Stretches of wind-swept meadow-land?

⋆

Oh, who can sound the human breast?
And this strange truth must be confessed;
That city do I love the best
Wherein my heart was heaviest!

In the Black Forest

I lay beneath the pine trees,
  And looked aloft, where, through
The dusky, clustered tree-tops,
  Gleamed rent, gay rifts of blue.

I shut my eyes, and a fancy
  Fluttered my sense around:
'I lie here dead and buried,
  And this is churchyard ground.

'I am at rest for ever;
  Ended the stress and strife.'
Straight I fell to and sorrowed
  For the pitiful past life.

Right wronged, and knowledge wasted;
  Wise labour spurned for ease;
The sloth and the sin and the failure;
  Did I grow sad for these?

They had made me sad so often;
  Not now they made me sad;
My heart was full of sorrow
  For joy it never had.

Captivity

The lion remembers the forest,
  The lion in chains;
To the bird that is captive a vision
  Of woodland remains.

One strains with his strength at the fetter,
  In impotent rage;
One flutters in flights of a moment,
  And beats at the cage.

If the lion were loosed from the fetter,
     To wander again;
He would seek the wide silence and shadow
     Of his jungle in vain.

He would rage in his fury, destroying;
     Let him rage, let him roam!
Shall he traverse the pitiless mountain,
     Or swim through the foam?

If they opened the cage and the casement,
     And the bird flew away;
He would come back at evening, heartbroken,
     A captive for aye.

Would come if his kindred had spared him,
     Free birds from afar —
There was wrought what is stronger than iron
     In fetter and bar.

I cannot remember my country,
     The land whence I came;
Whence they brought me and chained me and made me
     Nor wild thing nor tame.

This only I know of my country,
     This only repeat:
It was free as the forest, and sweeter
     Than woodland retreat.

When the chain shall at last be broken,
     The window set wide;
And I step in the largeness and freedom
     Of sunlight outside;

Shall I wander in vain for my country?
     Shall I seek and not find?
Shall I cry for the bars that encage me
     The fetters that bind?

The Two Terrors

Two terrors fright my soul by night and day:
The first is Life, and with her come the years;
A weary, winding train of maidens they,
With forward-fronting eyes, too sad for tears;
Upon whose kindred faces, blank and grey,
The shadow of a kindred woe appears.
Death is the second terror; who shall say
What form beneath the shrouding mantle nears?

Which way she turn, my soul finds no relief,
My smitten soul may not be comforted;
Alternately she swings from grief to grief,
And, poised between them, sways from dread to dread.
For there she dreads because she knows; and here,
Because she knows not, inly faints with fear.

The Promise of Sleep

Put the sweet thoughts from out thy mind,
        The dreams from out thy breast;
No joy for thee – but thou shalt find
        Thy rest

All day I could not work for woe,
        I could not work nor rest;
The trouble drove me to and fro,
        Like a leaf on the storm's breast.

Night came and saw my sorrow cease;
        Sleep in the chamber stole;
Peace crept about my limbs, and peace
        Fell on my stormy soul.

And now I think of only this,
        How I again may woo
The gentle sleep – who promises
        That death is gentle too.

The Last Judgement

With beating heart and lagging feet,
Lord, I approach the Judgement seat.
All bring hither the fruits of toil,
Measures of wheat and measures of oil;

Gold and jewels and precious wine;
No hands bare like these hands of mine.
The treasure I have nor weighs nor gleams:
Lord, I can bring you only dreams.

In days of spring, when my blood ran high,
I lay in the grass and looked at the sky,
And dreamed that my love lay by my side –
My love was false, and then she died.

All the heat of the summer through,
I dreamed she lived, that her heart was true
Throughout the hours of the day I slept,
But woke in the night, at times, and wept.

The nights and days, they went and came,
I lay in shadow and dreamed of fame;
And heard men passing the lonely place,
Who marked me not and my hidden face.

My strength waxed faint, my hair grew grey;
Nothing but dreams by night and day.
Some men sicken, with wine and food;
I starved on dreams, and found them good.

★

This is the tale I have to tell –
Show the fellow the way to hell.

The Lost Friend

The people take the thing of course,
They marvel not to see
This strange, unnatural divorce
Betwixt delight and me.

I know the face of sorrow, and I know
Her voice with all its varied cadences;
Which way she turns and treads; how at her ease
Things fit her dreary largess to bestow.

Where sorrow long abides, some be that grow
To hold her dear, but I am not of these;
Joy is my friend, not sorrow; by strange seas,
In some far land we wandered, long ago.

O faith, long tried, that knows no faltering!
O vanished treasure of her hands and face!
Beloved – to whose memory I cling,
Unmoved within my heart she holds her place.

And never shall I hail that other 'friend',
Who yet shall dog my footsteps to the end.

Cambridge in the Long

Where drowsy sound of college-chimes
    Across the air is blown,
And drowsy fragrance of the limes,
    I lie and dream alone.

A dazzling radiance reigns o'er all –
    O'er gardens densely green,
O'er old grey bridges and the small,
    Slow flood which slides between.

This is the place; it is not strange,
    But known of old and dear.
What went I forth to seek? The change
    Is mine; why am I here?

Alas, in vain I turned away,
          I fled the town in vain;
The strenuous life of yesterday
          Calleth me back again.

And was it peace I came to seek?
          Yet here, where memories throng,
Ev'n here, I know the past is weak,
          I know the present strong.

This drowsy fragrance, silent heat,
          Suit not my present mind,
Whose eager thought goes out to meet
          The life it left behind.

Spirit with sky to change; such hope,
          An idle one we know;
Unship the oars, make loose the rope,
          Push off the boat and go...

Ah, would what binds me could have been
          Thus loosened at a touch!
This pain of living is too keen,
          Of loving, is too much.

To Vernon Lee

On Bellosguardo, when the year was young,
We wandered, seeking for the daffodil
And dark anemone, whose purples fill
The peasant's plot, between the corn-shoots sprung.

Over the grey, low wall the olive flung
Her deeper greyness; far off, hill on hill
Sloped to the sky, which, pearly-pale and still,
Above the large and luminous landscape hung.

A snowy blackthorn flowered beyond my reach;
You broke a branch and gave it to me there;
I found for you a scarlet blossom rare.

Thereby ran on of Art and Life our speech;
And of the gifts the gods had given to each –
Hope unto you, and unto me Despair.

Oh, is it Love?

O is it Love or is it Fame,
          This thing for which I sigh?
Or has it then no earthly name
          For men to call it by?

I know not what can ease my pains,
          Nor what it is I wish;
The passion at my heart-strings strains
          Like a tiger in a leash.

In the Nower

To J. De P.

Deep in the grass outstretched I lie,
          Motionless on the hill;
Above me is a cloudless sky,
          Around me all is still:

There is no breath, no sound, no stir,
          The drowsy peace to break:
I close my tired eyes – it were
          So simple not to wake.

The End of the Day

To B.T.

Dead-tired, dog-tired, as the vivid day
Fails and slackens and fades away.
The sky that was so blue before
With sudden clouds is shrouded o'er.
Swiftly, stilly the mists uprise,
Till blurred and grey the landscape lies.

All day we have plied the oar; all day
Eager and keen have said our say
On life and death, on love and art,
On good or ill at Nature's heart.
Now, grown so tired, we scarce can lift
The lazy oars, but onward drift.
And the silence is only stirred
Here and there by a broken word.

★

O, sweeter far than strain and stress
Is the slow, creeping weariness.
And better far than thought I find
The drowsy blankness of the mind.
More than all joys of soul or sense
Is this divine indifference;
Where grief a shadow grows to be,
And peace a possibility.

A Wall Flower

I lounge in the doorway and languish in vain
While Tom, Dick and Harry are dancing with Jane

My spirit rises to the music's beat;
There is a leaden fiend lurks in my feet!
To move unto your motion, Love, were sweet.

Somewhere, I think, some other where, not here,
In other ages, on another sphere,
I danced with you, and you with me, my dear.

In perfect motion did our bodies sway,
To perfect music that was heard alway;
Woe's me, that am so dull of foot today!

To move unto your motion, Love, were sweet;
My spirit rises to the music's beat –
But, ah, the leaden demon in my feet!

At a Dinner Party

With fruit and flowers the board is deckt,
    The wine and laughter flow;
I'll not complain – could one expect
    So dull a world to know?

You look across the fruit and flowers,
    My glance your glances find
It is our secret, only ours,
    Since all the world is blind.

Philosophy

Ere all the world had grown so drear,
When I was young and you were here,
'Mid summer roses in summer weather,
What pleasant times we've had together!

We were not Phyllis, simple-sweet,
And Corydon; we did not meet
By brook or meadow, but among
A Philistine and flippant throng

Which much we scorned; (less rigorous
It had no scorn at all for us!)
How many an eve of sweet July,
Heedless of Mrs Grundy's eye,

We've scaled the stairway's topmost height,
And sat there talking half the night;
And, gazing on the crowd below,
Thanked Fate and Heaven that made us so;

To hold the pure delights of brain
Above light loves and sweet champagne.
For, you and I, we did eschew
The egoistic 'I' and 'you';

And all our observations ran
On Art and Letters, Life and Man.
Proudly we sat, we two, on high,
Throned in our Objectivity;

Scarce friends, not lovers (each avers),
But sexless, safe Philosophers.

★

Dear Friend, you must not deem me light
If, as I lie and muse tonight,
I give a smile and not a sigh
To thoughts of our Philosophy.

A Game of Lawn Tennis

What wonder that I should be dreaming
  Out here in the garden today?
The light through the leaves is streaming –
  Paulina cries, 'Play!'

The birds to each other are calling,
  The freshly cut grasses smell sweet;
To Teddy's dismay, comes falling
  The ball at my feet.

'Your stroke should be over, not under!'
  'But that's such a difficult way!'
The place is a springtide wonder
  Of lilac and may;

Of lilac, and may, and laburnum,
  Of blossom – *We're losing the set!*
'Those volleys of Jenny's – return them;
  'Stand close to the net!'

★

You are so fond of the Maytime,
  My friend, far away;
Small wonder that I should be dreaming
  Of you in the garden today.

To E.

The mountains in fantastic lines
Sweep, blue-white, to the sky, which shines
Blue as blue gems; athwart the pines
  The lake gleams blue.

We three were here, three years gone by;
Our Poet, with fine-frenzied eye,
You, stepped in learned lore, and I,
  A poet too.

Our Poet brought us books and flowers,
He read us *Faust*; he talked for hours
Philosophy (sad Schopenhauer's),
  Beneath the trees:

And do you mind that sunny day,
When he, as on the sward he lay,
Told of Lassalle who bore away
  The false Louise?

Thrice-favoured bard! To him alone
That green and snug retreat was shown,
Where to the vulgar herd unknown,
  Our pens we plied.

(For, in those distant days, it seems,
We cherished sundry idle dreams,
And with our flowing foolscap reams
  The Fates defied.)

And after, when the day was gone,
And the hushed, silver night came on,
He showed us where the glow-worm shone;
  We stooped to see.

There, too, by yonder moon we swore
Platonic friendship o'er and o'er;
No folk, we deemed, had been before
  So wise and free.

★

And do I sigh or smile today?
Dead love or dead ambition, say,
Which mourn we most? Not much we weigh
    Platonic friends.

On you the sun is shining free;
Our Poet sleeps in Italy,
Beneath an alien sod; on me
    The cloud descends.

A Ballad of Religion and Marriage

Swept into limbo is the host
    Of heavenly angels, row on row;
The Father, Son, and Holy Ghost,
    Pale and defeated, rise and go.
The great Jehovah is laid low,
    Vanished his burning bush and rod –
Say, are we doomed to deeper woe?
    Shall marriage go the way of God?

Monogamous, still at our post,
    Reluctantly we undergo
Domestic round of boiled and roast,
    Yet deem the whole proceeding slow.
Daily the secret murmurs grow;
    We are no more content to plod
Along the beaten paths – and so
    Marriage must go the way of God.

Soon, before all men, each shall toast
    The seven strings unto his bow,
Like beacon fires along the coast,
    The flame of love shall glance and glow.
Nor let nor hindrance man shall know,
    From natal bath to funeral sod;
Perennial shall his pleasures flow
    When marriage goes the way of God.

Grant, in a million years at most,
    Folk shall be neither pairs nor odd –
Alas! We shan't be there to boast
    'Marriage has gone the way of God!'

AMY LEVY

NOTES ON THE POEMS

Augusta Webster

Blanche Lisle and Other Poems

Webster's first collection, published under the name of 'Cecil Home', consists of lyrics and ballads clearly influenced by Keats' 'Eve of St Agnes' and Tennyson's 'Mariana'. Emerging from her replaying of Gothic conventions, though, can be seen early outlines of the themes that she would go on to explore in more challenging ways.

'Blanche Lisle' itself is a long narrative poem; the extract is taken from the opening section, 'Reveries'. The orphaned Blanche lives in Mariana-like seclusion with her aunt and uncle: one night, in the old family chapel, her own body in a coffin is revealed to her by a ghostly vision of her mother. Inevitably, her lover betrays her, and she fulfils the omen by dying of grief.

Dramatic Studies

'Sister Annunciata'
The poem is in two parts, extracts from the first of which are included here. The first part follows the emotions and memories of a nun through her vigil on the anniversary of becoming a 'bride of Christ'. As an eighteen-year-old, Eva was forced by her mother, at the command of the head of the family, to give up her lover Angelo. She enters a convent, partly giving in to family pressure, partly from her own pride and naïve sense of vocation. Her sister Leonora marries the prince she refused; Angelo too makes the marriage his family have planned for him. The first part ends with Annunciata's anguished vision of herself watching her lover drown. The second part of the poem, 'Abbess Ursula's Lecture', takes place after Annunciata's death. The Abbess tells her story to another unhappy novice as an example of pious resignation to God. In her version of the story, Annunciata is attended by visions of the saints, and dies at peace, although the convent is surprised that no miracles follow her death. Only the reader is aware of the memories that darken her last words, spoken to the Abbess who showed her long-forgotten kindness when she entered the convent: 'Mothers smile like you'.

p. 20 'Did Mary envy Martha?': in Luke 10.38–42, Mary sits and listens to Jesus, while her sister Martha continues with the domestic chores.

'By the Looking-Glass'
p. 31 'the red-bound book': the Peerage.

A Woman Sold and Other Poems

'A Woman Sold' dramatises the domestic tragedy of Eleanor Vaughan's wasted life. In the first part of the poem, she has succumbed to family pressure to renounce her lover, Lionel, and agree to marriage to wealthy, elderly Sir Joyce Boycott. Confronted by Lionel, she is persuaded by his contrary insistence that she defy parental wishes: the scene turns upon her cry, 'Oh Lionel / Do help me. Tell me what to do.' The second scene takes place six years later. Eleanor has broken her promise to Lionel for the second time and is now the widowed Lady Boycott. Lionel is a successful lawyer and, it emerges, about to marry Eleanor's friend Mary.

Portraits

Portraits opens with four monologues: 'Medea in Athens', 'Circe', 'The Happiest Girl in the World' and 'A Castaway', to which Webster added a fifth, 'Faded', in the 1893 edition. 'The Happiest Girl in the World' has not been included here, for reasons of space.

'Medea in Athens'
Medea, a priestess of Hecate, betrayed her father to help her lover Jason to secure the Golden Fleece. Finding that Jason plans to marry Glaucè, Medea sends her a poisoned garment that kills her. She then kills her own children in revenge against Jason. Webster's poem is set after Medea's escape to Athens, when she is married to King Aegeus.

p. 49 'Symplegades': dangerous rocks circumvented by Jason and the Argonauts.

p. 53 'my so loved brother': Medea's brother was sent to persuade her to return home and is murdered by her or, in another version, by Jason at her instigation.

p. 53 'credulous girls': two daughters of Pelias of Iolkos whom Medea duped into killing their father in another of her acts of revenge.

'Circe'
In the *Odyssey*, Odysseus's ship is blown off-course to the island of the witch Circe, who changes the crew into pigs when they eat the banquet she has prepared for them. Odysseus, as instructed by Hermes, bargains with Circe to secure the restoration of his men to human shape, before succumbing to her seduction. The men remain in the luxury of the island for a year, until the crew remind Odysseus of their mission to return home and they resume their voyage, with Circe's help. Webster's poem takes place as Odysseus' ship approaches. As in the *Odyssey*, the island is populated by Circe's earlier victims in the forms of animals that are both wild and pitiable. Like the island of Tennyson's *Lotos Eaters* (1832), Circe's island is a sinister and seductive distraction from the life of action and freedom – but in Webster's reimagining, it entraps Circe as much as the mariners.

'A Castaway'
Anna Howitt (1824–84), an artist whom Webster is likely to have known, since they mixed in the same feminist and Pre-Raphaelite circles and were neighbours in Cheyne Walk, had exhibited a painting entitled *The Castaway* at the Royal Academy in 1855, a symbolic depiction of a 'fallen woman' among trampled lilies.

'Eulalie', the name of Webster's castaway, is also the name of the priestess-poet in 'A History of the Lyre' (1829) by Letitia Landon (L.E.L.; 1802–38). Landon was a key figure for later Victorian women poets; her Eulalie is also a presence in Barrett Browning's *Aurora Leigh*.

p. 60 the speaker's recollection of her daily activities recalls Emily Davies' impatience with the dangerous inadequacy of girls' education: lacking the resources to occupy their time purposefully, '[girls'] energies are frittered away in minor attempts at petty improvement', until, defeated, they 'let themselves go drifting down the stream, despising themselves but listlessly yielding to what seems to be their fate' (*The Higher Education of Women*, Alexander Strahan, London 1866; pp. 43, 50).

p. 64 'Rahabs and Jezebels': names associated with prostitution, from Old Testament characters. 'Tartuffe': the religious hypocrite in Molière's play *Le Tartuffe, ou 'l'imposteur* (1664).

p. 66 'doing Magdalene': from the biblical Mary Magdalene, a figure who came to represent the penitent prostitute in Christian iconography. From the mid-1850s, refuges had been run by the Magdalene Society with the aim of reforming and rehabilitating prostitutes, giving them shelter and finding them domestic work. Christina Rossetti was a helper at the St Mary Magdalene Penitentiary in Highgate for some years from around 1859.

p. 66 'three per cents': Government stocks.

p. 67 'white work': embroidery finely worked in white thread on white cloth, used for both domestic linen and church vestments.

p. 68 'to ship us to the colonies for wives': Webster is alluding to real schemes such as Maria Rye's Society for Female Emigration, and W.R. Greg's proposals in his 1862 pamphlet 'Why Are Women Redundant?', proposed as solutions to the growing number of 'superfluous women' in the population. Greg suggested that emigration was particularly suitable for 'those who swell the ranks of "distressed needlewomen", those who as milliners' apprentices so frequently fall victims to temptation or to toil' (see Patricia Hollis, *Women in Public 1850–1900: Documents of the Victorian Women's Movement*, London 1979, pp. 31–40).

'Tired'
p. 89 'Duessa': the daughter of Deceit and Shame in Spenser's *Faerie Queen*.

A Book of Rhyme

'English Rispetti'
This sequence of thirty poems was originally called 'English Stornelli'. When

they were reprinted in *Selections from the Verse of Augusta Webster* in 1893, Webster changed the title in response to criticism that the verses more accurately followed the *rispetto* form. *Rispetti* consist of between six and twelve lines, with a rhyme scheme abababcc. They are conventionally love poems addressed by a man to a woman: Webster reverses the roles.

Mother and Daughter: An Uncompleted Sonnet Sequence

The sequence consists of twenty-seven sonnets in all. The introductory note to the work, written by William Rossetti, praises the sonnets in somewhat lukewarm terms ('nothing could be more genuine than these sonnets... the theme is as beautiful and natural a one as any poetess could select') but insists on Webster's stature as a dramatist, discussing (oddly, given the context) her play *The Sentence*, a 'thrilling and stupendous' three-act verse tragedy about the Emperor Caligula which, according to Rossetti, 'is the supreme thing amid the work of all British poetesses', surpassing the achievements of Elizabeth Barrett Browning and his sister Christina, and 'one of the masterpieces of European drama'.

p. 96   Sonnet XVII: 'frore': a poeticism for 'frozen' (the *OED* cites Elizabeth Barrett Browning, 'Loves lie frore').

Mathilde Blind

Poems by Claude Lake

Blind's first collection was dedicated to 'Joseph' (Giuseppe) Mazzini (1805–72). Mazzini, who spent most of his life in exile in France, Switzerland and England, was a charismatic figure who drew liberal sympathisers to his ideology of Italian freedom and heroic self-determination (notably, in this context, Elizabeth Barrett Browning). Garnett's 'Memoir' quotes one of Blind's letters in which she describes her 'especial veneration' for Mazzini: 'How this man, with his fire, his glowing eloquence, his holy zeal, carries one away! I hang with my whole soul upon his every word... and I should like to remember every single word for ever.'

The Heather on Fire: A Tale of the Highland Clearances

The poem is dedicated to Captain Cameron, 'whose glory it is to have thrown up his place rather than proceed in command of the steamer *Lochiel*, which was to convey the Police Expedition against the Skye Crofters in the winter of 1884'. Blind's Preface gives an account of the poem's origins in a visit she made in 1884 to a ruined village on the Isle of Arran. An old woman told her of the community's experience of the Clearances:

> Here, she said, and as far as one could see, had dwelt the Glen Sannox people... evicted by the Duke of Hamilton in 1832. The lives of these crofters became an idyll in her mouth. She dwelt proudly on their patient labour, their simple joys... and her brown eyes filled with tears as she recalled the day of their expulsion, when the people gathered from all parts of the island to see the last of the Glen Sannox folk ere they went on board the brig that was bound for New Brunswick in Canada. 'Ah, it was a sore day that,' she sighed, 'when the old people cast themselves down on the seashore and wept.' They were gone, these Crofters, and their dwellings laid low with the hillside, and their fertile plots of corn overrun with ling and heather... and to use the touching words of a Highland minister, 'There was not a smoke there now.' (*Poetical Works*, p. 91)

The poem tells the story of the crofters Mary and Michael, who meet and fall in love in the first duan, and marry in the second. The third duan takes place nine years later. The idyll is over. Mary is pregnant and nursing one of her four children, who is ill; Michael is at sea, fishing. Neighbours rush in with news that houses in the glen have been set on fire by the factor, the agent of the absentee landlord, forcing the crofters from their homes. The sick child dies during the night the family spends in the open air, and Michael's aged mother dies of burns. Michael arrives home with the other fishermen to discover the ruin of the community. In the fourth and final duan, Blind describes the horrors that follow the eviction. Hiding in a ruin, Mary gives birth during a storm: both she and the baby die. A hurried funeral at which another of Michael's children collapses and dies is broken up by the factor's men driving the crofters onto boats that will take them out to the waiting emigrant ship, the *Koh-i-Noor*. Michael's father Rory, who has descended into madness 'like a village Lear' (III, xlvi), evades the round-up only to witness the remnants of his family drown as the ship founders on rocks in the Sound of Sleat.

p. 115 'Duan': a Gaelic term for a canto, introduced into English by the poet James MacPherson (1736–96) in his Gaelic verse pastiche *The Epic of Ossian* (1765).

The Ascent of Man

The title is an allusion to Darwin's work on human evolution, *The Descent of Man* (1871).

The poem is a sequence in three parts. Part I traces human development from the origins of life, through human history to a spiritual oneness with creation in which 'no longer cramped and bound / By the narrow human round', 'Human lives dissolve, enlace / In a flaming world embrace'. In Part II, titled 'The Pilgrim Soul', the poet travels through scenes of human misery in a dark and violent city. These descriptions owe much to James Thomson's 'City of Dreadful Night' (Blind knew Thomson well), and almost certainly also draw on Blind's frequent visits to Manchester as a guest of the Madox Brown family between 1884 and 1886, while Ford Madox Brown was working on the murals for Manchester Town Hall. An abandoned child reveals himself as Love, and Part II ends with the stanza:

> And lo, as we went through the woe-clouded city,
> Where women bring forth and men labour in vain,
> Weak Love grew so great in his passion of pity
> That all who beheld him were born once again.

In Part III, the poet is led by Sorrow 'o'er the thickly peopled earth' to a peaceful 'white town dozing in the valley', to witness the effects of war.

'The Red Sunsets, 1883'
p. 144 Spectacular sunsets were observed around the world in the months following the eruption of Krakatoa in August 1883. Line 6 refers to St John the Evangelist, banished to the island of Patmos, where he wrote the Book of Revelation.

Dramas in Miniature

The collection was published with a frontispiece by Ford Madox Brown illustrating lines from 'The Message': 'The perfume of the breath of May / Had passed into her soul'. Arthur Symons, reviewing the collection in *The Athenaeum* (21 May 1892), wrote of the poems as 'tragedies of the kind which many people are apt to sum up… in the one word "painful" '; he also, strikingly, described them as 'flowers of evil' (quoted in James Diedrick, ' "My love is a force that will force you to care": Subversive Sexuality in Mathilde Blind's Dramatic Monologues', *Victorian Poetry* 40, 2002, pp. 359–86). Diedrick suggests that Swinburne's 1862 review of Baudelaire's *Fleurs du Mal* was a significant influence on Blind's poetry.

'A Carnival Episode'
Details in the poem recall descriptions of carnival in Rome and Naples (chs. IV, V) in *The Journal of Marie Bashkirtseff*, published in Blind's translation in 1890.

'Manchester by Night'
See note to 'The Ascent of Man', p. 257 above.

Birds of Passage: Songs of the Orient and Occident

The collection's title is echoed in the lines from Edward Fitzgerald's *Rubáiyát of Omar Khayyám* (1859, with four further editions), quoted in the epigraph: 'The Bird of Time has but a little way / To flutter – and the bird is on the wing' (VII).

'Sphinx-Money'
Blind's notes to the poem explain 'sphinx-money' as 'small fossil shells or ammonites, frequently found in some parts of the desert'.

'The Desert'
p. 167 'Beeshareen': a tribal group living between the Nile and the Red Sea in Egypt (and further south, where they had gained a fearsome reputation fighting against the British army led by General Gordon in the Sudan campaign of 1883–5).
p. 168 'A human form, indeed, but stone', annotated by Blind as an 'unfinished Colossus of red granite discovered by two English officers while riding in the desert round Assouan'.

Amy Levy

Xantippe and Other Verse

Levy's small first collection was published in Cambridge, while she was still a student at Newnham College. In addition to the title poem, 'A Prayer', 'Felo de Se' (not included here), the sonnet 'Most wonderful and strange it seems' and 'Run to Death' were all later reprinted in *A Minor Poet and Other Verse* (1884). The lines from Heine, in Elizabeth Barrett Browning's translation (1862), run 'Out of my own great woe / I make my little songs'.

'Xantippe'
The poem was written in 1878 (according to Oscar Wilde in his obituary of Levy), or 1879, just before Levy began her first term at Newnham, and was first published in *The Dublin University Magazine* in 1880.
p. 181 Xantippe was the notoriously bad-tempered wife of Socrates, almost a pantomime character in the standard versions of the story.
p. 185 Aspasia: the mistress of Pericles, admitted to the otherwise exclusively male circle of philosophers on account of her learning.
p. 187 'the time of horror': Socrates was sentenced to death and fulfilled the command by drinking hemlock.

'Run to Death'
The poem was first published in 1879 in *The Victoria Magazine* (although it may have been revised from a much earlier version). From its foundation in 1863, the magazine had been not only managed and edited, but also printed by women, at the Victoria Press in Russell Square, where women were trained and employed in a practical response to the problem of the destitution of 'surplus women'. Both press and magazine were the initiatives of an informal association of women who came to be known as the Langham Place Group, and the more formal Society for Promoting the Employment of Women which grew out of it. The group included in its orbit at different times many of the most notable women of mid- to late Victorian feminist

campaigning in education, employment and suffrage. The magazine, one of several that originated from within this circle, set out to broaden the knowledge and horizons of its readers, advising them on reading and encouraging them to engage with social issues. In this context, Levy's poem can be seen to be of a piece with the magazine's agenda of both sharpening women's sense of injustice, and warning them against the illusions of romantic convention – the picturesque medievalism of gallant huntsmen and fair ladies 'with their graceful nothings trifling all the weary time away' frames the hunters' hidden savagery to the gipsy mother and child.

'A Ballad of Last Seeing'
The poem was published in *The Cambridge Review*, 2 May 1883, p. 337, but Levy did not include it in any of her collections. It has been reprinted by Hunt Beckman, pp. 88–9, who links it thematically to a group of poems from *A Minor Poet*, 'To Sylvia', 'Sinfonia Eroica', and 'In a Minor Key'.

A Minor Poet and Other Verse

A second edition of the collection was published in 1891. After she left Cambridge, Levy made a number of extended visits to Europe between 1881 and 1885, travelling, studying and giving English lessons, and many of the poems in her second collection were written in Dresden. In addition to the frontispiece photograph of Levy, the book includes an illustration on the title page showing a despondent woman crouching beside a well, over which appears the legend 'Non in est veritas': 'Truth is not within'.

'To a Dead Poet'
The subject is James Thomson (1834–82). See p. 177 above. The poem forms the epigraph to the volume.
    p. 193 'I who had never seen your face': the line echoes the final sentence of Levy's essay on Thomson in *The Cambridge Review*: 'To us, who never saw his face nor touched his living hand, his image stands out large and clear, unutterably tragic: the image of a great mind and a great soul thwarted in their development by circumstance; of a nature struggling with itself and Fate; of an existence doomed to bear a twofold burden' (21 and 28 February 1883, pp. 240–1, 257–8, in New, pp. 502–9).

'A Minor Poet'
The epigraph is from *Hamlet*, III i 27.
    p. 195 'Prometheus' bard': Shelley
    p. 195 'one wild singer of today': in her essay on Thomson, Levy writes 'All through the work of James Thomson we hear one note, one cry, muffled sometimes, but always there; a passionate, hungry cry for life, for the things of this human, flesh and blood life; for love and praise, for mere sunlight and sun's warmth' (New, p. 506). See also p. 196 'I want the best: / Love, beauty, sunlight, nameless joy of life.'

'Medea'
For the story of Medea, see note to Webster's 'Medea in Athens', p. 254 above.

'Sinfonia Eroica'
One of a number of Levy's poems inspired by music (see notes to 'To Sylvia' and 'A June-Tide Echo', below), the poem takes its title from the Beethoven symphony. It was written in Dresden. The dedication to Sylvia in this and the following poem is conventional.

'To Sylvia'
The lines of 'the song you sang to me' are Levy's translation of the opening lines of the *lied* 'Lehn deine Wang' an meine Wang" ('Lean your cheek against my cheek'), one of a sequence of poems by Heine expressing the torment of unfulfilled love. There are a number of nineteenth-century settings, the best-known by Schumann (although Levy's musical quotation is not from this).

'Magdalen'
For the title, see note to Webster's 'A Castaway', p. 255 above.

'A Dirge'
A poem in the manner of Heine; Levy's translation of the Heine poem from which the epigraph is taken was published in *The Cambridge Review* in 1882 with the title 'From Heine' (26 April, p. 270). Her translation of the two lines runs 'My heart, my heart is heavy, / Yet May is bright in the land'.

'The Sick Man and the Nightingale'
This is one of two poems in the collection that are translations of *Lieder* by the German poet Nikolaus Franz Niemsch (1802–50), who wrote as Nikolaus Lenau.

'A June-Tide Echo'
'After a Richter concert': Hans Richter (1843–1916) was a Hungarian-born conductor who played a significant role in the musical life of late nineteenth-century England, as a conductor of Wagner and Beethoven in particular. In 1882 he conducted the first English performances of *Die Meistersinger* and *Tristan* in an influential Wagner series in London. One of these concerts is likely to have been the source of the poem. *A London Plane Tree* includes another poem with a Wagnerian inspiration, 'Lohengrin'.

'To Lallie'
Melvyn New suggests that 'Lallie' may be a diminutive for 'Violet', and hence a reference to Violet Paget (Vernon Lee), but although Levy did write love poems to her (included in *A London Plane Tree*), she did not meet her until 1886, during the months she spent in Florence. Levy used the British

Museum Reading Room when she was working on her translations of German poets; Eleanor Marx recalled how she used to meet her there when she herself was working in the Reading Room on her Ibsen translations. Clementina Black also frequented the Reading Room, and was a friend of the scholar Richard Garnett (1835–1906), the superintendent and Keeper of Printed Books, who reviewed Levy's first collection. The Reading Room was important to Levy and her female contemporaries as a space where they could meet and work that was neither domestic nor unacceptably public, and it recurs several times in her novels.

'A Farewell'
A poem inspired by Heine, rather than a translation.
p. 223   King's: King's College, Cambridge.

A London Plane-Tree and Other Verse

Levy checked the proofs of her third collection about a week before her death; the book was published posthumously. An American edition of the collection was published in 1891. The book includes two drawings by John Bernard Partridge (1861–1945), an illustrator and portrait painter of some distinction: of the Temple Church in London, and of a writer at a paper-strewn table, hand clasped to forehead (see p. 172 above). The book is divided into four parts: 'A London Plane-Tree', 'Love, Dreams and Death', 'Moods and Thoughts', and 'Odds and Ends'; the second and third have epigraphs from Fitzgerald's *Rubáiyát of Omar Khayyám* (stanzas XCIX and LXVI, 1872/1875 edn). The first epigraph is from Austin Dobson's 'On London Stones' (1876):

> On London stones I sometimes sigh
> For wider green and bluer sky; – …
> 'Pure song is country born' – I cry…
> In vain! – the woods, the fields deny
> That clearer strain I fain would try;
> Mine is an urban Muse…

The tone of Levy's London poems suggests the influence of Dobson's polished urban idylls: the whimsical, untroubled counterpart to Thomson's visions of the 'void agony' of the city (the phrase is Levy's, from her article on Thomson; New, p. 504).

'To Clementina Black'
Clementina Black had been a friend since Levy's schooldays. She was a novelist and campaigner, a close friend of the Marx family, involved in lecturing and trade unionism. In 1886 she became honorary secretary of the Women's Trade Union League. She was a supportive presence in Levy's life, although Levy never shared Black's radicalism. In 1886 Black was living with her sister Grace (also a trade unionist) in a flat where, as Levy wrote

with prim amusement to Vernon Lee, 'they do their own housework, and are quite and completely domestic, unless they are attending Socialist and Anarchist meetings. I confess, that my own Philistine, middle class notions of comfort wd. not be met by their ménage' (letter 26, Hunt Beckman, p. 255).

'A London Plane-Tree'
Levy never did live in a garret, but comfortably in the family home: 'the garret-pane' of line 5 contributed to a misconception that arose after her death.

'Ballade of an Omnibus'
The epigraph is from Andrew Lang's 'Ballade Amoureuse, after Froissart' from his *Ballades in Blue China* (1880, 1881).

The omnibus represented an extension of freedom and possibility to urban women, and is a frequent motif in fiction of the period: in Levy's novel *The Romance of a Shop* (1888), the determined, independent Gertrude is seen by her conventional aunt returning from a morning in the British Museum, 'careering up the street on the summit of a tall green omnibus, her hair blowing gaily in the breeze' (in New, p. 105).

Croesus and Lucullus: classical figures proverbial for wealth and luxury.

'Ballade of a Special Edition'
Levy's short story 'Sokratics in the Strand' (*Cambridge Review* 1884; in New, pp. 424–34) opens with a description of 'the crowded mazes of the Strand': 'newsboys were calling out the latest news with a grim emulation of horrors: "Terrible Railway Accident," bawled *Globe*; "Double Murder in Mile End," yelled *Echo*; "Loss of 2,000 Lives," shrieked *Evening Standard*, vague but triumphant' (p. 424). Levy uses the same image of the thrilling horrors of the city in her novel *The Romance of a Shop*: Gertrude Lorimer shudders with apprehension at 'the hoarse shriek of a man proclaiming a "special edition"' (New, p. 165). Mile End, in the East End of London, had long been associated with poverty, criminality and violence, although Levy's 'double murder' pre-dates the Whitechapel murders of 'Jack the Ripper' by some months.

'Straw in the Street'
Straw was laid in a street to dull the sound of traffic passing a house where someone was sick or dying.

'London Poets'
Hunt Beckman points out that Levy amended the last line of the poem on the proofs, changing the pronoun from 'she' to 'he' (p. 190).

'The Village Garden'
E.M.S. has been identified by Hunt Beckman as Euphemia Malder Stevens, a schoolfriend of Levy's.

'The Dream'
The epigraph is by the poet Agnes Mary F. Robinson (1857–1949). She was prominent in literary circles both as an admired poet and as an influential literary hostess (she was also a brilliant classicist who had studied Greek at University College London). Robinson was a friend, and probably lover, of Vernon Lee. Augusta Webster was unimpressed by Robinson's dreamy Pre-Raphaelite poetry (see pp. 13–14 above), although she did later praise the 'spontaneous yet skilled grace' of her *Retrospect and Other Poems* (*The Athenaeum*, 30 September 1893).

'The Birch-Tree at Loschwitz'
Hunt Beckman records that the manuscript of the poem is inscribed 'To Vernon Lee' (p. 257).

'A Reminiscence'
The content suggests Levy's visit to Vernon Lee in Florence. 'Perseus' refers to Cellini's bronze *Perseus with the Head of Medusa*.

'Alma Mater'
The epigraph is a paraphrase of the lines 'St Andrews by the Northern sea / That is a haunted town to me!' from Lang's 'Almae Matres (St Andrews, 1862. Oxford, 1865)', *Ballades in Blue China* (1880; 1881).

'Cambridge in the Long'
The title refers to the long summer vacation.

'In the Nower'
'Nower': an archaic form of 'nowhere' (*OED*). The dedicatee has been iden-tified by Hunt Beckman as Jennette de Pass, a Jewish friend. This poem, like 'A Wall Flower', was published by Oscar Wilde in the magazine *The Woman's World* (1890 and 1899 respectively).

'The End of the Day'
B.T. is Levy's friend the novelist Bertha Thomas.

'A Wall Flower'
This poem, from the short final section of the book, is one of three ('The First Extra', not included here, and 'At a Dinner Party'), headed 'Songs from *The New Phaon* (unpublished)' – presumably the title of a planned collec-tion. Phaon was Sappho's (male) lover.

'Philosophy'
Mrs Grundy: the proverbial figure of a prude.

'A Game of Lawn Tennis'
This verse first appeared in Levy's novel *The Romance of a Shop*, where it is written by Gertrude Lorimer and accompanies an engraving by the young

artist Frank Jermyn of the three Lorimer sisters and himself playing tennis. Its playfulness is more equivocal in context. Gertrude is proud to see it in print, but ruefully aware that 'It is rather a come down after *Charlotte Corday*, isn't it?' – the five-act tragedy that she has thrown away with her other writing in a bleak clear-out when she faces the practical responsibilities of providing for the family after the death of their father (in New, pp. 125–6, 67). Frank, true to his name, underlines the pragmatic compromises the poem represents: 'We all have to get off our high horse, Miss Lorimer, if we want to live. I had ten guineas this morning for that thing; and there is the *Death of Oedipus* with its face to the wall in the studio – and likely to remain there' (ibid., p. 126).

'To E.'
'E.' may be Eleanor Marx or, given the context, Vernon Lee.

Lassalle and the false Louise: Ferdinand Lassalle (1825–64), a German socialist of the 1848 generation, well known to the Marx family, whom he visited in London in 1862. More important here than the Marx connection, though, is Lassalle's death as a result of his entanglement with the daughter of a Bavarian diplomat who was already engaged to be married. Lassalle was killed in a duel as a result. The story became well known (and is the basis of Meredith's novel *The Tragic Comedians* (1880)). 'Louise' is an allusion to Héloïse, the lover of Abelard.

'A Ballad of Religion and Marriage'
The poem was not included in any of Levy's published collections. Twelve copies were printed in an undated, privately circulated pamphlet, possibly after her death. Two copies are held by the British Library. It has been reprinted in New, pp. 404–5.

FURTHER READING

Augusta Webster

Blanche Lisle and Other Poems, Macmillan, Cambridge and London 1860
Dramatic Studies, Macmillan, London and Cambridge 1866
A Woman Sold and Other Poems, Macmillan, London and Cambridge1867
Portraits, Macmillan, London 1870
A Book of Rhyme, Macmillan, London 1881
Mother and Daughter: An Uncompleted Sonnet Sequence, Macmillan, London 1895
Christine Sutphin (ed.), *Augusta Webster: Portraits and Other Poems*, Broadview Press, Ontario 2000

Susan Brown, 'Determined Heroines: George Eliot, Augusta Webster and Closet Drama by Victorian Women', *Victorian Poetry* 33, 1995, pp. 89–109
Robert P. Fletcher, ' "Convent Thoughts": Augusta Webster and the Body Politics of the Victorian Cloister', *Victorian Poetry* 37, 2003, pp. 295–313
Angela Leighton, 'Augusta Webster', in *Victorian Women Poets: Writing against the Heart*, Harvester-Wheatsheaf, Hemel Hempstead 1992, pp. 164–201
Patricia Rigg, 'Augusta Webster: The Social Politics of Monodrama', *Victorian Review* 26, 2001, pp. 75–107
— 'Augusta Webster and the Lyric Muse: *The Athenaeum* and Webster's Poetics', *Victorian Poetry* 42, 2004, pp. 135–64

Mathilde Blind

Poems by Claude Lake, Alfred W. Bennett, London 1867
The Heather on Fire: A Tale of the Highland Clearances, Walter Scott, London 1886
The Ascent of Man, Chatto and Windus, London 1889
Dramas in Miniature, Chatto and Windus, London 1891
Songs and Sonnets, Chatto and Windus, London 1893
Birds of Passage: Songs of the Orient and Occident, Chatto and Windus, London 1895
Arthur Symons (ed.), *The Poetical Works of Mathilde Blind*, T. Fisher Unwin, London 1900

Rosemary Ashton, *Little Germany: German Refugees in Victorian Britain*, Oxford University Press, Oxford 1989
Simon Avery, ' "Tantalising Glimpses": The Intersecting Lives of Eleanor

Marx and Mathilde Blind', in John Stokes (ed.), *Eleanor Marx (1855–1898): Life, Work, Contacts*, Ashgate, Aldershot 2000, pp. 173–87

Susan Brown, 'A Still and Mute-Born Vision: Locating Mathilde Blind's Reproductive Poetics' in Alison Chapman (ed.), *Victorian Women Poets* (English Association Essays and Studies 53), D.S. Brewer, Cambridge 2003, pp. 123–44

James Diedrick, '"My love is a force that will force you to care": Subversive Sexuality in Mathilde Blind's Dramatic Monologues', *Victorian Poetry* 40, 2002, pp. 359–86

Ford Madox Hueffer, *Ford Madox Brown: A Record of His Life and Work*, Longmans, Green and Co., London 1896

Amy Levy

Xantippe and Other Verse, E. Johnson, Cambridge 1881

A Minor Poet and Other Verse, T. Fisher Unwin, London 1884

A London Plane Tree and Other Verse, T. Fisher Unwin, London 1889

Melvyn New (ed.), *The Complete Novels and Selected Writings of Amy Levy 1861–1889*, University Press of Florida, Gainesville FL, 1993

Linda Hunt Beckman, *Amy Levy: Her Life and Letters*, Ohio University Press, Athens OH, 2000

Emma Francis, 'Amy Levy: Contradictions? Feminism and Semitic Discourse', in Isobel Armstrong and Virginia Blain (eds), *Women's Poetry: Late Romantic to Late Victorian: Gender and Genre 1830–1900*, Macmillan, Basingstoke 1999, pp. 183–206

Deborah Epstein Nord, ' "Neither Pairs Nor Odd": Women, Urban Community, and Writing in the 1880s', in *Walking the Victorian Streets: Women, Representation and the City*, Cornell University Press, Ithaca NY 1995, pp. 181–206

Cynthia Scheinberg, 'Recasting "sympathy and judgement": Amy Levy, Women Poets and the Victorian Dramatic Monologue', *Victorian Poetry* 35, 1997, pp. 173–92

— 'Amy Levy and the Accents of Minor(ity) Poetry', in *Women's Poetry and Religion in Victorian England: Jewish Identity and Christian Culture*, Cambridge University Press, Cambridge 2002, pp. 190–237

Background

Isobel Armstrong, *Victorian Poetry: Poetry, Poetics and Politics*, Routledge, London 1983

Joseph Bristow (ed.), *The Fin-de-Siècle Poem: English Literary Culture and the 1890s*, Ohio University Press, Athens OH 2005

Angela Leighton (ed.), *Victorian Women Poets: A Critical Reader*, Blackwell, Oxford 1996

Philippa Levine, *Victorian Feminism 1850–1900*, Hutchinson, London 1987

Dorothy Mermin, *Godiva's Ride: Women of Letters in England, 1830–1880*, Indiana University Press, Bloomington 1993

Angelique Richardson and Chris Willis (eds), *The New Woman in Fiction and in Fact: Fin-de-Siècle Feminisms*, Palgrave Macmillan, Basingstoke 2002

Ray Strachey, *The Cause*, G. Bell and Sons, London 1928, repr. Virago Press, London 1978

Martha Vicinus, *Independent Women: Work and Community for Single Women 1850–1920*, Virago Press, London 1985

Victorian Literature and Culture 34, 2006, 'Mapping Women's Poetries at the Fin de Siècle', special issue, ed. Marion Thain and Ana Vadillo

Victorian Poetry 33, 1995, special issue on women's poetry, ed. Linda K. Hughes

Fyfield*Books*

Two millennia of essential classics
The extensive Fyfield*Books* list includes

Djuna Barnes *The Book of Repulsive Women and other poems*
edited by Rebecca Loncraine

Elizabeth Barrett Browning *Selected Poems* edited by Malcolm Hicks

Charles Baudelaire *Complete Poems in French and English*
translated by Walter Martin

Thomas Lovell Beddoes *Death's Jest-Book* edited by Michael Bradshaw

Aphra Behn *Selected Poems*
edited by Malcolm Hicks

Border Ballads: A Selection
edited by James Reed

The Brontë Sisters *Selected Poems*
edited by Stevie Davies

Sir Thomas Browne *Selected Writings*
edited by Claire Preston

Lewis Carroll *Selected Poems*
edited by Keith Silver

Paul Celan *Collected Prose*
translated by Rosmarie Waldrop

Thomas Chatterton *Selected Poems*
edited by Grevel Lindop

John Clare *By Himself*
edited by Eric Robinson and David Powell

Arthur Hugh Clough *Selected Poems*
edited by Shirley Chew

Samuel Taylor Coleridge *Selected Poetry* edited by William Empson and David Pirie

Tristan Corbière *The Centenary Corbière*
in French and English
translated by Val Warner

William Cowper *Selected Poems*
edited by Nick Rhodes

Gabriele d'Annunzio *Halcyon*
translated by J.G. Nichols

John Donne *Selected Letters*
edited by P.M. Oliver

William Dunbar *Selected Poems*
edited by Harriet Harvey Wood

Anne Finch, Countess of Winchilsea
Selected Poems
edited by Denys Thompson

Ford Madox Ford *Selected Poems*
edited by Max Saunders

John Gay *Selected Poems*
edited by Marcus Walsh

Oliver Goldsmith *Selected Writings*
edited by John Lucas

Robert Herrick *Selected Poems*
edited by David Jesson-Dibley

Victor Hugo *Selected Poetry*
in French and English
translated by Steven Monte

T.E. Hulme *Selected Writings*
edited by Patrick McGuinness

Leigh Hunt *Selected Writings*
edited by David Jesson Dibley

Wyndham Lewis *Collected Poems and Plays* edited by Alan Munton

Charles Lamb *Selected Writings*
edited by J.E. Morpurgo

Lucretius *De Rerum Natura: The Poem on Nature*
translated by C.H. Sisson

John Lyly *Selected Prose and Dramatic Work*
edited by Leah Scragg

Ben Jonson *Epigrams and The Forest*
edited by Richard Dutton

Giacomo Leopardi *The Canti with a selection of his prose*
translated by J.G. Nichols

Stéphane Mallarmé *For Anatole's Tomb in French and English*
translated by Patrick McGuinness

Andrew Marvell *Selected Poems*
edited by Bill Hutchings

Charlotte Mew *Collected Poems and Selected Prose*
edited by Val Warner

Michelangelo *Sonnets*
translated by Elizabeth Jennings, introduction by Michael Ayrton

William Morris *Selected Poems*
edited by Peter Faulkner

John Henry Newman *Selected Writings to 1845*
edited by Albert Radcliffe

Ovid *Amores*
translated by Tom Bishop

Fernando Pessoa *A Centenary Pessoa*
edited by Eugenio Lisboa and L.C. Taylor, introduction by Octavio Paz

Petrarch *Canzoniere*
translated by J.G. Nichols

Edgar Allan Poe *Poems and Essays on Poetry*
edited by C.H. Sisson

Restoration Bawdy
edited by John Adlard

Rainer Maria Rilke *Sonnets to Orpheus and Letters to a Young Poet*
translated by Stephen Cohn

Christina Rossetti *Selected Poems*
edited by C.H. Sisson

Dante Gabriel Rossetti *Selected Poems and Translations*
edited by Clive Wilmer

Sir Walter Scott *Selected Poems*
edited by James Reed

Sir Philip Sidney *Selected Writings*
edited by Richard Dutton

John Skelton *Selected Poems*
edited by Gerald Hammond

Charlotte Smith *Selected Poems*
edited by Judith Willson

Henry Howard, Earl of Surrey *Selected Poems*
edited by Dennis Keene

Algernon Charles Swinburne *Selected Poems*
edited by L.M. Findlay

Arthur Symons *Selected Writings*
edited by Roger Holdsworth

William Tyndale *Selected Writings*
edited by David Daniell

Oscar Wilde *Selected Poems*
edited by Malcolm Hicks

William Wordsworth *The Earliest Poems* edited by Duncan Wu

Sir Thomas Wyatt *Selected Poems*
edited by Hardiman Scott

For more information, including a full list of Fyfield*Books* and a contents list for each title, and details of how to order the books, visit the Carcanet website at www.carcanet.co.uk or email info@carcanet.co.uk